St. Louis Community College

Library

5801 Wilson Avenue
St. Louis, Missouri 63110

Pushkin in 1827

ALEXANDER PUSHKIN

Collected Narrative

and Lyrical Poetry

Translated in the Prosodic Forms of the Original
by Walter Arndt

Ardis, Ann Arbor

Alexander Pushkin
Collected Narrative and Lyrical Poetry
Copyright © *1984 by Walter Arndt*
All rights reserved
Printed in the United States of America
No part of this publication may be
reproduced, stored in a retrieval system
or transmitted in any form or by any means,
electronic, mechanical, photocopying, recording,
or otherwise, without the prior permission
of the publisher

Ardis Publishers
2901 Heatherway
Ann Arbor, Michigan 48104

ISBN 0-88233-825-0 (cloth)
ISBN 0-88233-826-9 (paper)

Library of Congress Cataloging in Publication Data

Pushkin, Aleksandr Sergeevich, 1799-1837
  Collected narrative and lyrical poetry.

    I. Arndt, Walter W., 1916-   .   II. Title.
PG3347.A17   1983c   891.71'3   83-15029
ISBN 0-88233-825-0

ACKNOWLEDGMENTS

The author and publishers express their gratitude to the following for permission granted to reprint, adapt, or otherwise make use of materials previously published:

The South Atlantic Modern Language Association and the Northwestern University Press for introductory passages first published, respectively, in the *South Atlantic Bulletin,* Vol. XXIX, No. 3 (May 1964), and the *Tri-Quarterly,* No. 8 (Winter 1967).

To Dimitri von Mohrenschildt for eleven verse translations of poems by Pushkin, first published in the *Russian Review,* Vol. XXIV, No. 1 (January 1965).

The American Association for the Advancement of Slavic Studies for the verse translation of *The Gypsies,* first published in a slightly different version in the *Slavic Review,* Vol. XXIV, No.2 (June 1965).

HMH Publishing Co. Inc., holders of the copyrights 1965 and 1974 for *Tsar Nikita* and *The Gabri-iliad,* originally published in slightly different versions in *Playboy* magazine; and to *Canadian-American Slavic Studies* for permission to reprint *The Fountain of Bahçesaray,* first published in CASS 10, 2 (1977), pp. 161-74; *The Tale of the Golden Cockerel* and three poems, first published in CASS 11, 1 (1977), pp. 1-11; and *Poltava,* Canto III, first published in CASS 14, 1 (1980), pp. 62-73.

Russian Language Journal for permission to reprint *Poltava,* Cantos I and II, first published in RLT XXXIV, 117 and 118 (Winter and Spring 1980), respectively.

The editor and translator gratefully acknowledges the generous assistance in funds and facilities rendered him in his work on *Poltava* in Washington and abroad by the National Endowment for the Humanities Translation Program, the Institute for Advanced Russian Studies (Wilson Center, Smithsonian Institution), by the American Philosophical Society, and by the American Council of Learned Societies.

The author further records his warm sense of obligation to his revered late teacher, Roman Jakobson, to Edmund Wilson, René Wellek, George Steiner, and Vsevolod Setchkarev.

CONTENTS

To the living memory of

Roman Jakobson

ON READING PUSHKIN*

While reading in his verse it is as though
I were vouchsafed a sudden flash of wonders,
As if of some high harmony beyond us
Had been released an unsuspected glow.

Its sounds do not seem made in this world's fashion:
As if, pervaded with his deathless leaven,
All earthly stuff—emotions, anguish, passion—
Had been transmuted to the stuff of heaven.

A. N. Maikov

*1887, on the fiftieth anniversary of his death.

INTRODUCTION

I

Pushkin enjoys in his country a veneration comparable to that formerly accorded to Goethe in Germany and Mickiewicz in Poland—with the immense difference that, generation after generation, young people read him spontaneously and quote him with love and pride—and at great length. I have yet to meet the schoolboy in the U.S.S.R. who would lump Pushkin together with trig and M-L (Marxism-Leninism) among the "drags" of the school curriculum. It is doubly pleasant, therefore, to assume that a new collection of translations from Pushkin no longer needs an elaborate biographical-critical send-off to introduce the author to an American public.

To the extent that this is true, we are indebted for it to the progress achieved in the last twenty years of Slavic studies at American universities, building on the early pioneering efforts of a handful of senior scholars,[1] some of whom are fortunately still living and active. Those who still find it difficult, owing perhaps in part to a popular vodka advertisement, to "place" Pushkin are referred to the Pushkin biographies by E. Simmons, D. M. Mirsky, V. Setchkarev, and W. Vickery, and to P. Debreczeny's recent work on Pushkin's prose.

Before my own *Pushkin Threefold* (1972), there were to my knowledge no more than three sizable Pushkin anthologies for English readers, of which two closely resembled each other in purpose and design, did not contain Russian originals, and showed considerable overlap of contents. The older and more voluminous of the latter was Avram Yarmonlinsky's collection of 1936,[2] which has gone through several editions and revisions. A more recent and compact one was the Dell paperback volume edited and introduced by Ernest Simmons, which appeared twenty-five years later. Each of these contained forty-odd shorter poems; *Eugene Onegin* in full or in part; *The Bronze Horseman* and one of the rhymed fairy tales in the familiar Oliver Elton translations; one or two of the dramatic works; and a more or less extensive sampling of Pushkin's prose. Close to one-half of the contents of the two were quantitatively the same. In the Yarmolinsky volume, the translations of the short poems selected were almost all the work of Babette Deutsch. Professor Simmons sampled a great variety of translators for the lyrics and ballads he selected, drawing, for instance, on the artists, chiefly English, who had contributed Pushkin translations to the two *Books of Russian Verse* issued by Macmillan of London some twenty years ago, like Baring, Bowra, Elton, Jerrold, V. de S. Pinto.

The latest volume preceding *Pushkin Threefold*, confined to metric works and featuring the Russian originals with fine, accurate prose translations in small print below them, was edited and introduced by John Fennell of Oxford for the Penguin Poets series in 1964. The selections of shorter verse forms were about equal in number, but in balance more interesting and representative in their variety, than those of the two predecessors, avoiding, as they did, the better-known poems already chosen for the earlier *Penguin Book of Russian Verse*.

Pushkin Threefold, out of which the present collection grew, had an unusual format: form-true verse translations in the first third of the book, the Russian originals with facing line-by-line translations of the same items making up the rest. Since most reviewers and users of the book have thought this triple approach to a foreign poem the best solution of a very complex old problem, and I agree with them, it may be worth while to describe its rationale and some underlying facts of translation theory and practice, even though the format could not be observed in the present book.

To a reader with little or no knowledge of Russian it offered, by juxtaposing line-by-line prose versions with verse translations by one and the same hand, a fairer chance to assess the textual, though hardly the emotional and atmospheric, fidelity of the final product, the English imitation, and to make up his mind which he would rather follow if one or the other jarred on him. At worst, or in a sense at best, it supplied an incentive to take up Russian or learn it better. To those versed in Russian, on the other hand, it afforded an opportunity not merely to have originals and English imitations close together, but also, for what this might be worth to them, to follow the reconstitution process (which of course cannot aim or stop at a "literal" version in prose and deserve the name of translation) through two of its many interacting states or suspensions. Admittedly, this nonsequential and ultimately untraceable process was there somewhat artificially presented as though it consisted essentially of two stages. Actually, the creator of a verse translation generally does not interpose a full, or perhaps even a partial, prose version between the original and the English poem—*pace* the absurd postulate of "literalness"—any more than, say, an artist copying in tempera a painting in oils would necessarily make or want an intermediate etching such as Millet made of his *Reapers*. Nor is the translator's end product often likely to remain final in his mind. In fact, my contention is (as may be deducible from the foregoing and will I hope be obvious by the end of this introduction) that the final version in verse is not a further departure from the original, exacted by technical difficulties, than that represented by a "literal prose" version, but a difficult journey *back* toward the full impact of the original, toward the integral sound-rhythm-sense aggregate experienced in it or through it by the native reader or hearer. The point at which this journey starts is not a "literal prose" version at all, but a sort of colloidal suspension of the elements in a bilingual mind, from which the new poem ultimately precipitates into its new medium and idiom.

However this may be, at least the public of this new sort of verse reader was no longer a wholly captive one, as was true in the all-English anthologies enumerated, where Pushkin was more helplessly at the uncertain mercies of his translators; nor was it deprived entirely of the virtues and graces, such as they may be, of the metric form in English, as was the case with presentations like the Fennell volume, not to mention the sad ritual murder performed for the purposes of an ever more insatiable lexical necrophilia in the first volume of Nabokov's otherwise peerless commentary on *Onegin*. Among Pushkiniana of recent years is D. M. Thomas' collection of spaced-out English prose versions of narrative and lyric poems; testimony perhaps to an increasing interest of English writers in Pushkin and his translators.

The arrangement of the selections is chronological by years within each section, without consistent regard, however, for sequence within each year, which is often impossible to establish. Nor was any attempt made, despite strong temptation, to assign the shorter poems to modes such as classicist or romantic, or to "genres" such as lyric, civic, polemic, occasional, ribald, or any others that might be discernible in the opulent tapestry of Pushkin's total *oeuvre*. Despite some hesitancy over presenting some of the contents of my *Eugene Onegin* translation of 1963 and 1981, I have included here a small selection of sequential stanzas from each chapter, because an anthology of Pushkin's rhymed poetry cannot well ignore the novel in verse altogether.

Presented here for the first time are all the extant complete stanzas of the original Chapter VIII of *Onegin*, called "Onegin's Travels."

The design of *Pushkin Threefold* was not followed here because reasons of layout and cost forbade it with this much larger book. The volume of both narrative and shorter poems included has approximately doubled, which means that their presentation in the "threefold" mode would have required nearly one thousand pages. Only a small number of (incomplete or unsuccessful) translations have been excluded.

II

Traduttore, traditore—"translator, traitor"—mocks the Italian pun like a malicious echo; and it implies no question mark, but rather an exclamation point of *Schadenfreude*, a snigger of wicked enjoyment. From the safe port of criticism the expert who needs no translation hugs himself over the discomfiture of the wretch who set out to dismount a poetic artifact cast in an alien medium, and to reassemble it into a new poem of his own, calling the two the same—or seeming to. But as far as this Introduction is concerned, a boldly added question mark is the point of the citation; which one could translate, punning back etymologically at the Italian, "translator, traducer." To me the translators-traducers are (as Pushkin says of his fellow poets) "a brotherhood I can't condemn, because, you see, I'm one of them."

In using this occasion to examine some selected modes and dilemmas of poetic translation, my motive is not merely personal experience and involvement. It is the evident truth that all of us who acknowledge an emotional stake in literature are ultimately at the mercy of the brotherhood of traitors or traducers; quite directly when we wish to look beyond our own linguistic boundaries; indirectly if we wish to savor fully almost any of the major pieces of our own national literatures, which are invariably impregnated with a supranational tradition reaching back into untraceable antiquity. We cannot read Pope's translation of the *Iliad* or much of Dryden simply as English poems without confronting the question of how much of this poetry is Homer or Vergil, even how much of Vergil is Homer again. The massive borrowing by Milton from Salandra in the theme, characters, and structure of *Paradise Lost* was assuredly only the last and most wholesale of a series of loans. We cannot escape inquiry into the nature of the process of creative metamorphosis, when at its inception lies not an intricate blend of contemporary personal experience, but the already transmuted experience of another mind in an antecedent work of art, often continents and ages removed, and moving within its own associative and linguistic code. In such a case we find ourselves witnesses, to a degree proportionate to our linguistic sophistication, at both ends of the creative process. We are able, and tempted, to tell the artist "you cannot say this—you misrepresent your experience," for much of his experience is there for us to compare with his final product.

The poet is not so helplessly exposed to privileged eavesdropping as the translator or borrower; nor, on the other hand, is he a power behind someone else's throne. The translator is both of these—a gray eminence who helps decide what will reach the oligoglot public, and in what form; and a poor relation at the margin of letters, poorly regarded despite the fact that his handicaps are in some ways more stringent than the poet's: he must be a poet, if not a great one, and one who will put what light he has under a bushel.

Those aware of this constant admixture of translingual experience in seemingly "national" writing of caliber are bound to wonder about the ambiguous likenesses-unlikenesses, as teasing as an elusive family resemblance, between any work and its partial matrix. When such a matrix is not only acknowledged but explicitly claimed as a nearly congruent and equivalent model, more searching scrutiny, on the part of both artist and reader, must attend the process of transmutation or carrying-across—the *trans-lation*.

The store of images and emotions unlocked by words in intricate conjunction, the secret world of associative relays that are set to operate on each other in an instantaneous, yet almost infinite chain reaction—this whole complex system exists, for anyone, only in his own, at most in two or three languages. And *it* is the medium of poetic experience, it cannot be synthesized piecemeal by affirmation, description, and persuasion through a commentator's already interpretive diction in another language—in other words, by literary criticism. Hence, even an inferior associative orchestration, resembling it, in the hearer's language is superior to mere aural or visual reproduction of the original plus exegesis—"the cold way." This reproduction simply does not reproduce—it describes, analyzes, exhorts—it tries to teach rather than to transport the reader. Roland Barthes called prosodically faithful translation, where feasible, that ideal form of literary criticism which embodies the least distortion and redundancy.

The central problem, surely, is that of accuracy; or more basically, the problem of what constitutes accuracy. Within it are contained many others, such as that of the proper *unit of translation*—word, phrase, stanza, poem; that of the alleged enmity between form and content, which, it is claimed, makes verse translation resemble a constant arithmetical product of two factors, rhyme and reason. If you increase one, the other diminishes, the product remains constant—a constant of inadequacy. Then, to name another problem within the realm of accuracy, there is the dilemma of allusiveness or associative authenticity of a special sort.

A particular blend of these, where accuracy assumes a more fundamental dimension of meaning, may be labeled the problem of simplicity—one of the most disheartening in verse translation into English. It is posed by a certain frugality and calm—lexical and metaphorical—in the original that to the English mind borders on triteness; an intractable quality that in the long poetic run, through some magic of craftsmanship, by way of a rejuvenation of the reader's imagination, turns into a haunting inevitability, a disarming utter rightness. Verse translators into English from such media as Chinese, Greek, Russian, and at times German verse encounter this dilemma with especial force. Gilbert Murray's renderings or adaptations from Greek, Oliver Elton's from Pushkin, Heine translations, have all suffered from the fundamental contrast in poetic instrumentation, as well as in the nature of the aesthetic hearer-response labeled "poetic," between those verse traditions and the English, or at any rate the nineteenth-century English one. Edmund Wilson in his perceptive centenary essay on *Eugene Onegin* (1937) speaks to this problem in a vein similar to that of Maurice Baring's Introduction to the *Oxford Book of Russian Verse*:

... the poetry of Pushkin is particularly difficult to translate. It is difficult for the same reason that Dante is difficult: because it says so much in so few words, so clearly and yet so concisely, and the words themselves and their place in the line have become so much more important than in the case of more facile or rhetorical writers. It would require a translator himself a poet of the first order to reproduce Pushkin's peculiar combination of intensity, compression, and perfect ease. A writer like Pushkin may easily sound "flat," as he did to Flaubert in French, just as Cary's translation of Dante sounds flat. Furthermore, the Russian language, which is highly inflected and able to dispense with pronouns and prepositions in many cases where we have to use them, and which does without the article altogether, makes it possible for Pushkin to pack his lines (separating modifiers from substantives, if need be) in a way which renders the problem of translating him close to that of translating a tightly articulated Latin poet like Horace than any modern poet that we know. Such a poet in translation may sound trivial just as many of the translations of Horace sound trivial—because the weight of the words and the force of their relation has been lost with the inflections and the syntax.

Gilbert Murray was reduced to well-tempered despair by the refusal of his Greek originals to get excited, or to erupt into stylistic shock effects of the kind that his English-trained poetic sense kept demanding. This mildest of men could become *almost* exasperated on the subject; and even in print he ventured this mannerly half-complaint:

I have often used a more elaborate diction than Euripides did because I found that, Greek being a very simple language and English an ornate one, a direct translation produced an effect of baldness which was quite unlike the original.

Maurice Baring, the anthologist of the *Oxford Book of Russian Verse*, was struck forcibly by a similar difference in climate and orchestration between Russian and English. Edith Hamilton has analyzed with a wealth of illustration the striking contrast in the very stuff and temper of poetry between Greek and English. Both she and Baring emphasized the seemingly inbred need for expressive hyperbole in English—understood by everyone as not merely "poetic license" but part of the poetic essential of a verbally fresh view, the most conventional variety of estrangement (R. *ostranenie*, defamiliarization). Greek appears to abhor this device as cheap and needless. Our response mechanisms, says Edith Hamilton, are conditioned to "caverns measureless to man, down to a sunless sea," to "magic casements opening on the foam of perilous seas." To which anyone can add uncounted examples: rose-red cities half as old as time, skylarks that are, all in the same poem, blithe spirits, clouds of fire, poets hidden in the light of thought, highborn maidens in a palace tower, glowworms golden in a dell of dew. Intoxicating stuff, but as the poet says himself: "bird thou never wert...."

In the calmer realms of Greek, Russian, and much German poetry, such exuberant music of the spheres, still quiring to the young-eyed cherubim, takes on a dubious aroma of the overripe and overrich. A skylark is a skylark over there, the ocean may be wine-colored, but it is still recognizably the ocean; no slimy things do crawl with legs upon the slimy sea. Fancy is tight-reined: milk is white and good to drink, girls are *dulce ridentes, dulce loquentes*, wide-eyed, dark-lashed, ivory-browed even: but their faces launch no ships, let alone a thousand; they are never splendid angels, newly dressed, save wings, for heaven . . . . Consider how Pushkin, not insensitive to beauty, but like Pericles' Athenians, lover of beauty *with economy*, evokes the seasons with a sparing stanza of calm shorthand here and there in *Eugene Onegin*. The following is a passage that Edmund Wilson preferred to render in prose in his essay; and it may be verified in my *Pushkin Threefold* that in verse translation some of the English verbal decoration has already accrued to it:

> Autumn was in the air already;
> The sun's gay sparkle grew unsteady
> The heedless day became more brief;
> The forest, long in darkling leaf,
> Unclothed itself with mournful rustle;
> The fields were wrapped in misty fleece;
> A caravan of raucous geese
> Winged southward; after summer's bustle
> A duller season was at hand:
> November hovered overland.

And then he turns to sharp little genre pictures, all seen truly and calmly, never doped to overcharge the poetic nerve with imagery:

> Through frigid haze the dawn resurges;
> Abroad the harvest sounds abate;
> And soon the hungry wolf emerges
> Upon the highway with his mate.
> The scent scares into snorting flurry
> The trudging horse, and travelers hurry
> Their uphill way in wary haste.
> No longer are the cattle chased
> Out of the stalls at dawn, the ringing
> Horn-notes of shepherds do not sound
> Their noontime summons all around.
> Indoors the maiden spins, with singing,
> Before the crackling pine-flare light—
> Companion of the winter night.

Compare Byron, describing a high mountain:

> . . .the monarch of mountains.
> They crowned him long ago

On a throne of rocks, in a robe of clouds,
With a diadem of snow.

By way of more detailed illustration, one may select one of many short pieces by Heinrich Heine and despair over the mysterious alchemy of obscurely relevant irrelevancies, rhythmic mutations, and pivotal silences that transmutes commonplace lexical and semantic material into a memorable lyric evocation:

Es ragt ins Meer der Runenstein,
Da sitz ich mit meinen Träumen.
Es pfeift der Wind, die Möwen schrein,
Die Wellen, die wandern und schäumen.
Ich habe geliebt manch schönes Kind
Und manchen guten Gesellen.
Wo sind sie hin? Es pfeift der Wind,
Es schäumen und wandern die Wellen.

Here is the most hackneyed *Weltschmerz*, one is bound to say, in diction of well-worn pocket change, seemingly powerless to stab with any novelty of vision or insight. The poet sits on the seashore, musing on bygone love and friendship, as the wind whistles about his ears and the waves break and ebb below. The words for the most part are the most obvious at hand: *sea, wind, love, waves, sit*; the *schönes Kind* is quite faceless, and so are the *gute Gesellen*. There are, to be sure, three or four words of big magic, which carry what may be termed a suprasemantic charge of associations: *ragt, Runenstein, Träumen, wandern*; but at least two of these had long worked overtime for the romantic poets. They contrive to radiate diffuse associations all about them, but they neither ravish the imagination with metaphor nor dope the nerves with hyperbole; they transcend, yet do not upset the surface boundaries of reason and syntax. It is by their very lack of display, their refusal to stun or transport, that they imperceptibly draw the reader more deeply into the creative process itself, as part of the fresh vision or mood of the instant of experience regenerates itself within him as his own. And this precisely is the must of highest poetic effect: not a passive gaping at verbal fireworks, not a vicarious ecstasy, but the superior excitement of sharing a creative experience. How exactly is it brought about?

Of the charged words, the remotest from rational context, the most willful (though still fitting the contextual frame) is of course the *runestone*. Its enigma presides over the first line, and subtly over the whole poem, like one of the three wrinkled hags that spin out our fate, like the dead sailor over a certain passage in Eliot. This runestone need not be there so far as the cognitive content of the poem is concerned. And yet, it adds something, precisely the something which, with some formal elements, is essential to save the two quatrains from triteness: it casts a note of inscrutability and despair over what goes on there. Runes denote what is indecipherable, fateful, and ancient, and the irrelevant presence of the runestone reinforces from a subconscious realm two suggestions already contained in the body of the poem: the idea of an aloof inanimate environment, and the helpless questioning plaint of human transcience, powerless to cope with the riddle of existence. Beyond this, the associative connection between *Runen* and *raunen*, that mystery-charged word for "secretly whispering," adds its subterranean force to the tritely foaming waves and the tritely whistling seawind. On the surface, obvious agents do expected things: the wind whistles, the waves foam, the seagulls scream, the pretty flappers are loved, and so are the good companions. But all is estranged and newly charged under the secret auspices of the runestone's obscure despair; the stark loom (*ragen*) of its jutting into the sea; the "roving" of the waves (not aimless so much as "of unfathomed and unshareable purpose"), suggested in *wandern*, so banal a word in other contexts. The soothing and drugging effect of sea and wind, conjured up from earliest acquaintance, draws fresh magic even from the worn surface of *Träumen*. When I tackled Heine's provocative bit of sorcery for the sake of demonstration, I came up, rather bruised, with this:

> The runestone juts into the brine,
> I sit beside it dreaming.
> The seawinds hiss, the seamews whine,
> The waves, they go foaming and streaming.
>
> I have loved many a pretty miss
> And some of the best lads roaming.
> Where have they gone? The seawinds hiss,
> The waves, they go streaming and foaming.

I felt constrained to respect the three charged words as best I could; to render the surface lexical triteness of much of the rest; and most confining of all, to preserve the marvelously simple syntactic reversal of that keyline of the pulsing waves, which occurs in one order in line 4, in reversed order in line 8. It interrupts with its dreamy dactyls the iambic beat of the rest: first, *Die Wellen, die wandern und schäumen*—simple setting of the scene; and then, denying participation in the pathetic human query with a powerful echo of mocking repetition—*Es schäumen und wandern die Wellen*. This effect brings the tremor of recognition—suddenly there is real ache, real poignancy. But for the translator, at once there begins the winding path of painful compromise: there is no simple English term the equal of *ragen*, with its joint connotation of vertical looming and sharp cragginess. One has to settle for "jut." Because the subdued jingle of end rhyme is needed for the artful *Folklorelei* of the little piece, one may try "brine" for sea, despite its obnoxious Viking flavor, for the seamews cannot well "cry" or "scream" in English for reasons of rhyme and/or semantics. Only "whine/brine" lies at hand. Similarly with the "pretty miss" here brought in—she is far too pert for the dreamy, artless archetype of *schönes Kind*, but in response to "miss" the wind can "hiss," just as in response to "foaming," "many a good lad" has to yield to "some of the best lads roaming." Or is one to choose the more literal "many a good young fellow," and make the waves "bellow" indecently in the parting line—in which case they would duly have to bellow also in line 4, rudely bursting into the elegaic murmur that pervades the whole? The gray eminence of the translator may contrive to release an echo of the wistful music of the whole; but usually at a painful price.

It may now be clearer what a dragon there is to slay in the deceptive jejuneness of simplicity. Centuries of sophisticated English, stately, baroquely jeweled, evocatively obscure, rear up in revolt against perpetrating anything as flat and bland as "there I sit with my dreams" or "I have loved many a pretty maid." Remember Mr. Huxley's pathetic painter-poet, Lypiatt, who was laughed to scorn for using that inadmissible word, *dream—le rêve*—no really, it is far too late for that! Housman dared something similar and achieved the same pure, restrained pathos; but his is after all a very special product apart from the main tradition, and he was steeped in classical simplicity himself. Yet when we try to translate, do we dare to go back to the witches' caldron of the poetic laboratory itself (our own, necessarily, not Heine's or Pushkin's) and start the transformation process afresh with more gleaming and more cunningly startling words and similes? Shall we talk of the *ambient stupor of the surf*, in fastidious fear of *waves that go foaming and streaming?* What shall we betray, the irradiated simplicity of the German, or the zest and shock of the English word?

There is no set answer. But we must not wholly despair of achieving some of the careless, deceptively casual felicity of interrhyming and rhythmically interechoing tritenesses with similar materials in English—if we wish to call what we strive for a translation, and not an *imitatio*, a poem of the second order, a poem-inspired poem. Is not the true translator, after all, what the lamented Poggioli called in an essay the *added* artificer, *artifex additus artifici?* English resources of rhyme and rhythm, within the given range of lexical elements, may accommodate us—even unto half the kingdom—by a constellation of happy coincidence and restless ingenuity; and if we then make the unit of translation large enough, we may hope, through a kind of mosaic technique, to achieve a similarly harmonious pattern of linguistic building stones, associative relays, and rhythmic elements.

Such interlingual salvage operations, and their cost, can be illustrated, if not assessed, by a crude little experiment in which several translation processes are linked in a chain reaction. I once chose a random quatrain from Swinburne's "Chorus from Atalanta" and asked each of several sensitive and long-suffering friends to render it, successively, from English into French, from French into German, from German into Russian, and from Russian back into English. Here are three links in this cycle of cumulative compromises:

> For winter's rains and ruins are over,
> And all the season of snows and sins;
> The days dividing lover and lover,
> The light that loses, the night that wins.

> Car les pluies et les deuils de l'hiver ont cessé,
> Et le temps de la neige et le temps du péché;
> Les heures qui séparent l'amant de l'aimée,
> La lumière qui meurt, et la nuit couronnée.

> Denn Winterschauer, -trauer sind vergangen,
> Die Zeit, die Sünde mit dem Schnee gebracht;
> Die Stunden, da entrückt zwei Liebste bangen,
> Das Licht das stirbt, und die gekrönte Nacht.

> For winter's gusts and griefs are over,
> Snowtime weather and sin-time blight,
> Lone ache of lover for distant lover,
> The light that dies, and the throne of night.

The versions are like turns in a spiral, coiling out ever farther from the sprightly though undistinguished original in spirit, tone, and rhythm. We notice that the last coil, which is English again, has sprung back, after all these vicissitudes, into a skippy four-footed rhythm very like the original's; and it has salvaged the identical end rhyme of one couple. Otherwise one observes a certain loss of simplicity, accretion of material, some obscurity and loss of tension in the last line. "The night that wins" lost its innocence by way of "la nuit couronnée" and "gekrönte Nacht," for example. Still—the result is not as unrecognizable as was the rule in the similar post-office game of our youth, where a short message was hurriedly whispered from ear to ear in a circle of players, and the result was a hilarious shambles. After all, we deliberately courted here the cumulative effect of four subtle acts of "treason," and what emerged was by no means a complete travesty of the original.

A more general interlingual and intercultural translation problem than that of simplicity is that of allusiveness. Here a more or less esoteric allusion, or a whole sequence of intramural associations, more specific than those of linguistic hyperbole or estrangement, is to be set quivering and tittering in the reader's mind like a mobile. Here the translator has three choices, all distasteful: he may brave it out with high-handed, literal brevity; or he may have to expand a pregnant line or two into three or four lightly loaded ones; or he may have to give up the precious form and goad the reader up a pile of footnotes. The latter way, alas, was Nabokov's with his prose paraphrase of *Onegin*.

On this kind of dilemma I know of no better example than one that the late Dudley Fitts furnished in a thoughtful essay many years ago. It concerns an anonymous Greek epigram about a girl called Daphne:

> Léktron henòs pheugoûsa léktron polloîsin etúkhthē.

One may translate this, to a close equivalent of overt message and rhythm, as follows:

> She who fled from the bed of one
> A bed for many has become.

But this leaves the covert message, a multiple twinkling of simultaneous allusions, at the mercy of chance and faint hope. What to do? Shall one leave it at that and hope that the slow fuse will burn its meandering way by half-buried landmarks into those recesses of the reader's mind where his classical mythology languishes—and risk that when the spark arrives, there is nothing there to flash up in recognition? Or shall the allusive sentence be studded with essential little signposts, to lose all bite in the process? To quote Fitts:

> By the time we have reflected that the girl who owns the bed is named Daphne and that *daphne* is laurel in Greek, and that her bed is made of laurel, and that upon that bed, since she is a gallant lady, she entertains the men that visit her, and that for this reason she is inappropriately named for the original Daphne, a nymph, who, far from being a gallant lady, was so prim that she preferred to be turned into a laurel bush rather than to submit to the advances of a god, that god being inflamed Apollo himself....

By the time the fuse has burned this far, not secretly and in one flash of associative delight, but slowly and prosaically, and all of it has been pondered and savored and made explicit, nothing is left but a laborious learned exegesis, as dead as an explained joke. The reader will give the three widely spaced guffaws once attributed to Austrian field marshals when told jokes—one laugh when the joke is told, another when it is explained, and a third when it is understood.

The very opening lines of *Onegin* contain a similar headache of an allusion. The elegant young scamp, summoned to the bedside of a dying, moneyed uncle, ponders the legacy and its irksome price—a few weeks' attendance at the sickbed, feigned solicitude, dancing in and out with poultices and sympathy; and he begins an inner monologue like this: "My uncle of most honest principles ..." He invokes most clearly, to Russians of his and later ages, the start of a famous Krylov fable: "A donkey of most honest principles..." Where to go for an equivalent literary allusion in English? Provided you have caught the allusion in the first place?

By way of strategic retreat from the whole painful subject, let us consider the following attempts at Pushkinian stanzas; first in plain prose, then in my verse rendering:

Onegin, VII, 2

LITERAL TRANSLATION

How sad I feel at your appearing,
Spring, spring—season of love!
What languid stir
(Is) in my soul, in my blood!
With what a heavyhearted tenderness
I rejoice in the wafting of spring
As it breathes against my face
In the lap of rustic silence!
Or is enjoyment alien to me,
And all that gladdens, animates,
All that exults and glistens,
Brings boredom and languor
Upon the soul long dead,
And all seems dark to it?

VERSE RENDERING

How I am saddened by your coming,
O time of love, o time of *bud*!
What languid stir you send *benumbing*
Into my soul, into my blood!
What painful tender feeling seizes
The heart, as spring's *returning* breezes
Waft to my face *in silken rush*
Here in the lap of rural hush!
Have I become so alienated
From all things that exult and glow,
All things that joy and life bestow,
That now they find me dull and sated,
And all seems *dark as burnt-out coal*
To the long-since insentient soul?

Onegin, III, 14

LITERAL TRANSLATION

I shall recount the simple speeches
Of father and old uncle,
The children's appointed meetings
By the old lindens, by the brook:

The torments of luckless jealousy,
Separation, tears of reconciliation;
I shall set (them) at odds again, and at last,
I shall lead them under the wreath . . .
I shall cite the speeches of passionate tenderness,
The words of languishing love,
Which in days gone by
At the feet of a beautiful lady-love
Have come to my tongue,
Of which I have now lost the habit.

VERSE RENDERING

I shall recount the simple speeches
Of dad and Granddad *in my book*,
The children's trysts by ancient *beeches*,
Or on the borders of a brook;
The ravages of jealous torment,
Partings, reunion tears, *long dormant*,
I shall stir up once more, and then
In marriage soothe them down again . . . .
The language of impassioned pining
Will I *renew*, and love's *reply*,
The like of which in days gone by
Came to me as I lay *reclining*
At a dear beauty's feet, bemused,
And which of late I have not used.

I have juxtaposed a literal prose translation, conceding for the moment that even such a thing is possible, and my published version in the so-called Onegin stanza of the original. The stanza, as must be evident, is dismayingly intricate in its ordered interplay of masculine and feminine rhymes, and its three differently patterned iambic tetrameter quatrains with a couplet at the end. The italics mark the departures the translator was forced into: mostly padding necessitated by the shorter English breath, some rearrangement of the mosaic stones, some omissions. Predictably, most occur at the end of the lines.

Other offenses against literal fidelity occurred in substituting for the rhythmic and structural grandeur achieved by the long Russian words a careful modicum of the more semantic and metaphoric ornateness expected in English—but all of it only under dire duress. If the translator makes similar accommodations in his work, has he tacitly conceded that his enterprise has failed, or was impractical from the start? Has he falsified the poem? Or has he rather shown it the superior loyalty of a daring and creative sympathy? Is he a *traduttore*, or a *traditore*? For any corpus of poetry, only a handful of scholar-poets are qualified to say.

Nabokov's two-volume commentary in English on *Eugene Onegin* attempts to call into question again, not *a* verse translation, but verse translation itself. This happens once or twice in every literary period. The work illustrates this attitude of militant resignation by continually substituting exhaustive and highly imaginative exegesis for translation—while, however, retaining the word "translation" in its title. It will be clear now that I cannot regard the essential legitimacy of poetic translation—as distinct from the means and the areas and limits of tolerable compromise—as highly controversial. I would endorse the more challenging majority view of the task, which is that the task exists, and must be tackled. The goal is to create a poem in the target language, which should simulate, as near as may be, the total effect produced by the original on the contemporary reader. Total effect to me means *import* as well as *impact*, i.e., both what the poem imparts to the mind and how it strikes the sense; cognitive as well as aesthetic (stylistic, formal, musical, "poetic") values, pretending for just a moment that these two congruent entities can somehow be analytically separated. Again, "import as well as impact" means import *through* and *congruent with* impact; it does not mean a message in garbled prose, with subsequent assurances by way of stylistic and other commentary that the corpse in its lifetime was poetry. Eugene Nida has phrased the same postulate rather baldly like this:

> Translation consists in producing in the receptor language the closest natural equivalent to the message of the source language, first in meaning, and secondly in style.

I find precarious in this only the suggestion of consecutiveness or priority in the terms *first* and *secondly*. But then, Nida spoke of prose.

This disposes to my mind (at least for culturally kindred languages like German and English, and even Russian and English), of both counsels of insouciance and counsels of despair; that is, on the one hand, of remote imitations or adaptations in distant meters and, on the other hand, of the spavined pony of would-be "literal" prose.

The central problem of verse translation, then, in a sense the only one, is not whether there can and should be simultaneous fidelity to content and form, but rather how to decide, first, what constitutes double fidelity in a given case and how it can best be approximated. The proper formal frame of accuracy, i.e., the largest allowable unit of form within which maximum fidelity must be achieved, is a delicate matter of balancing the poetic pulse of the original against the stylistic sense of the reader in the target language, and against his syntactic comprehension span; but luckily a large enough unit *can* usually be chosen to afford desperately needed latitude for transposing and rearranging within it elements of message and lexical-stylistic effects. This latitude somewhat soothes the notorious enmity between form and content in the recasting process—what I am now tempted to call the Nabokov Relation of Fated Failure.

When I spoke of reproducing the total impact on the *contemporary* reader, I meant, in a sense, the reader contemporary to the author, not the author's present-day native public. I realize that here I am on more controversial ground. But I am convinced that the diction used in the target language, save for deliberate archaisms used by the author, should be essentially modern, as that of the original was modern at its first appearance. Here "modern" may embrace the still resonant linguistic strata of the past one hundred, perhaps one hundred and fifty years. The antiquarian pursuit of archaizing the language used, to approximate the surface quaintness or patina that the original may by now have acquired among its native readers, is tempting; but I feel it is not only a foredoomed quest—technically too formidable and treacherous—but essentially wrongheaded. It is not the translator's business to produce an imitation period piece, to fake up that "classic" of a translation, which at the time remained unborn because no Schlegel and Tieck or no Zhukovsky happened to pick up the original. No one should—and few could—try to make himself into a ghostly Heine because in his time Heine *might* have produced the ideal translation of his contemporary Pushkin's *Onegin*.

Let me go back for a moment to the "unit of fidelity." In prose, except for extreme cases that tend to depart from prose, the problem of the unit of fidelity is not acute. The unit is normally the sentence, and only extremes of syntactic yapping or hacking, as in some German expressionism, or of syntactic convolution, as in Thomas Mann or Tolstoi, raise the question of where the demands of naturalness must call a halt to close stylistic-syntactic imitation. But in poetry, especially rhymed poetry, the rigors of prosody bring "naturalness" and fidelity into conflict much sooner and oftener—in fact, sometimes at every step. "Meaning" acquires a more rigorous, because more comprehensive sense; freshness of vision and linguistic novelty are of the essesnce of what is stated, meaning *is* form and form meaning, over quite small units of discourse. To *just that* particular poetic impact of a line or phrase, there seem to be no alternative "plain" forms that could produce it. By the same token, literal translation, so-called (i.e., atomistic and sequential substitution of lexical pieces, morphological devices, and syntactic structures), not only runs into the hard wall of rhythm and rhyme, but is intrinsically absurd and self-defeating. Poetic utterance is not produced from some underlying, neutral, merely cognitive statement by linguistic manipulation; and if it were, the manipulations could not be the same in language A as in language B, or else they would be the *same* language. Hence sequential literalness becomes worse than irrelevant. All this would have been comically redundant to say again, had the notion of literalness as a technique not been resurrected by Nabokov in relation to a major work of world literature, and had it not been respectfully (or at least gingerly) handled by at least some critics.

The first and constantly recurring decision, then, which the translator of poetry faces, is that of choosing the unit of fidelity. In some short articulated forms like the sonnet or the quatrain, or in long narrative poems whose overall unity is as brilliantly quantified as Pushkin's *Onegin* into stanzas, each of which is a viable and substructured microcosm of mood and meaning, the obvious outer unit is the stanza; within it, the whole delicate balancing act of restructuring and tint-matching necessarily consummates itself. What original effects have not been caught up within the translated stanza have been lost and cannot be made up before or beyond it. Within the outer unit, almost invariably there are subordinate ones that should be preserved, but with a less degree of rigor; for the poetic *mora* of the whole statement has not lapsed till the end of the stanza or other unit of fidelity: the ear is still open, all is yet in suspense.

Thus a mosaic technique of reconstitution within the unit, somewhat independent of the original order of poetic effects and certainly of the kind and sequence of linguistic elements, is possible and not only possible, but necessary; and not only necessary *faute de mieux*, but often as a condition of fidelity. What the original, say, renders verbally (by verb) near the end of the first line, may or should be rendered adverbially, nominally, adjectivally, or even syntactically, say in the middle of the second line or still later—if thus the mosaic-making rules of the target language, its aesthetics and poetics demand it for the overall stanzaic impact. If, after a few days, the translator finds he cannot quite remember the stanza in the original, I submit this is not always a bad sign, or a symptom of a fatuous vanity.

Now if a line, or a larger subunit within the stanza, cries out for separate status as an integral felicity, or an inimitable local effect that cannot be moved or compensated elsewhere, it should be tackled in its place. But if move it must, then as likely as not it is the poetics and linguistics of the target language that demand it, not necessarily the denseness or stupor of the translator. The scar of the excision, or the local opaqueness caused in the image, may yet be partially remedied elsewhere; or the loss must simply be borne. It may be found that in such cases the light merely strikes another facet of the stanza; and the spatial sense of the reader may yet perceive, with luck, a refraction of the same jewel turned to another angle.

Walter Arndt

LYRIC POEMS

LIBERTY   [1817]

An Ode

Begone out of my sight and flee,
Oh, feeble princess of Cythera!
Thou, haughty muse of Liberty,
The bane of kings, come here, come nearer!
The flowered garland from me wrench,
Break in my hand the pampered lyre . . .
I sing of Freedom's conquering fire
Scourge vice enthroned on royal bench.

Reveal to me the noble path
Of that great Gaul whom in the wrongs
And terrors of the days of wrath
You would inspire to daring songs.
You, fickle Fortune's favored knaves,
The tyrants of the nations, tremble!
And you with manhood fresh assemble
And listen: Rise, oh fallen slaves!

Alas, where'er my eye may light,
It falls on ankle chains and scourges,
Perverted law's pernicious blight
And tearful serfdom's fruitless surges.
Where has authority unjust
In superstition's dense delusion
Not settled—slavery's dread effusion
And rank vainglory's fateful lust?

Unstained by human freedom choked,
A sovereign's brow alone is carried
Where sacred liberty is married
With mighty law and firmly yoked;

Where its stout roof enshelters all,
And where, by watchful burghers wielded,
Law's sword impends, and none are shielded
From its inexorable fall.

Before whose righteous accolade
The minions of transgression cower,
Whose vengeful hand cannot be stayed
By slavering greed or dread of power.
Oh, kings, you owe your crown and writ
To Law, not nature's dispensation;
While you stand high above the nation,
The changeless Law stands higher yet.

And woe betide the common weal
Where it incontinently slumbers,
Where Law itself is rendered feal
Be it to kings or strength of numbers!
To this one martyr witness bears,
Heir to his forebears' famous errors,
Who in the storm of recent terrors
Laid down his royal head for theirs.

Unto his death King Louis went,
His speechless offspring watching after,
His head bereft of crown he bent
To fell Rebellion's bloodied rafter.
Mute is the Law, the people too,
And down the axe of outrage rattles . . .
And an unholy purple settles
Upon a Gaul enchained anew.

Yes, I abhor thee and thy throne,
Oh, miscreant in despot's clothing!
Thy doom, thy children's dying groan,
I witness them with mirthful loathing.
Upon thy brow one reads the sign
Of subject peoples' degradation,
World's horror, blemish of creation,
Reproach on earth to the Divine.

When by Nevá the midnight star
Hangs sparkling on the somber waters,
And carefree sleepers near and far
Have drooped to slumber in their quarters,
The singer finds his gaze and thought
The tyrant's lonely statue roaming,
Its ominous torpor in the gloaming,
And the forlorn imperial court—

And Clio's awesome tones he hears
Behind those awesome casements tolling,
Caligula's last hour appears
Before his sight anew unrolling,
He sees, beribboned and bestarred,
By venom and by wine befuddled,
The clandestine assassins huddled
With brazen brow and wolfish heart.

And silenced is the faithless guard,
The drawbridge downed at midnight season,
In secrecy the gate unbarred
By hands of mercenary treason.
Oh, shame! Of horror newly found!
The janissars burst in, appalling
Like beasts, the impious blows are falling . . .
And slaughtered lies the miscreant crowned.

Henceforward, rulers, know this true:
That neither blandishments nor halters
Make trusty buttresses for you,
Nor dungeon walls, nor sacred altars.
Be ye the first to bow you down
Beneath Law's canopy eternal:
The people's bliss and freedom vernal
Will keep forever safe your crown.

◆◆◆

TO CHAADAEV[1]   [1818]

Love, hope, our private fame we banished
As fond illusions soon dismissed,
And Youth's serene pursuits have vanished
Like dreamy wisps of morning mist;
Yet 'neath the fateful yoke that bows us
One burning wish will not abate:
With mutinous soul we still await
Our Fatherland to call and rouse us.
In transports of impatient anguish
For sacred Liberty we thrill,
No less than a young lover will
Yearn for the promised tryst and languish.
While yet with Freedom's spark we burn
And Honor's generous devotion,
On our dear country let us turn
Our fervent spirit's fine emotion!
Believe, my friend: Russia will rise,
A joyous, dazzling constellation,
Will leap from sleep to life and fame;
On tyranny's stark wreck the nation
Will write for evermore our name!

◆◆◆

TO THE AUTHOR OF
HISTORY OF THE RUSSIAN STATE[1]   [1818]

In his *Historia* are proved and pointed out
With grace, simplicity, and judgment fair and cool,
The timeless need for autocratic rule
     And the charms of the knout.

◆◆◆

HISTORY OF A VERSIFIER   [1818]

He catches with accustomed ear a
    Tweet;
Bedabbles single-mindedly the
    Sheet;
Recites to settle everybody's
    Hash;
Then publishes, and into Lethe
    Splash!

IN THE COUNTRY   [1819]

I bid thee welcome, o, sequestered nook,
Refuge of quietude, of toil and inspiration,
Wherein my days meander like an unseen brook,
    Sunk in oblivious elation,
I'm thine—I have exchanged those shameful Circe's yokes,
Luxurious merriment, carousal, dissipation,
For the quiescent fields, the peace of murmurous oaks,
For heedless idleness, the friend of inspiration.

    I'm thine—I love this garden hush,
    To bloom and morning cool allotted,
This pasture green, by fragrant hayricks dotted,
Where in the glades and spinneys freshets gleam and rush.
The scene before my gaze abounds in lively graces:
On this side twofold lakes extend their azure spaces
Where every now and then a fisher's sail will shine,
Behind them quilted fields and rows of hillocks swelling,
    And farther, here and there a dwelling,
On luscious water-meadows wandering herds of kine,
Mills with their wings spread, drying-sheds with smoke-plumes
                    welling,
    Toil and content displaying sign on sign . . .

Here, freed from bonds of idle fuss and clutter,
I teach myself to taste of bliss without a flaw,
With spirit truly unconstrained to worship law,
To pay no heed to the untutored rabble's mutter,
With fellow-feeling to respond to bashful pleas,
     And not to grudge their fated ease
To fool or evildoer in their ill-got grandeur.

   Oracles of the ages, here I question you!
     In solemn and secluded splendor
     Your solace rings more clear and true.
     Sloth's sullen slumber is forsaken,
     To toil my ardent senses leap,
     And your creative thoughts awaken
     To ripeness in the spirit's deep.

But then a daunting thought casts gloom on mankind's lover:
     'Mid flowering crops and slopes
At every step his soul is saddened to discover
The infamy of ignorance that blights all hopes.
     Purblind to tears, deaf to entreaty,
    By destiny ordained for man's distress,
A barbarous barondom, devoid of law or pity,
By usurpation and the knout of ruthlessness
Preys on the peasant's goods and time and hardship.
Bent to a ploughshare not its own, subdued by rods,
Here hollow-chested servitude in furrows plods
     For an inexorable lordship.
Here all drag on the ponderous yoke unto the tomb,
Their souls too crushed to nourish hope or aspiration,
     Here in their freshness maidens bloom
    But for some brute's capricious inclination.
The dear support that every aging father craves,
His adolescent sons, companions of his labors,
Go from the native cabin but to join their neighbors
And swell the rosters of exhausted manor slaves.
Ah, that my voice could quicken hearts to indignation!
Wherefore into my breast were idle embers cast
Not to be bursting into fierce heroic blast?
Shall I behold, friends, an unshackled population,

And serfdom overthrown by an imperial hand?
Will there be ushered forth unto our fatherland
  A lovely dawn of liberty at last?

SECLUSION   [1819]

Blest he who in secluded leisure,
Far from the numskull's brazen ways,
Between hard work and slothful pleasure,
Old thoughts, new hopes, divides his days;
Whose friends by kindly fate were chosen
So as to save him, lucky pup,
Both from the bore that sends you dozing,
And from the boor that wakes you up.

TO A. B.   [1819]

What can I quickly say in verse to greet her?
  Set by the truth, all must be lame.
Well, unprepared I'll say there's no one sweeter;
  Well, and prepared I'll say the same.

EPIGRAM   [1821]

Prince G. is not aware of me; and I
Have never known a mix of such ingredients:
He's blended of conceit and vile expedience,
Conceit much overmatched by what is vile.
In hostels boor, in battle lines poltroon,
In antechambers cad, in drawing-rooms baboon.

◆◆◆

[1821]

I have outlasted all desire,
My dreams and I have grown apart;
My grief alone is left entire,
The gleanings of an empty heart.

The storms of ruthless dispensation
Have struck my flowery garland numb—
I live in lonely desolation
And wonder when my end will come.

Thus on a naked tree-limb, blasted
By tardy winter's whistling chill,
A single leaf which has outlasted
Its season will be trembling still.

◆◆◆

THE DAGGER   [1821]

By Lemnos'[1] god, avenging knife,
For deathless Nemesis wast fashioned,

The secret sentinel of Freedom's threatened life,
The final arbiter of rape and shame impassioned.

Where Zeus's thunder sleeps, the sword of law is drowsing,
    Thou art executor of curse and hope,
        In wait within the throne room's housing,
        Beneath the gleam of festive cope.

    Like Hades' ray, Jove's bolt, the villain sees
The silent steel flash in his eye and quiver,
        That makes him look behind and shiver
            Amidst his revelries.

For everywhere thy blade will carve a sudden path,
On land, upon the seas, in temple or in tavern,
        Thrice-guarded strong-room, hidden cavern,
        Upon his couch, by his own hearth.

Forbidden Rubicon[2] has suffered Caesar's tread,
Majestic Rome succumbed, the law inclined its head;
        But Brutus righted Freedom's damage:
You struck down Caesar—and he staggered, dead,
        Against great Pompey's haughty image.

The hordes of grim rebellion raise their outcry hoarse,
        Detested, black of visage, sanguine,
        Arose the misbegotten hangman
        On slaughtered Freedom's headless corse.

Henchman of death, to wearied Hades he
        With thumb-signs victims indicated,
        But a supreme tribunal fated
        For him the Eumenids[3] and thee.

Oh, righteous youth, the Fates' appointed choice,
        Oh, Sand,[4] you perished on the scaffold;
        But from your martyred dust the voice
        Of holy virtue speaks unmuffled.

In your own Germany a shadow you became
   That grants to lawless force no haven—
   And on your solemn tomb ungraven
   There glows a dagger for a name.

◆◆◆

CHRIST IS RISEN   [1821]

My sweet Rebecca, Christ is risen!
This Easter Day, devoutly true
To our Messiah's catechism,
I share this kiss, my heart, with you.
If more are reaped by rites archaic,
Tomorrow I will turn Mosaic,
So help me, and regret it not—
I'll even offer you that spot
By which one tells the true Hebraic
Believer from the other lot.

◆◆◆

NAPOLEON   [1821]

A wondrous fate is now fulfilled,
Extinguished a majestic man.
In somber prison night was stilled
Napoleon's grim, tumultous span.
The outlawed potentate has vanished,
Bright Nike's mighty, pampered son;
For him, from all Creation banished,
Posterity has now begun.

O hero, with whose bloodied story
Long, long the earth will still resound,

Sleep in the shadow of your glory,
The desert ocean all around . . .
A tomb of rock, in splendor riding!
The urn that holds your mortal clay,
As tribal hatreds are subsiding,
Now sends aloft a deathless ray.

How recently your eagles glowered
Atop a disenfranchised world,
And fallen sovereignties cowered
Beneath the thunderbolts you hurled!
Your banners at a word would shower
Destruction from their folds and dearth,
Yoke after yoke of ruthless power
You fitted on the tribes of earth.

When first from ancient serfdom's languor
The world awoke to hope new-grown,
And Gaul hauled down with hands of anger
The idol from its brittle throne;
When on the milling square in gory
Collapse the royal carcase lay
And brought the fated day of glory,
All-conquering freedom's shining day—

Then in the storm and strife of nations
An awesome lot you soon divined,
And nobleminded aspirations
You came to scorn in humankind.
The baneful augury of fortune
Would beckon to your lawless bent,
To self-rule unrestrained importune
The lure of disillusionment.

The risen people's youthful vigor
You knew to dissipate at length,
And liberty new-born, by rigor
Abruptly muzzled, lost its strength;
You poured, to slake the lust of chattel,
The drug of conquest in their veins,

You sped their musters into battle
And laurels wound about their chains.

France came to fasten her besotted
Young countenance—a slave to fame,
And grandeur's finer hopes forgotten—
Upon her scintillating shame.
You gorged her swords in the undoing
Of all who rose against their doom;
On Europe, brought to crashing ruin,
Now fell the silence of the tomb.

Lo, the colossus strode to crush her
Beneath his heel with baleful zest;
Then Tilsit! . . (but no more has Russia
At that vile name to beat her breast.)
True, Tilsit yielded him new treasure
Of majesty, a final toll;
But tedious peace, but torpid leisure
Galled that insatiable soul.

Vainglorious man! Where were you faring,
Who blinded that astounding mind?
How came it in designs of daring
The Russian's heart was not divined?
At fiery sacrifice not guessing,
You idly fancied, tempting fate,
We would seek peace and count it blessing;
You came to fathom us too late . . .

Fight on, embattled Russia mine,
Recall the rights of ancient days!
The sun of Austerlitz, decline!
And Moscow, mighty city, blaze!
Brief be the time of our dishonor,
The auspices are turning now;
Hail Moscow—Russia's blessings on her!
War to extinction, thus our vow!

The diadem of iron[1] shaking
In stiffened fingers' feeble clasp,
He stares into a chasm, quaking,
And is undone, undone at last.
Behold all Europe's legions sprawling . . .
The wintry fields' encrimsoned glow
Bore testimony to their falling
Till blood-prints melted with the snow.

Then Europe's shackles broke asunder,
Her fury burst like tempest racks;
The curse of nationhoods like thunder
Rolled on the fleeing tyrant's tracks.
He sees the Nemesis of nations,
Her all-avenging hand up-flung;
For maiming wounds and depredations
Now payment to the full is wrung.

Redeemed are now the blights and horrors
He spread with fabled victories
By the forsaken exile's sorrows
Amidst the gloom of alien seas.
At that dry isle of desolation
Some day a northern sail will dock,
And words of reconciliation
A hand will carve upon that rock

Where, as he watched the breakers' glitter,
The glint of swords would catch his glance,
Or northern blizzards, blinding, bitter,
Or clouds across the skies of France;
Where in the wilderness, forgetting
War and posterity and throne,
On his dear son he brooded, fretting,
In grievous thought, alone, alone.

Let us hold up to reprobation
Such petty-minded men as chose
With unappeasable damnation
To stir his laurel-dark repose!

Hail him! He launched the Russian nation
Upon its lofty destinies
And augured ultimate salvation
For man's long-exiled liberties.

◆◆◆

TO OVID   [1821]

Ovidius, I live not far from that still shore
To which you, banished here, brought centuries before
Exiled paternal Lares, and where you left your ashes. [1]
Your unconsoled lament has made these places precious;
Your lyre's caressing voice has not been silenced yet;
The region still resounds with you and your regret.
You roam, as if alive, in my imagination
This gloomy emptiness, the poet's desolation,
The heaven's misty vault, the ever-present snows,
The meads which grudging thaws but fleetingly disclose.
How often, beckoned by your grieving strings anew,
My heart has been abroad, my Ovid, trailing you!
I saw your galley heave, by sporting breakers tossed,
I saw your anchor cast off this ungentle coast
Which loured to pay the singer loving's harsh reward,
Hills that no grapes, crops that no shade afford;
Engendered in the snows for cruelty of arms,
There frozen Scythia's sons in ever ready swarms
Are crouched in ambush just beyond the Dniestr's water
To rake the settlements with random raid and slaughter.
No hindrance can withstand their daring and device,
They brave the swirling flood, they cross the ringing ice.
You, Naso, [2] marvel too how strangely fate has turned:
You, who from boyhood up the craft of weapons spurned,
Who was accustomed once to braid your hair with flowers
And pass in mellow ease uncounted carefree hours,
Now to go helmeted and, iron-clad entire,
To keep the fearsome sword next to the bashful lyre!

Here neither wife nor child, companions' faithful ring,
Nor muses, light-o-loves of former dallying,
Surround you still to soothe the banished singer's grief.
In vain did Graces crown your verse with laurel leaf,
In vain do youths and maids by heart recite them still:
For neither fame nor age, nor plaints and sadness will,
Nor timid verse, avail to wear Octavian[3] down;
In deep forgetfulness your dim old age must drown.
Aureate Italy's luxurious citizen,
On that barbarian coast alone, unknown to men,
Long out of hearing now of sounds of native speech,
Heavy of heart you write to friends far out of reach:
"O friends, restore me to our fathers' sacred city,
Ancestral gardens' shade return to me, for pity!
Oh carry to Augustus, friends, my meek imploring,
The castigating hand, stay it with tears outpouring!
But should the demigod be proved relentless still,
And while I live, great Rome denied me by his will,
Then let dread fate be dulled by yet a final plea:
My grave at least be close to lovely Italy!"
Whose frozen heart, poetic graces scorning,
Would dare upbraid your plaints, your bitter tears of mourning?
What swelled-up crudity could listen quite unstirred
To those pure elegies, last of your songs we heard,
       Where you bequeathed to time the moan that found no ears?

Myself, hardbitten Slav, I did not shed such tears;
I understood them, though; exiled for self-will vented,
With world of men, myself, existence discontented,
I visited, my soul in meditative mood,
The land where you endured your dolorous solitude.
Here, by your image first new-quickened fancy granted,
I sang, Ovidius, afresh the songs you chanted,
And came to find them true, those landscapes of your grief.
I had my mind beguiled by dreams which make belief;
That banishment of yours must have beshrewed my sight
Accustomed still to snows, septentrional night.
For here with longer glow celestial azure warms;
Here only briefly reigns the wrath of winter storms.
Here on the Scythian slopes a recent graft, the luscious

Fosterling of the south, the grape, in purple blushes.
By now on Russian meadows rough December squalls
Have showered blanketings of snow in fluffy shawls.
A scintillating sun here circles overhead;
There winter blights the air—in vernal warmth instead
Here withered pasture herb to brilliant greening yields;
The early plough has scored the liberated fields;
A breeze will barely breathe, and cooler grow at dusk,
Ice, on the lake a half-transparent husk,
Beneath its crystal holds unmoving streams confined:
Your timid enterprise recalling to my mind,
That day, by inspiration's rushing pinions marked,
When first, with some distrust, your halting foot embarked
Upon the element benumbed by winter's spell,
And over virgin ice—I seemed to see it well—
Your shade would glide before, and mournful notes intone
That wavered from afar like parting's smothered moan.

Be comforted; unwilting, Ovid's wreath has bloomed!
But I, alas, a bard lost in the crowd, am doomed
To soundlessness, and as this age of men goes by,
A nameless sacrifice, my feeble gift must die
With my sad life and but a murmuring of fame . . .
Yet if a distant scion yet heard of me and came
To search the length and breadth of these forsaken places
Near Ovid's fabled dust for my forgotten traces,
Then from the zone of gloom, oblivion's outer rim,
My grateful shade would rise and fly to welcome him,
And dear to me would be his kindly recognition.
May there live on in men your sanctified tradition:
For sentenced, as were you, to an unpitying lot,
In fate I was your match, albeit in glory not.
Here, livening with lays of north the vacant lands,
I wandered—while on banks of Danube firebrands
Of freedom by the great-souled Greek were hurled—
With not a single friend to hear me in the world.
But meadows, drowsy groves, and hillocks were beguiled
By my outlandish song, and placid muses smiled.

[1821]

I enter now, and not again,
Your chamber, tender one, and ours,
Our love was joy and never pain,
I came to share its final hours.
Henceforth, in lonely languor calling,
Await me not as dark is falling,
Keep not your candle burning bright
Till morning light.

THE TENTH COMMANDMENT   [1821]

To hanker for my neighbor's hoard
You most explicitly forbade me;
You know my limits, though, you made me!
How can I help some feelings, Lord?
I never wish my neighbor harm,
I do not want his land or chattel,
Have no designs upon his cattle;
I see all these with perfect calm.
His house, his ox, his handy man,
I contemplate them unafraid;
But should he have a handy maid
With shapely . . . Lord, I doubt I can!
And should he have a lovely wife,
Fair as an angel, but not flighty,
Forgive my weakness, God Almighty!
I may just envy him his life.
The heart is free; what is it worth
To undertake what can't be done,
Unlove what's loved by everyone,
Not covet paradise on earth?
I look, I yearn, but dare not offer
Defiance to the stern command;

I quash the heart's remonstrance and
Keep silent . . . and in secret suffer.

◆◆◆

EPIGRAM ON A. A. DAVYDOVA[1]   [1822]

One had Agláya by attraction
Of raven curls and martial stance,
One for his money (no objection),
A third because he was from France,
Cleon by dint of being clever,
Damis for tender songs galore;
But, my Agláya, say, whatever
Did your own husband have you for?[2]

◆◆◆

[EPIGRAM]   [1822]

Clarissa has but little wealth;
You're rich—so take her down the aisle.
She'll find that money suits her health;
You'll find that horns are just your style.

◆◆◆

TO A FOREIGN GIRL   [1822]

This valedictory effusion
Pleads in a tongue you do not speak,

And yet for it by fond illusion
Your understanding I would seek.
My dearest, till a pall may smother
These senses while we are apart,
While I can feel, you and no other
Will be the idol of my heart.
On strangers now your gazes bending,
Go on believing just my heart,
As you believed it from the start,
Its passions never comprehending.

A LITTLE BIRD   [1823]

In alien lands devoutly clinging
To age-old rites of Russian earth,
I let a captive bird go winging
To greet the radiant spring's rebirth.

My heart grew lighter then: why mutter
Against God's providence, and rage,
When I was free to set aflutter
But one poor captive from his cage!

NIGHT   [1823]

My murmurous soliloquy of thee oppresses
The hush of midnight with its languorous caresses.
Beside the couch whereon I drowsing lie there glows
A fretful candle, and my verse wells up and flows
Till purling streams of love, full-charged with thee, run through me.

Then, shimmering through the dusk, thy lustrous eyes turn to me,
They smile at me and make a whisper as they shine:
My dearest, tender one . . . my love . . . I'm thine . . . I'm thine.

◆◆◆

[1823]

> *"Forth went the sower to sow his seeds . . . "*

    As freedom's sower in the wasteland
Before the morning star I went;
From hand immaculate and chastened
Into the grooves of prisonment
Flinging the vital seed I wandered—
But it was time and toiling squandered,
Benevolent designs misspent . . .

    Graze on, graze on, submissive nation!
You will not wake to honor's call.
Why offer herds their liberation?
For them are shears or slaughter-stall,
Their heritage each generation
The yoke with jingles, and the gall.

FROM A LETTER TO WIEGEL[1]   [1823]

Ah, Kishinev, you thrice-damned town!
The tongue that curses you grows numb.
Your guilty roofs of filthy brown
Shall feel the Lord's wrath crashing down
One day, and of the whole rank slum

No smallest vestige shall be found!
Those blazes will curl up and fuse
Vile ghettos with Bartholomew's
Bedizened den of ill renown:
Thus, Moses tells us, Sodom fared.
But that engaging citadel
And Kishinev, the sink of hell,
I really should not have compared.
I've read the Bible more than twice,
And never was inclined to flatter.
Sodom was noted in the matter
Not just of amiable vice,
But of enlightenment, carouses,
All sorts of hospitable houses,
And friendly girls of charm and wit!
It was too bad, and still arouses
The blood, that Jahve ruined it.
In sin's bright glamor not unnerved,
A mortal by the Lord preserved,
I humbly might have held my stand
And as His privy councillor served
The Paris of the Bible land!
But Kishinev, we know, has no
Indulgent ladies, and as low
Supply of wenches as of books.—
Which moves me to bemoan your fate!
Who knows if there you still await
At dusk three lads of grace and looks?
In any case, I'll try, my dear,
The moment things allow it here,
To come to see you, and stand by you,
Glad to relieve this sorry pass;
With verses, prose, and comfort ply you,
But mind you, Wiegel—spare my arse!

ON COUNT VORONTSOV[1]   [1824]

One half Milord, one half in trade,
One half a sage, one half a dunce,
One half a crook, but here for once
There's every hope he'll make the grade.

♦♦♦

TO A. N. WULF[1]   [1824]

Be saluted, Wulf, my friend,
Come before the winter's end,
Take the poet on your journey,
Have Yazykov[2] by your side,
We shall take a merry ride,
Have a little pistol tourney.
Lionel, my curly brother
(Not my counting clerk, the other)
Will haul up the stock, you know;
Stock? A hamper of bordeaux!
We shall feast the hours away,
Wondrous life of anchorites,
At Trigorskoe all day,
At Mikhailovskoe nights.
Day will pass by love beglamored
While the beakers reign at night;
We'll be royally enamored
Or imperially tight.

♦♦♦

CONVERSATION BETWEEN BOOKSELLER AND POET
[1824]

Bookseller

You toss off verselets just for pleasure,
You only need sit down a bit;
Great news about your latest treasure!
The town's already full of it.
A poem's ready, runs their prating,
Fresh produce of your nimble wit;
Make up your mind, then, I am waiting,
Put any price you want on it.
The Graces' and the Muses' capers
We change to rubles in a flash,
Your little sheaf of airy papers
Becomes a stack of ready cash.
What was that sigh that you were heaving,
May one inquire?

Poet

              My soul was grieving
As it relived the distant time
When borne aloft in hope's light raiment,
A carefree bard, I used to rhyme
From inspiration, not for payment.
I saw again those rugged views,
The shaded haunts of isolation,
Where banquets of imagination
Used to unite me with the Muse.
More sweetness did my voice diffuse,
More often dazzling apparitions
Of beauty past the reason's ken
Would soar and whirl above me then
At time of night and intuitions! . .
All caused the feeling soul to swoon:
The wind-sough heard in sanctuaries,
A flowering field, a gleaming moon,
A country-woman's tale of fairies.

A kind of demon held in fee
My leisure hours, my merrymaking,
And everywhere it followed me
With whispered spells of poetry;
A heavy throb, a fevered aching
Within the crowded mind it stirred,
And wondrous images engendered,
As to harmonious form surrendered
Obediently word on word,
To be with tuneful rhyming ended.
In cadences my rivals were
The rustling forest, gale-winds whirling,
The oriole's vivacious note,
At night the ocean's rumbling rote,
A whispering freshet's quiet purling.
Enraptured thus, I would refuse
To have my silent toil invaded
By crowds; the bounty of the Muse
At marts of shame I never traded
But used to husband it and hide.
Exactly so with wordless pride
Secretes the superstitious lover
The love-gifts of his youthful bride
For others never to uncover.

Bookseller

But fame has ousted pride and banned
The privacy of secret dreams:
You have been passed from hand to hand,
While other authors' dusty reams
Of slightly shopworn prose and verses
In vain implore the readers purses
And glory's swift inconstant beams.

Poet

Blest who could give his mind's play room
Within his mind without recital,
And not to men nor yet the tomb

Looked for an echo or requital!
Blest is the mute bard who, by fame
As little martyred as by cavil,
Forgotten by the paltry rabble,
Forsook this world without a name!
More false than hope by dreams engendered,
What is renown? A reader's glance?
The hue-and-cry of ignorance?
Or homage by an idiot tendered?

Bookseller

Lord Byron voiced a like impatience,
Zhukovsky[1] used to say the same,
Yet men bought up and brought acclaim
To their melodious creations.
Come—enviable is your lot:
The poet crowns, or hurls contempt
At the transgressor and his plot,
Whom then late ages won't exempt.
The noble hero he consoles,
Next to Corinna[2] he extolls
His love onto the throne of Venus.
To you, acclaim is something heinous,
But fame appeals to ladies' souls;
To them write verses: such a hearer
Is flattered by Anacreon;
For roses to the young are dearer
Than laurels plucked on Helicon.

Poet

Bah—self-indulgent dreams, the poultice
Of youth in its deluded strife!
I too composed for beauty's notice
Amid the storm and stress of life.
Bewitching beauties have perused me
With eyes in which enchantment smiled,
And speeches sweet to hear have soothed me
From lips that flattered and beguiled.

Enough! No more the dreamer brings
His freedom there for sacrifice;
Let madrigals of youths suffice,
Kind nature's pampered fosterlings.
I take no part. In lonely hush
My life meanders on, unspeaking,
My true lyre's plaint no longer seeking
Against those flighty minds to brush.
Impure is their imagination,
We do not come within its range;
The mark of godhead, inspiration,
To them is laughable and strange.
When on my memory impinges
A line of verse inspired by them,
I flush with shame and reason cringes,
My former idols I contemn.
For what, poor bungler, have I striven?
To whom the lofty mind enslaved?
Of whom has my pure fancy raved,
To ignominious worship driven?

Bookseller

Great stuff! I like the way you fume.
I cannot guess why you're so tender,
But some among the charming gender
You do exempt, I may presume?
Is not a single one a dram's
Romance or inspiration worth?
Not one who tames your dithyrambs
By loveliness not of this earth?
You will not say?

Poet
                    Why with such babble
The poet's troubled sleep profane?
He flogs his memory in vain.
And how would it concern the rabble?
I live estranged. Who cares if this
Locked heart holds unforgotten pictures,

If it has tasted of love's bliss,
If by relentless bleak self-strictures
Were silent tears in secret shriven?..
Where is the one whose eyes of blue
Once smiled at me like very heaven,
Whom, all my life, two nights I knew?

. . . .

And so? Love's tedious threnody,
My words, will always seem to me
A madman's incoherent stammer.
One heart out there may pay them heed,
And that but with a mournful tremor.
Thus fate has once for all decreed.
The thought of her, for me departed,
Might have revitalized my soul
And live poetic fancies started
As bountifully as of old.
She would have held the wand divining
The treasures in my clouded themes,
Have kindled up her heart to shining
With love's intense and limpid beams.
Ah, idle yearnings, old frustration!
She spurned the toll of adoration,
And sad entreaty's, silent awe's;
No earthly worshipper's libation
Could move her, goddess that she was! . .

Bookseller

So, as from love, you now retire
From speech and call it needless prattle,
Withdrawing from the poets' battle
Ahead of time your gifted lyre.
The fads of style you sacrifice,
The muses, and the crowd's attendance;
What do you choose then?

Poet

                    Independence.

Bookseller

Superb. But here is my advice,
May useful truth find careful hearer:
Ours is a mercenary era,
And independence pays a price.
What's fame? A patch of many colors
Upon the singer's faded rags.
We go for dollars, dollars, dollars,
So rake in lucre, bags and bags!
I'll meet your standard protestation,
You gentlemen are all the same;
I know your sort and what you claim:
You cherish your detached creation
While on your labor's steady flame
Wells up and seethes imagination.
But time will cool it, and the same
Will happen to your composition.
Excuse me if I bluntly say
They will not buy your intuition,
It is for manuscripts they pay.
Why hesitate? Impatient readers
Already crowd about my shelves;
With journalists, "opinion leaders,"
Come in the hungry bards themselves.
Some seek here nourishment for satire,
Some for the soul, some for the pen;
I must confess I hope your lyre
May strum up lots of trade again.

Poet

You're absolutely right. Here, take my manuscript.
We are in business.

◆◆◆

TO THE SEA   [1824]

Farewell to you, unharnessed Ocean!
No longer will you roll at me
Your azure swells in endless motion
Or gleam in tranquil majesty.

A comrade's broken words on leaving,
His hail of parting at the door:
Your chant of luring, chant of grieving
Will murmur in my ears no more.

O homeland of my spirit's choosing!
How often on your banks at large
I wandered mute and dimly musing,
Fraught with a sacred, troubling charge!

How I would love your deep resounding,
The primal chasm's muffled voice,
How in your vesper calm rejoice,
And in your sudden, reckless bounding!

The fisher's lowly canvas slips,
By your capricious favor sheltered,
Undaunted down your breakers' lips:
Yet by your titan romps have weltered
And foundered droves of masted ships.

Alas, Fate thwarted me from weighing
My anchor off the cloddish shore,
Exultantly your realm surveying,
And by your drifting ridges laying
My poet's course forevermore.

You waited, called . . . I was in irons,
And vainly did my soul rebel,
Becalmed in those uncouth environs
By passion's overpowering spell.

Yet why this sorrow? Toward what fastness
Would now my carefree sails be spread?
To one lone goal in all your vastness
My spirit might have gladly sped.

One lonely cliff, the tomb of glory . . .
There chilling slumber fell upon
The ghost of mankind's proudest story:
There breathed his last Napoleon.

There rest for suffering he bartered;
And gale-borne in his wake, there streams
Another kingly spirit martyred,
Another regent of our dreams.[1]

He passed, and left to Freedom mourning,
His laurels to Eternity.
Arise, roar out in stormy warning:
He was your own true bard, o Sea!

His soul was by your spirit haunted,
In your own image was he framed:
Like you, immense, profound, undaunted,
Like you, nocturnal and untamed.

Bereft the world . . . where by your power,
O Sea, would you now carry me?
Life offers everywhere one dower:
On any glint of bliss there glower
Enlightenment or tyranny.

Farewell then, Sea! Henceforth in wonder
Your regal grace will I revere;
Long will your muffled twilit thunder
Reverberate within my ear.

To woods and silent wildernesses
Will I translate your potent spells,
Your cliffs, your coves, your shining tresses,
Your shadows and your murmurous swells.

[1824]

Rose-maiden, no, I do not quarrel
With these dear chains, they don't demean:
The nightingale embushed in laurel,
The sylvan singers' feathered queen,
Does she not bear the same sweet plight,
Near the proud rose's beauty dwelling,
And with her tender anthems thrilling
The dusk of a voluptuous night?

THE GRAPE   [1824]

No, not by fleeting roses saddened
That passing spring will fade and kill,
By clustered grapes will I be gladdened
That ripen on the sloping hill,
On my fair vale delight bestowing,
The golden autumn's richest pearl,
As supply-tapered, freshly-glowing
As fingers of a sweet young girl.

[1824]

Liza is afraid to love.
Or could this be just her fashion?
What if Dian's not above
Keeping dark her taste for passion?
Downcast lids, might they at all
Hide sly glances, holding wily

Muster of us, searching shyly
Which of us might help her fall?

◆◆◆

CLEOPATRA[1]   [1824]

Queen Cleopatra with her gazes
And voice adorned her splendid feast.
Exalting with a choir of praises
The chosen idol of the East,
Thronged to her throne the pleasure-seekers;
When all at once she stooped, and so
Fell still among the golden beakers,
Her wondrous forehead drooping low.

The rich assembly, never shifting,
Stands silently as in a daze . . .
Until the Queen announces, lifting
Her brow again, with solemn gaze:
"Hear me! This day it is my pleasure
To make us equals in my sight.
To you my love were highest blessing;
But you may buy this bliss to-night.
Behold the market-place of passion!
For sale I offer nights divine;
Who dares to barter in this fashion
His life against one night of mine?

Thus her decree. All breath abating,
The strange and stirring challenge looms.
Soon Cleopatra, coldly waiting,
With calm audacity resumes:
"Why are you silent? I am ready;
Or shall I see you all take flight?
Not few are here whose dreams were heady . . .
Come, purchase an enchanting night!"

Her haughty glances scan the verges
Of her admirers' silent throng . . .
There! of a sudden one emerges,
Two others follow soon along.
Their step is firm, their gaze unclouded.
The queen arises in her pride.
Three nights are bought: the couch is shrouded
For deadly pleasures at her side.

Once more they heard the Queen's imperious voice resound:
"Let none remember now I was in purple crowned!
I shall ascend the couch but as a common whore,
To serve thee, Lady Love, as no one has before,
And vow my nights' reward a novel gift to thee.
O awesome deities of Hades, hearken me,
Ye melancholy kings of nether realms forlorn!
Receive ye this my pledge: unto the languid dawn
I promise to obey my rulers' utmost wishes
With wondrous tenderness, strange arts, the deep, delicious
Cup ever newly filled with love's entrancing wine . . .
But when into my chamber through the curtains shine
Young Eos' early rays—I swear by your grim shade
Their heads shall fall that morn beneath the headsman's blade!"

By holy augury each sanctified in turn,
The lots assigned the three now issue from the urn:
First Archilaios' lot, of Pompey's noble guard,
Gone gray in his campaigns, in combat hewn and scarred.
His consort's chill disdain resolved to bear no more,
He haughtily stepped forth, the sombre son of war,
To heed the fateful lure, the last sweet test of mettle,
As earlier he had the glory-notes of battle.
Crito was second drawn, Crito the gentle sage
      Who, reared beneath the sky of Argolis,
Had glowing tribute paid, since barely come of age,
To Bacchus' fiery feasts, the Cyprid's fiery kiss.
The third one's name remains by annals unrecorded;
Unknown to all, unmarked, he would embrace his doom,
A downy youth as yet whose beard but faintly bordered
      His tender cheek with bashful bloom.

With love's consuming fire his eyes now gleamed,
For Cleopatra meant his very life, it seemed;
And long and silently the Queen rejoiced in him.

. . . .
[Uncompleted]

◆◆◆

[1825]

When first the roses wither,
Their breath ambrosia yields,
Their airy souls fly thither
To the Elysian fields.

And there, where waters vagrant
Oblivion bear and dreams,
Their shadows honey-fragrant
Bloom over Lethe's streams.

◆◆◆

EX UNGUE LEONEM   [1825]

One day I flicked my whip-o'-verse a little
And let the thing go out without my name;
Some scribbler pounced on it with ink and spittle
And had them print his piece unsigned, for shame.
Oh, Lord! The hack or I had never reckoned
That our generic marks gave us away:
He knew me by my talons in a second,
I knew him in an instant by his bray.

◆◆◆

TO . . .   [1825]

I recollect that wondrous meeting,
That instant I encountered you,
When like an apparition fleeting,
Like beauty's spirit, past you flew.

Long since, when hopeless grief distressed me,
When noise and turmoil vexed, it seemed
Your voice still tenderly caressed me,
Your dear face sought me as I dreamed.

Years passed; their stormy gusts confounded
And swept away old dreams apace.
I had forgotten how you sounded,
Forgot the heaven of your face.

In exiled gloom and isolation
My quiet days meandered on,
The thrill of awe and inspiration,
And life, and tears, and love, were gone.

My soul awoke from inanition,
And I encountered you anew,
And like a fleeting apparation,
Like beauty's spirit, past you flew.

My pulses bound in exultation,
And in my heart once more unfold
The sense of awe and inspiration,
The life, the tears, the love of old.

◆◆◆

WINTER EVENING   [1825]

Storm has set the heavens scowling,
Whirling gusty blizzards wild,
Now they are like beasts a-growling,
Now a-wailing like a child;
Now along the brittle thatches
They will scud with rustling sound,
Now against the window latches
Like belated wanderers pound.

Our frail hut is glum and sullen,
Dim with twilight and with care.
Why, dear granny, have you fallen
Silent by the window there?
Has the gale's insistent prodding
Made your drowsing senses numb,
Are you lulled to gentle nodding
By the whirling spindle's hum?

Let us drink for grief, let's drown it,
Comrade of my wretched youth,
Where's the jar? Pour out and down it,
Wine will make us less uncouth.
Sing me of the tomtit hatching
Safe beyond the ocean blue,
Sing about the maiden fetching
Water at the morning dew.

Storm has set the heavens scowling,
Whirling gusty blizzards wild,
Now they sound like beasts a-growling,
Now a-wailing like a child.
Let us drink for grief, let's drown it,
Comrade of my wretched youth,
Where's the jar? Pour out and down it,
Wine will make us less uncouth.

[1825]

What if life deceives and baits you,
Never bridle, never grieve!
Bide the dismal day, believe
That a day of joy awaits you.

By the future lives the heart;
And if dreary be the present,
All is fleeting, will depart,
And departed, will be pleasant.

◆◆◆

BACCHIC SONG   [1825]

Who laid our gay revel to rest?
Resound, bacchanalian cadence!
A toast to the amorous maidens
And tender young lovelies who loved us the best!
    Pour full every glass to the edges!
        The bottoms shall sing
        With rings that we fling
    In rich wine as our reverent pledges!
Up beakers as one, and a flourish in season!
Salute to the Muses, salute to man's reason!
    Thou holiest sun, be aglow!
    As this candelabrum has faded
    Before the bright dawn, even so
Shall flicker and die every sophistry jaded
    At reason's unperishing spark.
Salute to the sunrise, and vanish the dark!

◆◆◆

[1825]

The season's final blossoms bring
More dear delight than buds of spring.
They stir in us a live communion
Of sorrowfully poignant dreams.
Thus oft the hour of parting seems
More vivid than a sweet reunion.

TEMPEST   [1825]

You saw perched on a cliff a maid,
Her raiment white above the breakers,
When the mad sea reared up and played
Its whips of spray on coastal acres
And now and then the lightnings flush,
And purple gleams upon her hover,
And fluttering up in swirling rush,
The wind rides in her airy cover?
Fair is the sea in gales arrayed,
The heavens drained of blue and flashing,
But fairer on her cliff the maid
Than storms and skies and breakers crashing.

TO FRIENDS   [1825]

My foes—just for the nonce I may seem frozen,
And my quick wrath extinguished like a light;
But you have not escaped my field of sight,

Someone, some day, will all at once be chosen:
He shan't evade my penetrating claws
When for my swift, relentless swoop I picked him.
Thus the fierce hawk **marks** hen and goose for victim
As in the clouds his hazy rounds he draws.

PROSE AND POETRY   [1825]

Why, writer, toil with plodding prose?
Give me whatever thought you chose:
To pointed sharpness I will edge it.
With wingèd meters will I fledge it,
Will fit it to the tautened thew,
And bending my obedient bow,
Will send it flashing far and true,
And woe betide our common foe!

[1825]

You're the kind that always loses,
Bliss and you are all at odds:
You're too sweet when chance refuses
And too clever when it nods.

♦♦♦

[1825]

O Muse of satire, breathing fire!
Oh, come and heed my urgent call!
I do not need the thundering lyre,
Hand me the scourge of Juvenal!
Not the pedestrian imitators,
Not the penurious translators,
Nor rhymesters echoless, poor lambs,
Shall fester from my epigrams!
Peace to the poet wan with hunger,
Peace to the journals' gossipmonger.
Peace unto every harmless fool!
But as for you, my scoundrels cool,
Come forward! I shall surely hook one,
Hook all you scum with piercing pen,
And if by chance I overlook one,
Please do remind me, gentlemen!
Ah, mugs with sallow slander horrid,
Ah, forehead after brazen forehead,
All due from my avenging hand
The ineradicable brand!

TO VYAZEMSKY   [1825]

Stuck in the sticks, my life a bore,
I suffer from pernicious sloth;
I vegetate in lenten cloth,
A hawk in moult who cannot soar.

Estranged from every muse, on masses
Of virgin paper I am treed;
I never visit Mt. Parnassus
Except in case of urgent need.

And yet your artful excrement
Intrigues my nose; its pleasing scent
Puts me in mind of old Khvostov,
Whose doves were bred with stinging beaks;
My spirit strains and would be off
To take its customary leaks.

ON ALEXANDER I   [1825]

Reared as he was to drum and banner
Our Emperor was no mean commander:
At Austerlitz ran out of breath,
In Eighteen-Twelve was scared to death,
(Albeit a fair frontline professor).
The front, though, proved unpicturesque...
Now he's collegiate assessor
Behind some Foreign Office desk.

[1826]

Beneath the azure heaven of her native land
    She gently languished, gently faded . . .
She waned away at last and her young shade has fanned
    Its wings o'er me, I am persuaded;
Between us, though, a secret gulf has come to be.
    In vain I sought a sense of sharing:
Words from uncaring lips announced her death to me,
    And I took note of it uncaring.
So this was she whom I had loved with heart on fire,
    With strain of passion unto sadness,

With such slow ache of languishing desire,
    With such long agony, such madness!
Where is my pain, where is my love? Alas, my soul
    Relives those sweet dead days no longer;
It pays that luckless, all too trustful shade no toll,
    Be it of tears, be it of anger.

◆◆◆

TO VYAZEMSKY   [1826]

So Ocean, man-devourer strident,
Has fanned your genius with fire?
You serenade with golden lyre
Hoar Neptune's awe-inspiring trident.

Recant! Our age's savage bent
Has allied earth and Neptune wizened.
Man is in every element
Tyrant or traitor or imprisoned.

◆◆◆

TO YAZYKOV   [1826]

Yazykov, tell us from what source
Wells up your word of wild elation,
Now sweet, now like a gamboling horse,
Abrim with feeling, reckless force,
And young impulsive exaltation!
No—not Castalia's limpid blue
Has fed the notes of your Camoena,[1]
A vastly different Hippocrene[2]
Did Pegasus strike forth for you:

Not cooling waters calmly pouring,
With turbid ale afroth and soaring,
It's potent stuff and highly strung,
Like that new potion nobly rounded,
From rum and wine conjointly sprung,
With water's vileness uncompounded,
Which at Trigorsk our thirst unbounded
Revealed to us when we were young.

◆◆◆

CONFESSION   [1826]

I love you—though I rage at it,
Though it is shame and toil misguided,
And to my folly self-derided
Here at your feet I will admit!
It ill befits my years, my station,
Good sense has long been overdue!
And yet, by every indication,
Love's plague has stricken me anew:
You're out of sight—I fall to yawning;
You're here—I suffer and feel blue,
And barely keep myself from owning,
Dear elf, how much I care for you!
Why, when your guileless girlish chatter
Drifts from next door, your airy tread,
Your rustling dress, my senses scatter
And I completely lose my head.
You smile—I flush with exultation;
You turn away—I'm plunged in gloom,
Your pallid hand is compensation
For a whole day of fancied doom.
When to the frame with artless motion
You bend to cross-stitch, all devotion,
Your eyes and ringlets down-beguiled,
My heart goes out in mute emotion,

Rejoicing in you like a child!
Dare I confess to you my sighing,
How jealously I chafe and balk
When you set forth, at times defying
Bad weather, on a lengthy walk?
And then your solitary crying,
Those twosome whispers out of sight,
Your carriage to Opochka plying,
And the piano late at night . . .
Aline! I ask but to be pitied,
I do not dare to plead for love;
Love, for the sins I have committed,
I am perhaps unworthy of.
But make believe! Your gaze, dear elf,
Is fit to conjure with, believe me!
Ah, it is easy to deceive me! . . .
I long to be deceived myself!

TO . . .   [1826]

You're the Madonna—no confusion,
Though, with the one whose charm at most
Sufficed to snare the Holy Ghost,
You're dear to all, without exclusion;
Not she who managed Jesus' birth
Without her husband's intercession.
There is another god, on earth,
And Beauty dwells in his possession;
By him I ache, am soothed—like Moore,
Parny, Tibullus, many another.
He looks like you—you're Eros' mother,
You the Madonna I adore!

TO I. I. PUSHCHIN[1]   [1826]

My oldest friend, companion peerless!
I too blessed fate when far up north
In my retreat remote and cheerless,
Adrift in dismal snow, so fearless
Your little sleigh bell tinkled forth.

Now providential dispensation
Grant that my voice may bless, I pray,
Your soul with equal consolation,
And bear into your prison station
Of bright Lyceum days a ray!

◆◆◆

STANZAS[1]   [1826]

In hopes of fame and bliss to come
I gaze ahead with resolution;
The dawn of Peter's sun was glum
With turmoil and with execution.

But he used truth to conquer hearts,
Enlightenment to soften manners;
He honored Dolgoruki's[2] arts
Above wild janissaries' banners.

He with a sovereign's fearless hand
Lit page on page of learning's story;
He did not spurn our native land,
Aware of its predestined glory.

He was now sage, now hero-king,
Now wright, now mate, as might determine
His spirit all-encompassing—
Eternal craftsman born to ermine.

Hold, then, your kin in proud regard,
Your life in all to his comparing,
Unflagging be like him, and hard,
And like him, of resentment sparing.

◆◆◆

TO THE EMPEROR NICHOLAS I   [1826?]

He was made emperor, and right then
Displayed his flair and drive:
Sent to Siberia a hundred-twenty men
And strung up five.

◆◆◆

WINTER JOURNEY[1]   [1826]

Brightly from its watery swathing
Sallies forth the lunar horn,
Yonder mournful clearings bathing
In its mournful light forlorn.

Down the dismal snow-track swinging
Speeds the troika, and the drone
Of the sleigh-bell's tuneless ringing
Numbs me with its monotone.

Something stirring, something drowsing
Haunts the coachman's singsong too,
Chanting now of wild carousing,
Now of lovers' plaintive rue.

No black hut, no hearth-light sparkling,
Snow and desolation reign,
Mileposts only flash their darkling
Stripes and hurry past and wane.

Waste and gloom . . . but back tomorrow,
By your chimney, love, at will
Shall I muse, forget all sorrow,
Gaze, and never gaze my fill.

When the clock's unhurried finger
Rounds its beat and strikes adieu,
Bidding strangers not to linger,
Midnight will not part us two.

Cheerless, love, the sleigh bell's ringing,
Drear my path across the fen,
Stilled the coachman's drowsy singing,
Dim the watery moon again.

THREE SPRINGS   [1827]

In this world's wasteland, borderless and bitter,
Three springs have broken forth with secret force:
The spring of youth, abubble and aglitter,
Wells up and runs its swift and murmurous course.
Castalia's spring of flow divine is letting
In this world's wasteland exiles drink their fill.
The last, cool spring, the spring of all-forgetting,
Will slake the burning heart more sweetly still.

♦♦♦

ARION   [1827]

We sailed in numerous company.
A few of us drew fast the sheeting,
The rest with mighty oar were beating
The brine; while, calm on slumbrous sea,
Our skillful helmsman clasped the rudder
To guide the laden vessel's thrust,
And I, at ease in carefree trust,
I sang to them . . . A sudden gust
Swept down and set the deep ashudder,
And crew and helmsman, all were lost!—
I only, secret singer, tossed
Upon the coast by seas in torment,
I sing my anthems as before,
And by a boulder on the shore
Dry in the sun my sodden garment.

◆◆◆

THE POET   [1827]

When on the poet Lord Apollo
Does not for mystic homage call,
To worldly bustle, pastimes hollow,
He lives in petty-minded thrall;
Then the celestial lyre is muted,
Chill torpor does his heart befall,
Amid life's idle and unsuited
He seems the idlest wretch of all.

Yet once the god-engendered word
But touches on the vivid senses,
The poet's soul awakens, tenses
Its pinions like an eagle stirred.
He chafes in worldly dissipation,
From human colloquy he flees,

Before the idol of the nation
He is too proud to bend his knees.
Then will he rush, uncouth and somber,
Astir with sounds and wild unease,
Toward the shores of desolate seas,
To murmuring wildwoods' vast penumbra.

THE TALISMAN   [1827]

Where the sea forever dances
Over lonely cliff and dune,
Where sweet twilight's vapor glances
In a warmer-glowing moon,
Where with the seraglio's graces
Daylong toys the Mussulman,
An enchantress 'mid embraces
Handed me a talisman.

'Mid embraces I was bidden:
"Guard this talisman of mine:
In it secret power is hidden!
Love himself has made it thine.
Neither death nor ills nor aging,
My beloved, does it ban,
Nor in gales and tempest raging
Can avail my talisman.

"Never will it help thee gather
Treasures of the Orient coast,
Neither to thy harness tether
Captives of the Prophet's host;
Nor in sadness will it lead thee
To a friendly bosom, nor
From this alien southland speed thee
To the native northern shore.

"But whenever eyes designing
Cast on thee a sudden spell,
In the darkness lips entwining
Love thee not, but kiss too well:
Shield thee, love, from evil preying,
From new heart-wounds—that it can,
From forgetting, from betraying
Guards thee this my talisman."

♦♦♦

TO DAWE, ESQ.[1]   [1828]

Why does your wondrous pencil strive
My Moorish profile to elicit?
Your art will help it to survive,
But Mephistopheles will hiss it.

Draw Miss Olenin's face. To serve
His blazing inspiration's duty,
The genius should spend his verve
On homage but to youth and beauty.

♦♦♦

REMEMBRANCE[1]   [1828]

When for us mortal men the noisy day is stilled,
        And, the mute spaces of the town
With half-transparent nightly shadow filled,
        Sleep, daily toil's reward, drifts down,
Then is it that for me the gloom and quiet breed
        Long hours of agonized prostration;
On my noctural languor more intently feed

The asps of mortal desolation;
The fancies seethe at will and the despondent mind
    Groans with excess of grim reflection;
Relentless Memory will wordlessly unwind
    Her long, long scroll for my inspection;
With loathing I peruse the record of my years,
    I execrate, I quail and falter,
I utter bitter plaints, and hotly flow my tears,
    But those sad lines I cannot alter.

THOU AND YOU   [1928]

The pale "you are" by warm "thou art"
Through careless slip of tongue replacing,
She sent within the love-struck heart
All sorts of happy fancies racing.
I stand before her all beguiled;
I stare at her, and the old Adam
Blurts out: You are all kindness, Madam!
And thinks: God, how I love thee, child!

YOUNG MARE   [1828]

Whither, mettlesome young filly,
Pride of the Caucasian brand,
Wildly bolting? Willy-nilly
Bridle time is close at hand.
Squint affrighted at my shadow,
Kick your hooves up in the air,
Down the smooth and spacious meadow

Freely canter all you care:
Tarry; soon I shall direct you,
In my thigh-grip meekly bound,
And with shortened rein deflect you
To an even-tempered round.

◆◆◆

PORTRAIT   [1828]

With soul on fire and blazing forth,
With passion's turbulent invasion,
She makes her entry on occasion
Amongst you, ladies of the North,
And strains her forces to their summit,
Ignoring all the worldly bars,
As does a law-defying comet
Amidst the calculated stars.

◆◆◆

THE CONFIDANT   [1828]

For your soft plaints, for your confessions,
Each outcry, greedily I reach:
Those frenzied and oblivious passions,
How mind-bewitching is their speech!
But curb, dear girl, your recollection,
Your dreams keep to yourself alone:
I dread their fiery infection,
I dread to know what you have known!

EGYPTIAN NIGHTS   [1828]

The Italian's first improvisation[1]

The poet walks: his lids are open,
But to all men his eyes are blind;
Then by a ruffle of his robing
Someone detains him from behind . . .
"Why do you roam so void of purpose?
Your eye no sooner scales a height
Than you recall it to the surface
And netherward direct your sight.
Your view of this fair world is blurred,
You are consumed by idle flames;
Each moment you are lured and stirred
By petty subjects' fancied claims.
A genius soars above the earthy,
The genuine poet ought to deem
Of his inspired anthems worthy
None but an elevated theme."

"Why does the wind revolve inanely
In hollows, raising leaves and dust,
While vessels in the doldrums vainly
Await its animating gust?
Why, spurning mountain crag and tower,
Does the great eagle's fearsome power
Light on a withered stump? Ask him!
Ask Desdemona why her whim
Did on her dusky moor alight,
As Luna fell in love with night?
Like wind and erne, it is because
A maiden's heart obeys no laws.
Such is the poet: like the North,
Whate'er he lists he carries forth,
Wherever, eagle-like, he flies,
Acknowledging no rule or owner,
He finds a god, like Desdemona,
For wayward heart to idolize."

CLEOPATRA   [1828]

(From "Egyptian Nights")

The palace gleamed. From jubilant choirs
Of bards re-echoed hymns of praise;
The joyous strains of lutes and lyres
The Queen enhanced by voice and gaze.
All hearts in transports thronged to seek her,
When of a sudden she stopped short
And mused above the golden beaker,
Her wondrous forehead drooped in thought.

The festive turmoil ceases shifting,
The choir stands mute as in a daze;
At last the Queen pronounces, lifting
Her brow again, with cloudless gaze:
"Is it not my love your dreamed-of treasure?
Well—you may buy such bliss divine:
Hear me! This day it is my pleasure
To grant you equal rank to mine.
Behold the market-place of passion!
For sale is now my love divine;
Who dares to barter in this fashion
His life against one night of mine?"

Thus she. All hearts are set aflutter
By passion blent with dreadful qualm.
To their abashed and doubtful mutter
She listens with a brazen calm.
Her scornful glances sweep the verges
Of her admirers' silent throng . . .
There—of a sudden one emerges,
Two others follow soon along.
Their step is bold, their eyes unclouded;
The Queen arises to their stride;
Three nights are bought: the couch is shrouded
For deadly raptures at her side.

"Thee, Holy Goddess of the Senses,
I vow to serve like none before,
A venal passion's recompenses
To gather like a common whore.
Oh hearken Thou, Our Cyprian Lady's
High Grace, and hear, in realms forlorn,
Ye dreaded deities of Hades,
My oath: unto the morning's dawn
My sovereign rulers' burning wishes
With rich fulfillment I will quench,
Slake them with ecstasies delicious,
With magical caresses drench.
But mark! as soon as to Aurora's
Renascent blush this night shall fade,
The happy heads of my adorers
Shall leap beneath the deadly blade."

By holy augurs blessed and chosen,
There issue from the fateful urn,
While the assembled guests stand frozen,
The lots assigned to each in turn.
First, Flavius, grayed amidst the laurels
And scars of Rome's historic quarrels;
His pride resolved to bear no more
A female's challenge to his mettle,
He bridled, as in days of war
He used to rise to calls of battle.
Crito was next, young sage who, raised
In shady groves Epicurean,
Had chosen Love his god and praised
The Graces and the Cytherean.
Appealing both to eye and heart,
The last to have his doom awarded,
Like vernal petals shy to part,
Has never had his name recorded
By scribes. His tender cheek a start
Of downy beard but faintly bordered . . .
Untasted passion flared and tested
His heart with unaccustomed blaze . . .
And softly touched, the Queen's eyes rested

Upon him with a gentler gaze.

Already daylight, swift to fade,
To Luna's golden horn surrenders,
And Alexandria's high splendors
Lie sunken in a balmy shade.
The lights are glowing, fountains spraying,
Sweet incense wafting from a hearth,
A breeze, voluptuous cool conveying,
Is promised to the gods of earth.
And in that velvet dusk, all heady
With lures of luxury untold,
The gleaming ottoman of gold,
In purple canopied, stands ready.

FOREBODING   [1828]

Once again there hang beclouded
My horizons, dark with rain;
Envious Fate, in malice shrouded,
Lies in wait for me again.
Will I find the strength to treat it
With disdain and, head unbowed,
Go with fortitude to meet it
As I did when young and proud?

Calmly, though my sails are riven,
I await what lies in store;
Once again I may be driven
Safely to a placid shore.
But foreboding, I confess it,
Brings me parting's fearful knell;
To your hand I fly to press it,
Angel, for a last farewell.

Angel meek and undefiant,
Gently whisper me good-bye,
Mourn: your loving gaze compliant,
Cast it down or raise it high.
In your heart enshrined forever,
I shall not grow faint or old:
Shall be young in hope, and never
Aught but gay and proud and bold.

[1828]

Raven doth to raven fly,
Raven doth to raven cry:
Raven, where is fallen meat?
What shall be the morning's treat?

Raven answers raven thus:
Well I know of meat for us;
On the fallow, by the willow
Lies a knight, a clod his pillow.

Why he died, who dealt the blow,
That his hawk alone can know,
And the sable mare that bore him,
And his bride who rode before him.

But the hawk now sails the air,
And the foe bestrode the mare,
And the bride a wreath is wreathing
For a new love, warm and breathing.

[1828]

Capital of pomp and squalor,
Stately jail of souls unfree,
Firmament of greenish pallor,
Frost and stone and misery—
Still you set my heart to throbbing,
For at times there, down a street,
Comes a golden ringlet bobbing,
Trips a pair of slender feet.

THE UPAS TREE   [1828]

On acres charred by blasts of hell,
In sere and brittle desolation,
Stands like a baleful sentinel
The Upas, lone in all creation.

Grim Nature of the thirsting plains
Begot it on a day of ire
And steeped its leaves' insensate veins,
And filled its roots, with venom dire.

The poison trickles through its bark
And, melting in the noonday blazes,
It hardens at the fall of dark
In resinous translucent glazes.

That tree of death no bird will try
Or tiger seek: the storm wind vicious
Alone will darkly brush it by
And speed away, its breath pernicious.

And should a rain cloud overhead
Bedouse the brooding foliage, straying,

The boughs a lethal moisture shed,
The glowing sands with venom spraying.

Yet to that tree was man by man
With but an eyelid's flicker beckoned,
Sped duly forth that day, and ran,
And brought the poison by the second:

Brought waxen death back, and a bough
With leaves already limp and faded,
And from his wan and pallid brow
The sweat in clammy streams cascaded.

He brought it, faltered, and lay prone
On reeds beneath the vaulted tenting
And, luckless slave, died at the throne
Of that dread magnate unrelenting.

And on this venom arrows fed,
Obedient to the prince's orders,
And death and desolation spread
On fellowmen beyond the borders.

[1828]

The dreary day is spent, and dreary night has soon
In leaden-colored draperies the heavens shrouded,
And over firry groves has risen all beclouded
A wan and spectral moon;
All these in me a mood of dark unease engender . . .
Up yonder far the moon ascends in splendor,
There is the air with sunset warmth replete,
There would the ocean like a sumptuous sheet
Beneath a sapphire sky enfold us . . .
This is the time, I know, she walks the mountain brow

Toward the strand besieged by surging, plunging shoulders,
There, at the foot of hallowed boulders
Forlornly and alone she must be sitting now . . .
Alone . . . no one to weep before her, none to languish,
No one to kiss her knees in rapt, oblivious anguish . . .
Alone . . . and no one's lips she suffers to be pressed
Upon her shoulders, her moist lips, her snowy breast,
No one is worthy of the heaven in her arm . . .
You surely are alone . . . in tears . . . than I am calm.
But if . . .

◆◆◆

[1828]

Blest he who at your fancy's pleasure
Your dreamy, languid ardor won,
Whose every glance you heed and treasure,
Before all eyes by love undone;

But pity him who, heart and bowels
With love's consuming flame ablaze,
Must hear in silence your avowals,
While jealous anguish clouds his gaze.

◆◆◆

OMENS   [1829]

I drove to you—vivacious dreams
In playful throng behind me dancing;
The moon at right with steady beams
Accompanied my brisk advancing.

I drove away—quite other dreams . . .
The lovesick spirit sorely smarted;
The moon at left with steady beams
Accompanied me heavyhearted.

We poets thus by common trait
Are prone to endless silent dreaming,
The signs of superstition seeming
To suit the feeling soul's estate.

◆◆◆

[1829]

Winter. What's there to do for us here in the country?
I greet the man who brings my morning tea with sundry
Enquiries: is it milder? has the blizzard stopped?
Is powder on the ground or not, and may one opt
For saddle over bed, or had one best belabor
Till luncheon aged journals borrowed from the neighbor?
There's powder snow. We rise, and mount, and are away—
Brisk trot across the range at early light of day,
Long hunting-whips in hand, the hounds behind us streaking,
We scan the pallid snow, with avid gazes seeking,
Encircling, scouring fields, till, afternoon long past,
Two hares both raised and lost, we jog it home at last.
A load of fun! Night falls, the snowstorm howling madly,
A dismal candle burns, the heart is strangled sadly,
And boredom slowly, drop by poison drop I sip.
I try to read, my eyes atop the letters slip
While thoughts are far away . . . At last I stop pretending,
Take up the pen and sit . . . incontinently rending
Some ill-joined gibberish from the enslumbered Muse.
Sound will not match with sound . . . for at such time I lose
All governance of Rhyme, my curious serving-maiden:
My verses limp and stumble, cold and vapor-laden.
Exhausted, I break off my struggle with the lyre

And seek the sitting-room; there I can hear the Squire
Discuss a sugar mill, elections in the county;
The Mistress wears a scowl to match the weather's bounty;
Her knitting needles click by stormy fits and starts,
When she's not saying sooth upon the king of hearts.
Ennui! day follows day in dreary isolation!
But if at evenfall our sleepy rustic station,
As I am sitting in a corner playing draughts,
Stirs to a two-in-hand or sledge and cob in shafts
And springs some guests on us, a matron and two girls,
A shapely pair of sisters, trim and fair of curls,
How it invigorates the place till then so numb!
How full, dear heaven, life will suddenly become!
At first there only pass alert but sidelong glances,
A word or two ensues, a chat then as it chances,
In turn the friendly laugh, the after-supper sing,
Vivacious waltzes next and whispered words which bring,
Those trysts of sultry gazes, those flirtatious speeches,
Prolonged encounters up a stairway's narrow reaches;
At sundown then the girl, unmuffled neck and bust,
Steps on the porch, her face whipped by the snowy gust!
But lost are northern gales upon the Russian rose.
How burningly a kiss will glow amid the frost!
How fresh the Russian maid blooms in the powdery snows!

[1829]

I loved you—and my love, I think, was stronger
Than to be quite extinct within me yet;
But let it not distress you any longer;
I would not have you feel the least regret.

I loved you bare of hope and of expression,
By turns with jealousy and shyness sore;

I loved you with such purity, such passion
As may God grant you to be loved once more.

[1829]

As down the noisy streets I wander
Or walk into a crowded shrine,
Or sit with madcap youth, I ponder
Bemusing reveries of mine.

I say: the years speed by unhalting,
And we, as many as are here,
Will pass beneath the eternal vaulting,
And someone's hour is drawing near.

Or gazing at an oak tree lonely,
I muse: this patriarchal sage,
Did not outlast my forebears only,
It will outlive my own dim age.

Or fondling some dear child is reason
For me to think: I make thee room,
Farewell to thee! It is the season
For me to fade, for thee to bloom.

Each day, each passing year of aging,
In deep abstraction now I spend,
At pains among them to be gauging
The year-day of the coming end.

And where, fate, is my death preparing?
At sea, a-roving, in the fray?
Or will this nearby vale be bearing
Within its earth my feelless clay?[1]

Although my flesh will be past caring
About the site of its decay,
Yet would I gladly still be sharing
The dear haunts of my earthly day.

And close to my sepulchral portals
I want young life to be at play,
And Nature, unconcerned with mortals,
To shed its beauty's timeless ray.

AT THE BUST OF A CONQUEROR[1]   [1829]

You're wrong to think his likeness garbled:
The eye of art has truly seen
Upon his lips that smile enmarbled,
Wrath on his forehead's frigid sheen.
No wonder that his bust reflected
This potentate's internal strife:
His feelings ever were bisected,
A harlequin in face and life.

THE MONASTERY ON MT. KAZBEK   [1829]

  Above thy brother summits' rows,
Kazbek, thy royal tentment glows
Aloft with everlasting lusters.
Thy monastery, past cloudy musters,
An ark afloat in vaporous height,
Just shows above the mountain clusters.

Oh, far-away, oh, longed-for site!
Could I but leave behind this canyon
And, soaring far beyond those shrouds,
Withdraw, with God for my companion,
Into a cell above the clouds! . . .

◆◆◆

THE SNOWSLIDE   [1829]

On frowning boulders dashed to spray,
The waters roar and foam away,
Aloft the murmuring wildwoods sway,
    And eagles scream,
And through the watery haze of gray
    The summits gleam.

A slide broke off this mountain face
And in its thundering downhill pace
Dammed up the gorge's narrow space
    With ponderous force,
And Terek's mighty water race
    Choked in its course.

Abruptly then becalmed and caged,
Your clamor, Terek, was assuaged;
But stubborn onslaught grimly waged
    The rearward ranks,
Broke through the snow bar, while enraged
    You swamped your banks.

And long the ruptured barrier so
Lay on, a thawless hulk of snow,
And sullen Terek ran below,
    His watery dust
Bedewing in his lathered flow
    The icy crust.

Across it lay a pathway wide,
There palfreys pranced and oxen plied,
And traders of the steppe would guide
      Their camels there,
Where sky-born Aeol, none beside,
      Now cleaves the air.

[1830]

What use my name to you, what good?[1]
It will die down like the sad jingle
Of waves awash on distant shingle,
Like night sounds in the toneless wood.

Upon your mind it will for long
Leave but a lifeless trace, unspoken
Like on a tomb the lacy token
Of an unfathomable tongue.

What use is it? Long since suppressed
By fresh and turbulent emotion,
It will not stir within your breast
Old thoughts of tender, pure devotion.

But one still day, forlorn, bereft,
Pronounce it as your tears are welling;
Say: memory of me is left,
A heart on earth for me to dwell in!

[1830]

At moments when your graceful form
In my embrace I long to capture,
And from my lips a tender swarm
Of love's endearments pour in rapture—
Without a word your supple shape
From my encircling arms unfolding,
You make your answer by escape
And smile at me, all trust withholding;
Too keenly mindful in your heart
Of past betrayal's doleful mention,
You bide in listless inattention
And hear me not and take no part . . .
I curse the cunning machinations
That were my sinful youth's delight,
Those hours awaiting assignations
In gardens, in the dead of night.
I curse the lover's whispered suing,
And tuneful verse's magic aids,
Caress of rashly trusting maids,
Their tears, and their belated ruing.

FOUNTAIN AT TSARSKOE SELO   [1830]

Out of her fingers the urn must have slipped and burst on a boulder.
    Sorrowing there she sits, holding the useless shell.
Lo! from the jagged urn the jet springs still, and the maiden
    Over an endless flow leans in unending dismay.

◆◆◆

CONJURY[1]   [1830]

Oh, if it's true that in the night,
When quietude the living covers,
And liquidly the lunar light
Glides down and on the tombstones hovers,
Oh, if it's true that then appear
Their tenants on the ghostly common,—
Leyla I wait, her shade I summon:
To me, my love, come here, come here!

Appear to me, beloved shade,
As you appeared before we parted,
In pallid wintry chill arrayed,
By deathly agony distorted.
Come like a star of outmost sphere,
Like a faint sound, an emanation,
Come like a dreadful visitation,
I care not how: Come here, come here!

I call you—not because I crave
To chastise those before whose malice
My love took refuge in the grave,—
Or as my spy in Hades' palace,
Or yet because I know the fear
Of doubt . . . but sorrowing above you,
I want to say that still I love you,
And still am yours: Come here, come here!

◆◆◆

[1830]

Bound for the distant coast that bore you,
You left behind this alien clime,
And long that hour I wept before you,
That unforgotten, mournful time.

With fingers chill and numbed of feeling
I clutched you, begged you not to leave,
Parting's fierce pangs with moans appealing
To nourish still and let me grieve.

But from our sorrowing embraces
You tore away your lips and hand,
And from an exile's prison-places
You called me to another land.
"Let us await another meeting
'Neath skies of everlasting blue,
In olive shades," you kept repeating,
"Love's kisses, friend, we shall renew."

But there, alas, where heaven's quarters
Are steeped in azure lucence deep,
Where olives shade the sheltered waters,
You fell into eternal sleep.
Now all your beauty, all you suffered,
Are lost in the sepulchral urn,
And those reunion kisses proffered—
But I shall claim them, comes my turn.

MY PEDIGREE [1830]

The tribe of Russian scribblers, mocking
A confrère with malignant wit,
Calls me "aristocratic." Shocking,
The sheer absurdity of it!
I am no officer, assessor,
Seigneur by dint of chest décor,
Academician or professor:
A Russian commoner—no more.

I know that times may topple classes,
A fact to which I calmly bow:
They grow peers faster, and one passes
The newest for the noblest now.
Hung from an ever brittler line
(With other such precarious ends),
Of hoar Boyars I am the scion;
I am a commoner, my friends.

My grandsire was no pancake-frier,
Did not grease emperors' boots or mince
Cantatas in the Palace choir,
Or jump from yokel straight to prince;
He was no pawn on French vacation
From some bepowdered Austrian squad;
So what fits *me* for noble station?
I am a commoner, thank God.

St. Nevsky's arms, with might determined,
My forebear Racha carried north;
His progeny was spared the ermined
Malignance of Ivan the Fourth.
The Pushkins were by tsars befriended,
And more than one earned glory's nod
When with the Polish levies fended
The commoner of Nizhgorod.

Intrigue and strife brought to submission,
And havoc of tempestuous wars,
The people by their own petition
Called the Románovs to be tsars.
That roll had *our* names, too, upon it,
The martyr's son let favors flow.
There was a time when we were honored;
There was . . . I am a commoner, though.

A fatal penchant for defiance
We all share: stiffnecked, as was fit,
My ancestor refused compliance
To Peter, and was hanged for it.

By this an insight may be fostered:
A potentate dislikes retort.
Prince Yakov Dolgoruki prospered,
And humble commoners—are smart.

My grandsire, when revolt was calling
At Peterhof, still kept his word,
As Minikh did, and in his falling
Supported Peter, crowned the Third.
From this Orlovs emerged with luster,
My grandsire—under lock and ban.
Our roughhewn kin subdued their bluster,
And I was born a common man.

Beneath my crested seal now moulders
A stack of parchments, undisturbed,
With our new lords I don't rub shoulders,
My arrogance of blood is curbed.
I am a versewright and a bookman,
As Pushkin, not -Musín, am known,
No financier, no titled footman,
A commoner: great on his own.

◆◆◆

AT KUTUZOV'S GRAVE   [1831]

Before the hallowed burial-stead
I linger here with lowered head . . .
All sleep, save in the twilight solemn
The temple candelabra gild
Tall granites, column after column,
And rows of standards, pendent, stilled.

Beneath them lies that lord of clans,
That idol of the northern lands,
The mighty realm's revered defender,

Who all its enemies subdued,
The last of that illustrious gender,
Imperial Catherine's eagle brood.

Live ardor in your grave-site glows!
From it a Russian story flows,
Relates that hour when by the nation
Your silver-templed age was bid
With voice of trustful invocation
To "come and save!" You rose—and did.

Now hark again the voice of trust,
Arise and save the Tsar and us,
One instant, ancient grim preserver,
Appear at the sepulchral cleft,
Appear, and breathe new dash and fervor
Into the regiments you left.

Appear, and with your sacred hand
Point out among our leaders' band
Your true inheritor, your chosen . . .
But mute the temple chambers loom,
In calm, eternal slumber frozen
Sleeps the indomitable tomb.

TO THE SLANDERERS OF RUSSIA[1]   [1831]

Bards of the Nations, say, what set you seething,
Threats of Anathema at Russia breathing?
What roused your wrath? That Poland stirs again?
Desist: this strife pits Slavs against each other
It has been weighed by Fate, like many another
In an old dispute, past your scope and ken.

Long since these tribes of hostile brothers
Have vied among themselves and warred,
And now the ones and now the others
Have had to bow before the sword.
Who shall outlive that grim commotion,
The boastful Pole, the stalwart Russ?
Shall Slavic brooklets merge in Russia's ocean,
Shall it dry out? Leave it to us!

Desist: to you these bloodstained tables
Remain unread, the clannish fables
Of this our internecine feud
Are undeciphered, unreviewed;
The voice of Kremlin, Praga,[2] calls you
But stirs no echo; the mystique
Of desperate fortitude enthralls you,
And then your hatred of us . . . Speak:

Is it for this, perchance, you hate us
That Moscow's blazing shell defied decrees
Of a vainglorious dictator's,
While you were writhing on your knees?
Or that we smashed that idol towering
Above the realms, so Europe gained release
And, saved by Russian blood, is flowering
Anew in freedom, honor, peace?

Come, challenge us with deeds, not ringing quarrels!
Is the old hero, resting on his laurels,
Unfit to mount the Ismail[3] bayonet?
Has then the Russian Tsar's word lost its omen?
Are we unused to Western foemen,
With Russian triumphs sated yet?
Are we too few? From Perm to Tauris gleaming,
From Finnish crags to ardent Colchis teeming,
From Kremlin, rocked upon its stand,
To China's battlements unshaken,
Bright steel her bristles, shall not waken,
Shall not rise up the Russian land?
Send on, then, sacred mischief-makers,

Send your embittered sons and braves:
There's room for them in Russian acres
Amid not unfamiliar graves.

◆◆◆

ECHO[1]   [1831]

Where beasts in trackless forests wail,
Where horns intone, where thunders flail,
Or maiden chants in yonder vale—
    To every cry
Through empty air you never fail
    To speed reply.

You listen to the thunder knells,
The voice of gales and ocean swells,
The shepherd's hail in hills and dells
    And you requite:
But unrequited stay . . . This spells
    The poet's plight.

◆◆◆

[1831]

No, no, those fierce delights I do not treasure,
That sensuous ecstasy, oblivious, frenzied pleasure,
The young bacchante's moaning cry and quake
In my embrace, when writhing like a snake,
With wounding lips, caresses' fiery river
She speeds the instant of the utmost quiver!

Oh, how much dearer is your shy appeal!
What ache of happiness I come to feel
When after long entreaty you surrender,
By no intoxication drugged, yet tender,
Still cool with modesty, to my quick glow
Barely responding, all your senses slow,
And then awaken, more and more—until
You share my flame at last against your will!

◆◆◆

IN A BEAUTY'S ALBUM [1832]

All harmony, all wondrous fairness,
Aloof from passions and the world,
She rests, with tranquil unawareness
In her triumphant beauty furled.
When, all about her, eyes hold muster,
Nor friends, nor rivals can be found,
Our other beauties' pallid round
Extinguished wholly by her luster.

And were you bound I know not where,
Be it to love's embraces bidden,
Or what choice vision you may bear
In heart's most private chamber hidden,—
Yet, meeting her, you will delay,
Struck by bemusement in mid-motion,
And pause in worshipful devotion
At beauty's sacred shrine to pray.

◆◆◆

[1833]

But for my soul's obscurely asking
And pining for I know not what,
I would stay here forever, basking
In bliss at this forgetful spot:
Desire's vain tremors never missing,
I'd count the world a dreamy wisp,
Those slender feet forever kissing,
Forever hearing that sweet lisp.

[1833]

Don't let me lose my mind, o God;
I'd sooner beg with sack and rod
   Or starve in sweat and dust.
Not that I treasure my poor mind,
Or would bemoan it should I find
   That part from it I must:

If they but left me free to roam,
How I would fly to make my home
   In deepest forest gloom!
In blazing frenzy would I sing,
Be drugged by fancies smoldering
   In rank and wondrous fume.

And I would hear the breakers roar,
And my exultant gaze would soar
   In empty skies to drown:
Unbridled would I be and grand
Like the great gale that rakes the land
   And mows the forest down.

But woe befalls whose mind is vague:
They dread and shun you like the plague,
   And once the jail-gate jars,
They bolt the fool to chain and log
And come as to a poor mad dog
   To tease him through the bars.

And then upon the evenfall
I'd hear no nightingale's bright call,
   No oak tree's murmurous dreams—
I'd hear my prison-mates call out,
And night attendants rail and shout,
   And clashing chains, and screams.

◆◆◆

AUTUMN   [1833]

(A fragment)

> What will not enter then into my pensive mind?
> *Derzhavin*

      I

October—and the groves already shaking
From naked boughs what foliage clings there still;
The road congeals beneath the fall-wind's raking;
The stream still courses babbling past the mill,
But icebound lies the pond; my neighbor's taking
His hunt in haste to fields far overhill,
The fall crop suffers from their reckless playing,
And drowsing woods wake to the hounds' sharp baying.

II

This is my season: spring is not for me;
The thaw nags; slush and smells—spring makes me vapid;
The blood's in sap, both head and heart unfree.
Remorseless winter finds me more intrepid,
I love her snows; in moonlit nights, what glee
In sleighrides with a friend, so light and rapid,
When fresh and cozy under sable fur
She grips your hand, all glowing and astir!

III

What fun on sharpened irons to be curving
The level gloss of an encrystalled lake!
And winter balls' resplendent stir and swerving? . . .
But draw the line: six months of flake on flake
Our very troglodyte must find unnerving,
The northern bear. One can't forever take
Young charmers gliding through the snows, or cower
'Twixt stove and double windows, turning sour.

IV

Fair summer—ah! But can I call you friend,
By heat and dust and flies and midges harried,
When, draining all fine faculties, you rend
Our vitals like parched fields, and leave us arid?
Keep cool is all we think of, and we end
By wishing drab old wintertime had tarried;
Ashamed of wine and pancakes at her wake,
We now clink frosted glasses for her sake.

V

The fading autumn almost none admires,
Yet, reader, I am fond of her, I own,
Fond of her muted glow of half-banked fires.
Like a poor child unloved among her own
She calls to me. If anyone enquires,

Her of all seasons I hold dear alone.
There is much good in her. A frugal wooer,
My whim finds some appeal quite special to her.

VI

What is her hold? It may be—let me try—
Like a consumptive girl's who, meek and ailing,
Endears herself to you. Condemned to die,
She droops, poor thing, without revolt or wailing;
Upon her bloodless lips a smile will lie,
The very grave-pit's yawning hollow failing
To blanch the cheek that flushes play upon.
Today she is alive, tomorrow gone.

VII

I find you eye-beguiling, mournful season,
Your valedictory splendors make me glad—
For sumptuous in her death is nature, pleasing
The forest all in gold and purple clad;
The wind-sough's whisper in the treetops breezing,
The brooding sky with swirling vapor sad,
The virgin frost, the sun's infrequent glinting,
And hoary winter's distant ominous hinting.

VIII

With each new autumn I come fresh in bud;
The Russian winter makes my nature stronger;
With newfound zest I chew old habits' cud,
Slumber descends on time, on time comes hunger;
Serene and brisk beats in my heart the blood,
Desires well up, I'm gay again and younger,
I'm full of life—my organism's such
(If you will pardon this prosaic touch).

XI

They bring a steed to me; through open spaces
It bears the rider on with tossing mane,
Beneath the gleaming hooves' impatient paces
The sheet-ice crackles, rings the frozen plane.
The brief day spent, the orphaned fireplace's
Dead embers come to life—now flare amain,
Now smolder low; before it I sit reading
Or in my pensive mind long fancies feeding.

X

And in sweet silence I forget the world,
Imagination drugs me with its sweet slow current,
And poetry is in my soul unfurled:
It grows embattled with its lyric warrant,
It stirs and throbs and, yet in slumber curled,
It gropes to clear its way, an uncurbed current—
And then guests call on me, invisible swarms,
My fancy's fruit, in long familiar forms.

XI

And in my mind conceits grow bold and caper,
Light rhymes fly out to meet them on the wing,
And fingers itch for pen, and pen for paper,
And in a moment verse will freely ring.
Thus dreams a ship becalmed in stagnant vapor,
Till, look! she crawls with sailors, scampering
Up, down, the sails swell out and swing to quarters,
The great hulk gathers way and cleaves the waters.

◆◆◆

[1834]

It's time, friend, time! For peace the spirit aches—
Day chases day, each passing moment rakes
Away a grain of life, and while we, you and I,
Would rather have lived on, lo, all at once we die.
Here happiness is not, but peace and freedom are.
A dreamed-of lot long since has lured me from afar—
Long since, a weary slave, have I conceived of flight
To that far-off retreat of toil and pure delight.

◆◆◆

[1835]

Bitterly sobbing, the maid chid the youth with jealous reproaches;
    Facing her, propped on a shoulder, sleep took him all
                                                        unawares.
Straightway the maiden was still, lulling his gossamer slumber,
    Letting her tears flow on, quietly smiling at him.

◆◆◆

THE COMMANDER   [1835]

    One of the Tsar's palatial halls is an apartment
With neither gold nor velvet rich; here no assortment
Of coronation gems, kept under glass, is found;
But up and down, throughout its length and all around,
An artist has embellished it from floor to ceiling,
His ranging brush instinct with free and generous feeling.
No maidenly madonnas, nymphs on sylvan lawns,
Full-blossomed beauties, goblet-waving fauns,
No dances, hunting scenes—instead, all cloaks and sabres

And countenances marked by war's resolve, war's labors.
In serried throng the painter magicked back to light
The high commanders of our nation's warlike might:
All laureates of that campaign of wondrous glory,
Heroes of eighteen-twelve's imperishable story.
At times, astroll amongst them, as my gaze was caught
By the familiar likenesses, I idly thought
That I could hear their warrior notes ring down those spaces.
Yet many are no longer, and the rest, whose faces
In bloom of youth still grace this canvas, lively-hued,
Grown old by now, incline in modest quietude
Their laureled heads . . .
           But of this somber band of brothers
One always draws my mind more strongly than the others;
Bemused anew each time, I stop and cannot spare
A glance elsewhere, and then, the more I brood and stare,
The more I feel my heart in leaden sadness buried.

He is portrayed full-length.[1] Bald like a skull's, his forehead
Gleams loftily and, you would say, betrays the blight
Of some great suffering. Deep gloom enshrouds the site;
The background shows a host encamped. Calm in dejection,
He seems abstracted in disdainful recollection.
The artist either drew no more than he had seen
In choosing to portray him with just such a mien,
Or by some insight not his own it was engendered;
No matter, it is this expression Dawe has rendered.

Luckless commander! Ah, your fate was bitter gall:
The alien soil in sacrifice you brought your all.
By gaze of savage ignorance unpenetrated,
You strode alone, your mind with lofty concepts freighted;
But, fastening on your name's outlandish sound for bait,
And letting loose on you its hue-and-cry of hate,
As it was being rescued by your craft, the nation
Reviled your venerable head with execration.
And He, whose mind was shrewd enough to be exempt,
Found it more politic to join them in contempt . . .
And long, your mighty heart upheld by strong conviction,
Undaunted, you outfaced the cretinous affliction;

Until, but half-way home, you were compelled at length
To yield without a word the laurel wreath, the strength
Of high command, and that design so deeply pondered—
To vanish in the lines and see your glory squandered.
There, lord of hosts no more, young ensign now instead,
Who never heard before the merry hiss of lead,
You charged the firing line and sought the death you craved—
In vain! —

. . . .
. . . .

Ah, men! A wretched tribe, both tears and laughter worth!
Priests of the momentary, the success of earth!
How often in his passing may a man be seen
At whom a blind and hectic age will vent its spleen,
But whose exalted face within a generation
Draws poets into rapt and loving contemplation!

◆◆◆

[1835]

I was assured my heart had rested
Its urge to suffer long before;
What used to be, I had protested,
Shall be no more! shall be no more!
Deceitful dreams forever hidden,
Forsaken raptures, sorrows banned . . .
Yet here afresh they stir me, bidden
By Beauty's sovereign command.

◆◆◆

CLEOPATRA   [1835]

Fragment from
"We Were Spending the Evening at Princess D.'s Dacha"

Why is a melancholy racking
Her soul? Whatever could be lacking
The heir to Egypt's wealth of ages?
Securely walled by guards and pages,
Her highness holds by languid reins
The jewel of the coastal plains.
The deities of earth attend her,
Her palaces abound in splendor.
Let blaze with heat the Nubian day,
Let cool nocturnal breezes play,
What art with luxury dispenses
Combines to court her dreamy senses,
All lands, the swells of every sea
Bear her their toll of finery,
An endless choice of rich attire;
Now she will gleam with ruby fire,
Now robed and cloaked in purple shades
Aglow with dyes of Tyrian maids;
Then she may board her golden bark
And in the sail's translucent dark
Hoar Nilus' silver waters roam,
Like Aphrodite born of foam.
Her days are gorged with sights and sounds
By feast on feast in ceaseless rounds,
Her nights—no fancy yields the keys
To all their sultry mystery. . .

But all in vain! Her heart is wrenched
By nameless thirsting, never quenched;
Her oversated senses sicken,
With barrenness of feeling stricken . . .

Bedazed, the guests fall silent now;
But once again she lifts her brow,
And searing fire is in her gaze

As with a haughty smile she says:
"Am I not worth your love like Venus?
Mark what I choose to tell you, then.
I may forget the gulf between us
And make you happiest of men.
Here is my challenge—who will meet it?
For sale I offer peerless nights.
Who will step forward—I repeat it—
And pay with life for his delights?"

◆◆◆

[Between 1827 and 1839]

She looks at you with such soft feeling,
Her artless chatter so appealing,
Her gaiety so full of sap,
Her eyes replete with melting sweetness,
Last night she snuggled with such neatness
Beneath the sheltering table-nap
Her pretty foot into my lap!

◆◆◆

FROM PINDEMONTE[1]   [1836]

I have but little use for those loud "rights"—the phrase
That seems to addle people's minds these days.
I do not fault the gods, nor to a soul begrudge it
That I'm denied the bliss of wrangling over a Budget,
Or keeping king from fighting king in martial glee;
Nor do I worry greatly if the Press is free
To hoax the nitwits, or if censors-pokers
Spoil journalistic games for sundry jokers;

All this is merely "words, words, words," you see.
Quite other, better rights are dear to me;
I crave quite other, better liberation:
To be dependent on a king, or on a nation—
Is it not all the same? Good riddance! But to dance
To no one else's fiddle, foster and advance
One's private self alone; before gold braid and power
With neither conscience, thought, nor spine to cower;
To move now here, now there with fancy's whim for law,
At Nature's godlike works feel ecstasy and awe,
And start before the gifts of art and inspiration
With pangs of trembling, joyous adoration—
There's bliss for you! There are your rights . . .

RUSLAN AND LIUDMILA: INTRODUCTION

Ruslan and Liudmila, which did for Pushkin's career what *Die Leiden des jungen Werther* did for Goethe's, is so wildly polyphyletic (as geneticists would say), so elusive a literary hybrid, that a determined attempt to classify it might result in a label as terse as "a mock-romantic fairy-tale ballad parady of pseudo-Kievan sham-Chivalry." The poem was begun in 1817, before Pushkin's graduation from the Lycée at Tsarskoe Selo, and completed in draft on March 16, 1820. This was a few weeks before the twenty-year-old sybarite and brilliant literary sniper was packed off to the south on penal reassignment, having escaped Siberia through the intervention of high-placed friends.

The same day one of these, Vasily Zhukovsky, most illustrious poet of the era and Pushkin's mentor and patron, gave Pushkin his portrait with the much-cited inscription, "To a victorious pupil from a defeated master." This showed not only Zhukovsky's unfailing generosity—he was after all a prime target of the graceful but irreverent lampoon—but also his literary judgment and insight. It was not long after this that his star as a poet was forever eclipsed by Pushkin, and he turned—not for this reason so much as lured by new interests—to quite different literary pursuits, in which again he excelled.

The epilogue to the poem was written in the south in July, 1820. Its rather mawkish strain of youth decayed and inspiration withered strongly suggests the hope that some influential reader might implore those in authority to pardon Pushkin before brain fever or a decline should carry him off. As it turned out, such interventions were unsuccessful; but Pushkin's "southern exile" was not, on the whole, a desperate predicament, and it certainly proved one of his most productive periods.

Ruslan and Liudmila was widely taken seriously by both admirers and detractors as the first native example of a "new romanticism"—as distinct from the preromantic and Gothic modes introduced to Russia earlier by Zhukovsky, and not generally so labeled. At the same time, critics very plausibly discerned kinship with products not simply identifiable with romanticism, such as Wieland's three works on the theme of noble quests abandoned for the natural sensuous life, and his celebrated fairy-tale in verse, *Oberon*; and of course, Ariosto's mock-epic. Such critics as were able to swim against the torrent of popular acclaim redoubled the strictures of literary conservatism which had met Zhukovsky's work earlier: scandalously unbuttoned diction and a subject matter which combined chaotic structure with barbarity of taste.

A convenient way, as well as an amusing one, to understand the delight and, as it were, relief with which Pushkin's poem was greeted by some, and the pained indignation it evoked from others, is to compare it with the work of Pushkin's most immediate predecessor in its ostensible genre, Zhukovsky. Within Zhukovsky's work, one should turn to the famous poem which was to some slight degree the direct target of Pushkin's good-natured ridicule in *Ruslan and Liudmila*. It will then be clearer, perhaps, that "The Twelve Sleeping Maidens," and all that Russia's imported romanticism up to then represented in terms of poet's viewpoint, prosodic originality and assumed state of public taste, was not being "programmatically" attacked by the 20-year-old prodigy, as it might be in the name of French *raison*, or in the spirit of the experimental realism of his thirties, or even on behalf of a more lighthanded, native-flavored romanticism that he might have meant to launch. It was rather that the 18th century scoffer in him conspired with the amateur historian and folklorist, and with the man of taste allergic to solemn fustian, to make fun of his mentor's fashionable "antiquing" of Russian poetry with mock-medieval wormholes and feudal verdigris.

This is most explicit at the point in Canto Four where after a graceful bow to Zhukovsky and a genial plot summary of the soul-stirring "Twelve Maidens," Pushkin confronts young Ratmir with a crenelated castle. This is, not accidentally, the only false "Western" prop in the poem. Unforced European notes, by contrast, abound in the chit-chat which the detached singer intersperses between, and pertly sets off against, the mock-serious episodes of the fable. Maidens in white muslin, some gazing skyward, some chin on chest, commute up and down the keeps in Zhukovsky's poem. So they do, more briskly, in Pushkin's, and one sings a (derisively trite) Loreley ditty extolling the amenities of the castle and its inmates. But far from breaking their enchantment as Vadim had done, then freezing in chaste rapture before the head-maiden for some stanzas, then getting married in a derelict friary magically restored and refitted for the purpose, and finally running a sacred errand or two—Ratmir enters a voluptuary's dream. He finds himself gently divested of his ironmongery and led by the assembled strength of seductive maidens into a Russian-cum-Oriental bathhouse and massage parlor. There, it is clear, wisps of vapor are his sole screen from caressing eyes, "cast down" but full of eager interest, and heaping armfuls of "all-but-nakedness" which throng about his couch to perform delightful ministrations, with his increasingly fervent cooperation.

Yet Pushkin, like his circle and most of the literary public, rightly stood in awe of Zhukovsky's achievement and was aware of his historic role. In some moods, long after the period of *Ruslan and Liudmila*, he accuses himself (1830) of puerile impudence for having aimed a squirt gun at his patron and friend:

> ...*Ruslan and Liudmila* was favorably received on the whole...Nobody even noticed that it is a frigid work. It was charged with being immoral because of a few sensuous descriptions, some lines which I deleted from the second edition:

> > O dreadful sight! The feeble wizard
> > Caresses with a wrinkled hand...

> the introduction to I don't remember which canto:

> > In vain you nestled in the shadow, etc.

> and because of the parody of "The Twelve Sleeping Maidens." For this last I deserved to be soundly reproved, as betraying a lack of aesthetic sensibility. It was inexcusable, particularly at my age, to parody a work of pristine poetry in order to please the mob. There were other criticisms which were fairly shallow. Is there a single passage in *Ruslan* which could be compared, where the ribaldry of its humor is concerned, to the pranks of, say, Ariosto, of whom I was constantly being reminded? Even the passage I deleted was a very toned-down imitation of Ariosto (*Orlando*, Canto V, oct. viii).[1]

But spontaneous modern taste, unwarped by comparison with Zhukovsky's predecessors like Bogdanovich, would tend to judge that Pushkin blamed himself needlessly. "The Twelve Sleeping Maidens," subtitled "An Olden Tale in Two Ballads," is, of all bleak auspices, of Saxon inspiration, the plot being lifted from *Die zwölf schlafenden Jungfrauen* by Christian Heinrich Spiess,[2] a late 18th-century best-selling Gothic novelist and playwright. A three-word acknowledgment of this debt is followed by an untitled introductory poem in four octaves, dated 1817, which is an (unacknowledged) close paraphrase or imitation of Goethe's "Zueignung," the poem musing on the resumption of his 30-year-old labors on *Faust* which the old poet placed at the very head of the huge drama. The relevance of this translation to Zhukovsky's poem is obsure.

Then, after some more epigraphs and dedications, follow over 150 monotonous stanzas of six identical iambic couplets each. This stanza is derived by borrowing the static first quatrain of Bürger's famous "Lenore" stanza (cf. Pushkin's "Bridegroom" and "Drowned Man") and repeating it ad infinitum, for there is nothing metrically to mark the onset of a new stanza from that of any internal couplet. The effect is deadening, as the involved story, unrelieved by a spark of humor or grace and sticky with religiosity, goes clacking along, tapock-tapock-tapock-tapock, tapick-tapick-tapick-tapickah, like wheels passing over the rail-gaps on a very steady local train.

But the chief tedium of this and other specimens of Drawing-Room

Sepulchral, once the charm of absurdity has worn off, is its inherent lack of surprise, be it in narrative viewpoint, in incident, or in idiom. By sowing surprise with a lavish and mischievous hand, Pushkin carves a deeper grave for the antecedent mode than by any digs of outright parody. The mode is so "square" (as we said in the sixties), so "straight" (as we shall presently stop saying) because its conventions rest on wish-fulfilling romantic assumptions about the age of chivalry, or a remote facsimile of it trimmed with outright fairy stuff. Knights, fairies, witches, rescued maidens, rejected suitors, have to behave in typecast ways to cater to the illusions, or at any rate the voluntarily suspended disbelief, of the public regarding the rectilinear morals and mores of feudal society. Poignant, unstylized tragedy, comic pratfalls, complexities of character, appealing evil, repellent virtue, humdrum humanity, did not fit into the mold, and injecting them would destroy its main escapist virtues—romantic distance in time and space, picturesque piety, moral simplicity, heroic identification, thaumaturgic excitement. For the fifteen years or so that Zhukovsky and a few other prospectors were mining this vein, it was heady stuff, and the public developed a veritable addiction to it. But, in keeping with the notorious telescoping of time scales in Russian literature of that period, the fashion was overripe by the second decade of the century; and instead of being followed by another foreign fad, perhaps still better russicized, it was followed by that unclassifiable all-recasting phenomenon which was Pushkin. And Pushkin's cutting edge was *Ruslan and Liudmila*.

Did Pushkin then, with malice aforethought, forever unmagic these fairy lands forlorn by loosing a troupe of alien, complex, unbridled characters into the medium, and letting them gambol all over it? Did he, moreover, in his canto send-offs and asides personally laugh it to scorn? Not at all; nor should we assume that he had any such intention. His characters, too, are at best sketchy and start out, at least, as stereotypes.

The excitement in his story does not lie in any suspense about its outcome, hardly in even a momentary identification with hero or heroine, nor in any moral indignation at its human villains, who are pardonable or farcical—a sure sign of precocious realism. Instead, it lies in the teasing turns of the author's impish mind, the stylized intimacy with it to which we are admitted, the sure expectation of the joltingly unexpected, the delightful scandal of an overblown genre deflated, and more than anything, the infectious gaiety and effortless brilliance of the verse, which somehow translate a gifted prank into the realm of aesthetic elation.

Something of the difference in form and spirit between Zhukovsky's poem and Pushkin's may emerge from just one juxtaposition of very short parallel passages—from Vadim's encounter with the redeemed Sleeping Maidens, and from Ratmir's with his unredeemed ones:

Zhukovsky:

And all that here to us is dim,
To faith discovered only,
Abruptly stood revealed to him,
Blent in one image lonely.

They gaze to Heaven, shedding tears,
Devoid of speech with rapture;
Then, lo, the group of maidens nears,
Released from magic capture:
Like stars shine forth reopened eyes,
Alight with joy their faces,
With newly quickened beauty's prize,
With fresh redemption's graces.

Pushkin:

They spread rich fabrics of Iran,
Whereon reclines the weary Khan;
Fine wisps of steam about him loop;
Fond eyes cast down, the lovely troupe,
All eagerness to serve him, press
Their charming all-but-nakedness
About his couch, a playful group.
Above him, one of them is waving
The supple birch-twig's tender points,
His frame with fervent freshness laving;
Another cossets, silky palms
Perfumed with rose, his stiffened joints.

Fairness demands the acknowledgment that Zhukovksy too, or perhaps his model, the philistine from Saxony, felt impelled to provide some decorously erotic relief, a brief peepshow or centerfold to quicken the stoutly virtuous reader's circulation and cheer him on that isometric rail journey. Vadim en route to the cryptful of cataleptic maidens has occasion to maim a giant and scoop in a freshly abducted princess of Kiev from him. They are presently caught in a dreadful thunderstorm in the forest, thoroughly soaked and knocked about against trees and cliffs, and take refuge in a cave. There Vadim is impelled to apply what we must assume are standard measures of chivalrous first-aid, including mouth-to-breast resuscitation; and the princess, already stimulated no doubt by the earlier prospect of fate-worse-than-death, is silent but not unresponsive:

And to his bosom's safe repose
The young princess he presses,
He swabs away the rain that flows
From out her golden tresses.

> His lips in gentle touch, he warms
> The maiden breast with breathing,
> And heat invests the chilly forms;
> With silent tremors seething,
> Beneath the brushing lips they woke;
> An arm about him throwing,
> The quiet maiden never spoke
> But for her fingers' glowing.

At such rare moments of proximate humanity on Vadim's part, however, a ghostly tolling comes from the distressed gentlewomen's far-off dorm, like the bell signalling that creative play-period is over; and Vadim resumes his pious quest with a start and perhaps an inaudible sigh.

Beyond such casual comparisons, which are less than fair or conclusive, we should make some attempt to account more fully for the astonishing success of Pushkin's rather exotically blended confection. There are at least two, slightly farcically, "Byronic" devices appearing here, years before Pushkin's acquaintance with Byron: the pre-climactic suspension of the narrative, and authorial intrusion. But more than such devices in themselves, it is the fresh air of spontaneity and zest which breathes from these unshriven cantos, and the pleasantly unsettled feeling, akin to the rise of guilty but delicious laughter, which it induces from the start. This bubbles up in the sure anticipation, raised by faint hints in the initial diction, that musty "Gothic" stereotypes will be infused with saucy natural life, to play fast and loose with the stodgy genre's conventions. These atmospheric elements alone not merely distinguish, but transsubstantiate *Ruslan and Liudmila* from any of the forms Zhukovsky had transplanted to Russia from various Highland heaths, English churchyards, Rhinish blue-flower stands, and Saxon kitchen-plots of Western romanticism.

The antecedent mode chiefly relevant to *Ruslan and Liudmila*, and briefly sampled by us earlier, may be termed the "folklore Gothic." This comprises high-minded, moderately spine-tingling, often lachrymose verse romances or ballads, some redolent of a certain meretricious purity, a lily-browed pseudo-ingenuousness one is tempted to call Preraffaelite or Wagnerian, or more broadly, decadent. These often featured for characters denizens—sacred, profane, or supernatural—of a book-derived feudal society set in as ill-defined an age of vassail, quest and gadzooks as those tales of an avian entity American children call "robinhood." This milieu of romanticized chivalry, in West or East, had little to do with historical feudalism, and less with the Ukrainian principality of Kiev, or the Russian duchies of the high middle ages, or the living tradition of epic tales. But East Slavic names and settings associated with these were at once adopted when the romantic ballad was naturalized by Zhukovsky, starting with his first "Lenore" imitation (actually titled "Liudmila"), in 1808, and by his followers. These touches then took the place of the onomastic and toponymic links which, however tenuously and distantly, lent locale and lineament to the epigone form in Europe. Examples are the ancient Roland plots echoed in the fables of the Sicilian *pupi* bards to this day, and the slight flushes of life and color which filter even into Clemens Brentano's anaemic lays through transfusions of blood and iron across seven hundred years from Picardy and Provence.

Zhukovsky's masterly adaptations and, seldom, original ballads of the period from 1808 to 1820 did not alone account for this naturalized genre as such, but most probably for its immense vogue. And some of it, like some of the Scottish balladry and the rich German output of a century from Bürger to Count Strachwitz, Lulu v. Strauss u. Thorney, Fontane, C. F. Meyer, has the verve, mystery and noble vigor which supplant tawdry historical reality and enchant the adolescent or romantic mind. Anchorites and wizards, knights and chatelaines, devils and damozels disported themselves against backdrops of Standard Western Chivalric or Slapdash Slavonic—or a blend of both. Fable and motivation worked with strong color and contrast, inky guilt and snowy innocence, sin and retribution, betrayal or pitfall and rescue by exploit or miracle. The language was consiously archaic, though by no means less limber or mellifluous for that. On the contrary, in keeping once more with the remarkable foreshortening of literary stages in this "catch-up" period, the language that had been a genuine and contemporary, if ponderous and over-rich, medium only a generation or two earlier in the hands of Derzhavin and Shikhmatov (and still was for Krylov) was already available to skillful hands as an optional resource for literary pathos or archaizing stylization.

A great many of the gross tangible elements of the Zhukovskian romantic ballad were retained by Pushkin in *Ruslan and Liudmila*. The effect of his brilliant dabbling in the genre was not assault and overthrow, but infiltration and subversion from within by the subtle solvents of classicist sobriety and proto-realist debunking. One hastens to concede that *Ruslan and Liudmila* is anything but sober and owlish; but its buoyant fancy and madcap parody are at least partially, and at least half consciously, *reductio ad absurdum* in the service of taste and measure. Abstract literary concepts are apt to creak piteously under the weight of metaphor. But the thought does sugggest itself that classicism in him reached forward, and incipient realism reached back, to kill the consumptive genre with insidious kindness.

We have pointed to a quantum leap in the ease and vigor of poetic diction, and to a bracing suspense due to the minefield quality of the mock-epic mode. What else made *Ruslan and Liudmila* different from its precursors? Half a dozen quite definable elements, not all new, went into the delicate mobile, and their balancing rather than jangling and collapsing in Pushkin's hands helps account for the unforeseen *succès fou* of the poem, and for the gracious surrender inscribed by Zhukovsky on the portrait he sent him on this occasion.

One of these elements was the panoply of Kiev and its court—as thoroughly mythistorical by then as Barbarossa's Kyffhäuser or King Arthur's war cabinet, but still evocative. Another was a dose of the romantic opulence and menace of Islamic and Mongol cultures—here purveyed by Scheherezade and perhaps Voltaire's second-hand Orient rather than by the bloody shades of Russian history; but blending in so well as actually to strengthen the "Russian scent" claimed in the lilting, misleading foreword. Still another was the elegant, rosy-pink yet thin-blooded *salon* carnality of Boucher and Watteau, echoed in verse by Parny and others, and sparingly injected into this poem by way of teasing suggestion only; partly for Pushkin's own amusement, partly for the usual mock-epic purpose of comic incongruity, as in the episode of Ratmir in the massage parlor. A fourth was a quasi-romantic note of lyricism, with delicate 18th century pastoral echoes, which is occasionally sounded: not in sentimental communing with nature or rapturous portraiture of landscape, but in gemlike, totally conventional miniatures, like jade and mother-of-pearl inlays of Fujiyama, such as Liudmila's view of the arctic range from Chernomor's castle; or in such golden-age motifs as the idyll of Ratmir and the fisher-maiden, and the description of Chernomor's glacier-guarded pleasaunce, which might have inspired Hilton's Shangri-La. Among still other shapes in the mobile are some genuinely evocative of the Russian fairy-tale and heroic legend and the chapbooks of *Bova* and *Eruslan*: Ruslan's name, some details of his quest, the magic sword and beard, the vanishing cap, the bleached bones of horses and warriors on the ancient battlefield, recalling the site of Oleg's death; the reek of barbarous Indo-European antiquity, redolent of Old Irish or East Slavic imagination, that hangs about the Head; while the anti-climactic slap dispels it at once, it returns with an aura of pathos at the death scene.

Each of these quite disparate elements had a settled constituency in public taste; but they could only have been merged in the medium which Pushkin alone commanded: light, swiftly paced, lucidly phrased verse that tasted of the present while moving gaily in a mythic past, in a series of graceful stage sets which—blessed relief—one was not expected to take solemnly or milk for edification. Among the catalyzers of the fusion must surely be recognized the stance of humorous, tolerant detachment taken by the author from the outset—discounting the wide-eyed Folklorelei of the Prologue which he added eight years later, like a baby-food label on a can of fire crackers. In this atmosphere, the reader feels, it becomes graceless and pedestrian to raise considerations of time, space, continuity, plausibility—and modesty.

The long afterglow, reaching well into the present, shed by Pushkin's ambiguous masterpiece of 1820 is well documented by V. G. Belinsky's comments many years later. From his sober and somehow drab redoubt of realism and local color, he first judiciously praises Pushkin with faint damns. Then his own first reading of *Ruslan and Liudmila*—at nine? at fifteen?—surges up in his mind, he is bewitched again, and off he soars, ending in such a rainbow froth of rapture that one wonders what a "warm" poem would have done to him, if a "cold" one did this:

> Not one of Pushkin's works caused as much noise and outcry as *Ruslan and Liudmila*. Some saw in it the finest product of creative genius, others a violation of all canons of poesy, an insult to sound aesthetic taste. Both opinions might now appear equally fatuous if one failed to place them in historical perspective, where it becomes clear that there was sense in both of them and both were to some degree tenable and well-founded.
>
> Nowadays *Ruslan and Liudmila* is no more to us than a fairy-tale, void of any coloring of locale, epoch, nationality, and hence lacking verisimilitude; regardless of the fine verse it is written in, and the gleams of poetry that strike one at times, it is cold, by the author's own testimony . . . Hardly anyone is apt to contest this these days. Yet at the time this poem burst upon the scene, it was in fact bound to appear an uncommonly great work of art. Remember that until then an unconscionable respect was still accorded Bogdanovich's "Dushenka" and Zhukovsky's "The Twelve Sleeping Maidens"; how wonderstruck the readers of that time must have been by Pushkin's fairy poem wherein all was so new, so original, so alluring—the verse, which was quite without precedent, light, tuneful, harmonious, alive, buoyant; the diction, the bold brushwork, the vivid colors, the graceful capers of young fancy, playful *esprit*, the very freedom of the immodest but nonetheless poetic tableaus . . .
>
> When all is said and done, *Ruslan and Liudmila* is the kind of poem which by its appearance marked an epoch in the history of Russian literature . . . As a fairy-tale written when its time had come, it can even now stand as proof of the fact that our predecessors were not in error when they saw in it living revelation of the advent of a great poet in the Russian land.

RUSLAN AND LIUDMILA

DEDICATION

For you alone, enchanting beauties,
Queens of my spirit, for your sake
Did I convert to scribal duties
Some golden leisure hours, and make,
To whisperings of garrulous ages,
Once-on-a-time my faithful task.
Accept them, then, these playful pages;
And no one's praises do I ask
From fate, but shall be pleased to thank it
If one young girl should love, and pine,
And peep, perhaps beneath her blanket,
At these unshriven songs of mine.

An oaktree greening by the ocean;
A golden chain about it wound:
Whereon a learned cat, in motion
Both day and night, will walk around;
On walking right, he sings a ditty;
On walking left, he tells a lay.

A magic place: there wends his way
The woodsprite, there's a mermaid sitting
In branches, there on trails past knowing
Are tracks of beasts you never met;
On chicken feet a hut is set
With neither door nor window showing.
There wood and dale with wonders teem;
At dawn of day the breakers stream
Upon the bare and barren lea,
And thirty handsome armored heroes
File from the waters' shining mirrors,
With them their Usher from the Sea.
There glimpse a prince, and in his passing
He makes a dreaded tsar his slave;
Aloft, before the people massing,
Across the wood, across the wave,
A warlock bears a warrior brave;
See Baba Yaga's[1] mortar glide
All of itself, with her astride.
There droops Kashchéy,[2] on treasure bent;
There's Russia's spirit...Russian scent!
And there I stayed, and drank of mead;
That oaktree greening by the shore
I sat beneath, and of his lore
The learned cat would chant and read.
One tale of these I kept in mind,
And tell it now to all my kind...

CHANT THE FIRST

The lore of ages long gone by,
In hoar antiquity compounded.

A ducal wassail-chamber high;
By stalwart sons and friends surrounded,
Vladimir-Sun³ sat feasting there;
To valiant Prince Ruslan his fair
Young maid in wedlock he was linking,
And from a heavy tankard sinking
His mead in honor of the pair.
Our forebears were no hasty eaters,
Not speedily, you would have found,
The jars and silver pledging-beakers
Of wine and ale went foaming round.
High cheer of spirit they would pour them,
The spume rose lisping to the brim,
With gravity the bearers bore them
To guests and deeply bowed to them.

Now speeches merge in hum and hubbub;
Abuzz the revelers' gay round;
When tuneful singing of a sudden
Blends with the gusli's nimble sound;
A hush descends; all hark Bayan,
The sweet-voiced bard, for praise to sound
                         them
Of fair Liudmila's grace, Ruslan,
And of the garland Lel had wound them.

But overwhelmed by fiery passion,
Ruslan takes neither drink nor ration;
Upon his heart's-love fixed his gaze,
He is now sigh, now scowl, now blaze,
And gnaws away, impatience mounting,
At his moustache, each moment counting.
With brow beclouded, untoward,
About the clamorous wedding-board
Three other youthful knights are seated;
Their sulking leaves the ladle bare,
The bumpers of their circling cheated,
They take no pleasure in the fare.
They do not hear the bard Bayan;
Their troubled gaze is downward bent:
They are the rivals of Ruslan;
Deep in their luckless hearts is pent
Of love and hate a venom blent.
One is Rogdai, the valiant lord
Who clove wide open with his sword
The bounds of Kiev's fields of gold;
The next—Farlaf, poltroon conceited,
In toping contests undefeated,
But in the sword-clash less than bold;
Fierce young Ratmir, intently brooding,
The Khazar khan, is last, not least:
All three are pale of cheek and moody,
No feast to them, this merry feast.

And now it ends. The diners, surging,
Arise, in noisy swarms converging,
All gazing at the newly wed:
The bride looked down, her color altered,
As if her modest spirit faltered,

The happy bridegroom cheered instead.
But nature lies in shadows huddled,
The hush of midnight drawing on;
The boyars, lately mead-befuddled,
Made their obeisance and are gone.
The groom, in rapturous elation,
Lets his enflamed imagination
Caress his lovely, bashful fair;
While, secret rue his heart o erstealing,
The Duke confers with tender feeling
His blessing on the youthful pair.

And here they lead the bridal maiden
To couch her on the marriage-bed;
And Lel, as other lamps are fading,
Lights his nocturnal torch instead.
Now readies Love his gifts to lovers,
Long-cherished hopes are winning home;
And downward sink the grudging covers
Upon the rugs of Eastern Rome...
Can you not hear the lovelorn whispers,
The dulcet sounds of kisses there,
The gently intercepted lisping
Of final shyness?... Tokens fair
Of ecstasy beforehand given,
The groom now tastes it... Flash! By glare
Of lightning, thunderpeal, is riven
The dusk, the flame dies, smoke is drifting,
All's sunk in sooty murk, all shifting,
Ruslan struck senseless in the gloom...
Then all died down, a voice half broke
The fearsome silence, twice resounding,
A shape from out the depths of smoke

Loomed darker than the haze surrounding...
The chamber hushed in mute repose,
The bridegroom, terrified, arose,
Cold sweat still coursing down his face;
His trembling fingers, chill and stark,
Went out to probe the soundless dark...
Woe! of his lovely friend no trace!
He seizes but on empty air,
Dense gloom: Liudmila is not there—
Snatched in a nameless power's embrace.

Ah, if love's martyrdom condemns
A sufferer to hopeless passion,
Though sad his lot, he still, my friends,
May live to bear it in some fashion.
But let embrace, past endless years,
Close on your love and feel her in it,
The goal of longing, pining, tears,
And have the bride of but one minute
Snatched off and lost forever...I,
For one, my friends, would rather die!

Ruslan, though, worse for him, is living.
What did the Great Duke have to say?
Crushed by the fearful tiding given,
To fury at Ruslan a prey,
"Where, where's Liudmila?" asked he, trembling,
Dread glare of wrath upon his brow.
Ruslan is deaf. "Sons, vassals all!
Your former merits I recall,
Take pity on an old man now!
Well then, which one of you engages
In quest to save my daughter's life?

His exploit shall not lack for wages:
To him—yes, villain, wail and writhe!
Not man enough to guard his wife!—
Liudmila's hand I hereby proffer,
With half my ancestors' domain.
Who, sons and noble friends, will offer?.."
"I!" spoke the brokenhearted swain.
"I!" "I!" Rogdai's cry reinforces
Those of Farlaf and glad Ratmir.
"Straightway we saddle up our horses;
We'll ride the world through; do not fear,
Our Sire, a lengthy separation;
We'll fetch her from the earth's four ends!"
The aged prince to them extends,
By anguish bowed unto prostration,
In wordless gratitude his hands.

All four emerge—Ruslan appearing
Half dead from misery, and grim,
The thought of his lost consort searing
His soul and mortifying him.
And now they mount their mettled horses;
Along the Dnieper's smiling courses
They canter on in dusty swirls;
In haze afar their image furls;
And lost from sight are horse and man...
But long the Great Duke gazes, scanning
The face of the now empty land,
His anxious thought the distance spanning.

Ruslan pined mutely, in a limbo
Where memory and sense are lost.
Behind him rode, one arm akimbo,

Head arrogantly sideways tossed,
Farlaf, puffed up and all-defiant.
He crows: "It almost came too late,
This quest at large—I couldn't wait!
How soon will they bring up a giant?
Then, ahh...let streams of gore be poured,
The pledge that jealous ardors merit,
Rejoice, exult, my faithful sword,
Rejoice, exult, my steed of spirit!"

The Khazar khan, who clasped already
Liudmila in his mind's embrace,
Was fairly dancing in the saddle,
Youth's fervent spirits in him race;
Hope lighting up his gaze with cheer,
He now streaks on in full career,
Now falls to curveting, now teases
His eager stallion, makes him rear,
And charge the hillocks as he pleases.

Grim is Rogdai and mute—what squeezes
His idly jealous heart is fear,
Fear of a dark fate that awaited;
He feels the most unease of all,
And oftentimes his scowl of hatred
On Prince Ruslan will darkly fall.

Throughout that day the rivals travelled
By Dnieper's bank a common trail,
Till shades of night from orient levelled
The sloping banks and filled the vale;
Deep Dnieper lies in mist; the horses
Must needs be rested now and fed.
On yonder a broad highway crosses

A highway wide that slopes ahead.
"Here it is time to part," they voted,
"And chance the fated aftermath."
Each charger then, by steel ungoaded,
In freedom chose its random path.

What now, Ruslan, our luckless farer,
Alone in desert hush? It seems,
Liudmila and that night of terror
Are but the stuff of distant dreams.
Bronze helm on brow more tightly pressing,
From mighty hands the reins dismissing,
You walk your steed amongst the fields,
And in your soul there slowly yields
Faith to despair—hope barely glimmers.

But there! A cave before him shimmers
With light within. Straightway he marches
Beneath its brooding vaults and arches,
With very Nature jointly raised.
He entered moodily, and gazed:
There sits an elder, bright of dome,
Of tranquil mien and whiskers white,
A lamp before him sheds its light
Upon an open parchment tome,
Which he is diligently reading.
"I bid you welcome here, my son,"
He hospitably greets Ruslan.
"I whiled my twilight age away
In here these twenty years preceding;
Now I have lived to see the day
Which I have long anticipated.
This our encounter, son, is fated;

Sit down and hear what I shall say.
From you Liudmila has been wrested;
Your hardy spirit, sorely tested,
Would flag; yet woe will swiftly flee;
Brief is your clash with destiny.
Pluck up your faith and hope, serenely
Brave all, do not despond; fare forth,
And brace your heart and sword more keenly
To carve a pathway to the North.

  Know then, Ruslan: your foul offender
Is the magician Chernomor,
The northern ranges' dread commander,
Fair maidens' predator of yore.
Not ever has his mansion's splendor
Been pierced by human gaze before;
But you, vile artifices' ender,
Shall beard the malefactor, and—
He is to perish by your hand.
No more than this may I uncover,
My son: your future, understand,
Henceforward is your own to govern.

  Crouched at the elder's feet, the knight
Now kissed his hand in exultation.
The world before his eyes turned bright,
Forgot his spirit's sore vexation.
Then he bethought himself; again
Upon his flush a cloud descended.
"That qualm—I know its cause—be ended,"
The elder said, "for it is vain
And easily dispelled. Your terror
Is of the grizzled wizard's love;

But calm yourself, you are in error,
It has no force to harm your dove.
He plucks the stars from heaven's reaches,
He whistles, and the moon will quake,
But what the law of eons teaches
That all his magic cannot shake.
That jealous palpitating warder
Of his unyielding locks and gates
Is but an impotent marauder
To the sweet captive that he baits.
About her chambers mutely slinking,
He execrates his fate unblest...
But goodly knight, the sun is sinking,
And you are much in need of rest."

Before the flame, now slowly dying,
Upon a yielding bed of moss,
Ruslan would plunge in sleep...but toss
And turn is all he does; and sighing,
At last he calls the elder here:
"Sleep, father, shuns my couch, I fear!
No wonder, for my soul is ailing;
Where life is torment, slumber flees;
Accord me for my spirit's ease
Your saintly speech. Forgive my failing
If too uncouth be my address:
Who are you, man of kind intention,
Fate's intimate, past comprehension,
Who sent you to this wilderness?"

Then with a rueful smile replying:
"I scarce recall the darksome earth
Of my far land," he said with sighing;

"A Finnish shepherd lad by birth,
In valleylands unknown to strangers
I drove the flocks of nearby granges
And knew in boyhood free of care
But streams, the brooding forest's rustle,
The caverns of our cliffsides bare,
And rustic poverty's gay bustle.
But not for long was it my lot
To haunt that gay and tranquil spot.

At that time in a nearby clearing,
Like a lone wildwood flower endearing,
There lived Naina. She outshone
All maidens like the day at dawning.
One day I drove at early morning
My flocks to graze, and played upon
The bagpipe as the herd assembled;
A brook ran babbling through the heath,
By which a fair young beauty rambled
Alone, and wove a flowery wreath.
I was foredoomed by having seen her...
Ah, goodly knight, it was Naina!
I joined her—and a fatefull spell
Repaid the forward gaze with capture,
And love came in my heart to dwell,
Love seized it with his heavenly rapture
And with his agonies of hell.

My heart, as month on month succeeded,
Drove me in tremors to her side.
'I love you,' I confessed, and pleaded
My grief—but only selfish pride
Received the bashful plea I muttered.

Her beauty was her only joy,
And with indifference she uttered:
'I do not love you, shepherd boy!'

Then all was turned to gloom and folly,
My native groves, the sylvan shade,
The merry games the shepherds played—
No ray would pierce my melancholy,
In withering grief the spirit pined.
Then I bestirred my wounded mind
To leave the Finnish fields behind,
To scour with a fraternal band
The faithless billow of the oceans,
To stir Naina's proud emotions
By warlike fame, and win her hand.
Audacious boatmen I assembled
To quest for perils and for gold;
Then first the tranquil homeland trembled
With clash of chiseled sabres bold
And thudding of the warlike oar.
With my intrepid band I threaded
My eager way twixt main and shore,
Ten years we quested thus and redded
The seas and snows with foemen's gore.
The tiding spreads: the foreign princes
Grow fearful of our daring raids,
Each vaunted band of champions winces
And wilts before the northern blades.
Thus gaily, cruelly, we battled,
The spoils and gifts to share increased,
With each defeated foe we settled
To share a hospitable feast.
My heart, though, mindful of Naina,

Amid both gaiety and gore,
Nursed secret sorrow, ever keener
To seek the native Finnish shore.
'Home beckons, fisherman and farmer,'
I cried, 'it's time for idle armor
'Neath native eaves to hang in store.'
I spoke and forthwith called to quarters,
And, mortal terror in our wake,
We sailed with pride and joy to make
The shelter of our homeland's waters.

Now were the dreams of old fulfilled,
Now slaked desires so fiercely burning!
Here was the moment, sought with yearning,
For ardor to be sweetly stilled!
At proud Naina's feet I scattered,
Atop my sabre blood-bespattered,
Of coral, gold, and pearl the prize.
In front of her, my mind confounded
With passion's thrall, I stood, surrounded
By girlish envy and surmise,
A bondsman meek to serve her truly;
The maiden, though, withdrew with cold
Sufficiency, announcing coolly:
'I do not love you, warrior bold!'

Why strain, my son, to tell or think
What it is torment to remember?
Why, now, alone, and at the brink
Of death, my spirit numbed, I tremble,
By grief resurging newly seared,
And then from memory's deep sources
At times along my frosty beard
A tear of desolation courses.

But listen: in my native fen,
Among the lonely fishermen
Are hid miraculous traditions:
In timeless hush past human ken,
In farthest forest darkness dreary,
There live the silver-haired magicians;
In steadfast quest of wisdom eery
All potency of mind they spend.
By their dread voices all is driven
That ever breathed below, above;
Into their awesome will is given
Both life and death, and very love.
Love's hunted huntsman unto madness,
I thought in my despairing sadness
To bend Naina's heart to me
And warm her chill disdain to gladness
At my pursuit—through sorcery.
I sped away where freedom beckoned,
The twilight of the trackless wood,
And there in long apprenticehood
I dwelt, for years untold, unreckoned.
At last I knew the dreamed-of second
When nature's fearful spell, long sought,
Was grasped by my illumined thought:
High magic to my mind accorded!
Love garlanded, desire rewarded!
Now, proud Naina, you are mine,
I thought, achieved the fond design!
Instead, though, the triumphant suitor
Was fate, my stubborn persecutor.

My hopes still youthfully alive,
And parched with passion to the marrow,

My spells I hastily contrive,
I call on spirits—and an arrow,
Like lightning, parts the leafy gloom,
A gale sets all awhirl, aboom,
A quaking seizes earth and tree...
Before me all at once I see
A snow-haired crone, decrepit, shrunken,
Her rheumy blinkers deeply sunken,
Hunched over, agued piteously,
Embodiment of senile blight—
It was Naina, goodly knight!..
Bereft of speech, I stood aghast.
My eyes, the loathly phantom ranging,
Would not accept the horrid changeling;
Then bursting into tears, I asked:
'You—my Naina? You!..' I faltered,
'Naina—where did beauty flee?
Oh answer me—how could it be
You were so pitilessly altered?
Was it long since,' I asked in tears,
'That far from life and love I wandered?
How long ago?' 'Just forty years,'
The maiden's fateful tones responded;
'My age is seventy today.
Such is the way of things,' she quavered,
'In swarms the years have flown away.
My spring, or yours, will not be savored
Afresh—we both are old and gray.
But friend, is life without allure
Because inconstant youth forsook it?
My hair is white now, to be sure,
Perhaps I am a little crooked,
A trifle slower to entice,
Not quite as lively, quite as nice;

But then (she mouthed), let me confess:
I have become a sorceress!'

   And in good earnest it was true.
I stood and stared at her, dumbfounded,
An imbecile for all I knew,
For all the lore I had compounded.

   There's worse to come! My sorcery
Took full effect, to my misfortune.
My wizened idol warmed to me
With passion, started to importune.
On withered lips a ghastly smile,
In churchyard tones she would beguile,
Avowals, hoarsely wheezed, she offered...
Can you imagine what I suffered?
I shuddered, looked away, while she
Poured out, as best she could for coughing,
A sultry, slow soliloquy:
'Yes, now I know my heart—for loving,
For tender passion it was fated;
My friend, whose heart devoutly waited,
My feelings are aroused, in anguish
Of sensuous agony I languish,
Come, thrill to my embraces, soon,
Ah, dearest, dearest, now! I swoon...'

   And all through this, her gazes lingered
On me so mooningly, Ruslan;
And all through this, she feebly fingered
The shrinking folds of my kaftan;
And all through this, I closed my eyes,
Revulsion rising strong and stronger,
Till I could stand for it no longer

And broke away with stifled cries.
She started after. 'Shame!' she spattered,
'My maidenly repose you shattered,
Besieged my virginal retreat!
You begged Naina's love—you gain it—
And now—how like a man!—disdain it!
You all are steeped in vile deceit!
Alas, I am myself to blame;
He flattered me, seducer fashion,
And I succumbed to reckless passion...
Deceiver, profligate! Oh shame!
But tremble, heartless libertine!'

With this we parted. Since that scene
I've lived in solitude and quiet;
The disenchanted soul's surcease,
The aging spirit's soothing diet,
Are nature, scholarship, and peace.
By now I bide the grave's release;
And yet the crone's repressed desire
Is not forgotten all the same,
And thwarted love's belated flame
Now fuels not chagrin but ire.
To malice prone her spirit's night,
I have no doubt, the old enchantress
Will make you too endure her spite;
But then, no grief on earth is endless."

With rapt attention did our knight
Drink in the elder's tale, not hearing
The quiet winging of the night
In his bemusement; neither blearing
Nor drowsing blurred his lucid sight.

But day is breaking, rainbow-hued...
Ruslan in rueful gratitude
Embraces his magician friend;
His spirit buoyed with hope again,
He walks away. His thighs, astraddle,
With firmness grip the whinnying steed,
He whistles, straightening in the saddle—
"Be with me, father, in my need!"—
And canters down the empty clearing,
The silverhaired enchanter cheering
His pupil on: "God speed your ride!
Farewell, enjoy your lovely bride,
And grant the elder's counsel hearing!"

CHANT THE SECOND

Competitors for martial glory,
Let not your rivalry abate;
Bring up your sacrifices gory,
Be inexhaustible in hate!
Let peace still gaze aghast upon you,
At your dread banquets freeze in fear:
No one will waste compassion on you
Or stir himself to interfere.
Competitors of different station,
You knights of the Parnassian hills,
Try not to entertain the nation
With shameless clash of brawling quills;
By all means quarrel—but discreetly.
And you, competitors in love,
If you can manage, take it sweetly!
To whom unchanging fate above—
You may believe me, friends—assigns
A maiden's heart, he willy-nilly
Will thwart the whole wide world's designs;
Then anger is a sin—and silly.

When first Rogdai, the knight undaunted,
By nebulous forebodings haunted,
Had left his way-companions, and
By rugged trails of random choosing
Rode through deserted forest land,
His mind engrossed in heavy musing—

The evil spirit plagued and snared
The soul in ruminating labor;
The heartsick knight abruptly flared:
"I'll slash all barriers—with my sabre!
Ruslan...now you shall find me out...
We'll see a maiden weeping sadly..."
At once he reined his steed about
And urged it back, and spurred it madly.

Meanwhile, the valorous Farlaf,
The morning sweetly slumbered off,
Has settled by a brook to eat;
Well sheltered from the noonday heat,
He solaces his moral tissues
In lone repose. But as he issues,
He sees a horseman down the mead
Come charging up on foaming steed;
Whereon, with all convenient speed,
Abandoning both lunch and gear,
His armor, helmet, gloves, and spear,
He gallops off and takes no chance
On venturing a backward glance.
"Rein in, dishonored, craven wooer!"
He hears the voice of his pursuer;
"Just wait till I catch up with you,
I'll trim you down a foot or two!"
Farlaf took in the voice, and finding
It was Rogdai, curled up with dread,
And sensing certain death behind him,
Lashed on his horse still more instead.
Just so a rabbit, wildly bolting,
His ears in panic downward folding,
Will streak through paddock, copse, and mound,

Ahead of the pursuing hound.
The spring had melted into torrents
The thawing snows along the crest,
And where the chase went, turbid currents
Were furrowing earth's dampened breast.
The mettled charger faced the ditch,
Flicked tail and snowy mane at it,
Took in his teeth the iron bit,
And leapt across without a hitch.
Less venturesome, the portly rider
Diverged into the turbid flood;
Legs weaving like a foundered spider,
He plumped inertly in the mud,
And gave up life with earth and sky...
Here came, with sword upraised, Rogdai;
"Now perish, coward; die!" he thundered;
Then saw it was Farlaf, and wondered,
And looked again, and dropped his sword,
Surprise, chagrin, and rage compounded
Upon his troubled features warred;
The hero ground his teeth, dumbfounded,
Then wheeled about, head low, and fairly
Raced from the runnel's muddy shelf.
He fumed, he cursed...yet barely, barely
Could keep from laughing at himself.

Then, riding up a hill, he found
A little crone, all feeble-jointed,
Hunched over, snowy-haired; she pointed
Her crutch to send him northward bound.
"There you will come on him," she urged him.
Rogdai, his confidence resurging,
From sheer elation caught his breath

And galloped off to certain death.

And our Farlaf? Still deep in mud,
Feet up, distrustful of survival,
Afraid of breathing lest his blood
Be forfeit to his raging rival...
But now he hears just overhead
The crone's sepulchral tones instead:
"Get up, my gallant: fear no more,
No further trials are in store.
Here, I have brought your charger too.
Get up, I have to speak to you."

The knight's bedraggled residue
Crawled from the ditch; still on all fours,
His strange surroundings shyly eying,
In blithe relief he uttered, sighing:
"Well, God be praised—no bumps, no sores!"

The crone went on: "Liudmila's search
Sets quite a riddle to unravel;
That bird is on a distant perch,
Too far for you or me to travel.
It's risky work to quest and roam,
Why, you yourself might come to suffer;
Accept the sound advice I offer
And amble peacefully back home.
Near Kiev, such is my opinion,
In your inherited dominion,
You'll prosper free of fear or fuss:
Liudmila won't escape from us."

This said, she vanished. All abustle,

Our knight, judicious man he was,
Set off for home without a pause,
Forgotten dreams of hardihood,
And those of love at least withstood;
The slightest murmur in the wood,
A babbling brook, a bluetit's rustle,
Sufficed to make him sweat and hustle.

Ruslan, far off by now, is coursing
Ahead through fields and forests wide,
His mind's insistent custom forcing
His pace toward his lovely bride.
He cries: "My love, my consort sweet!
How shall I win you back, where meet
Your gaze again of bright caress,
Your converse gay with tenderness?
Are you by grudging fate imprisoned
Forever in this warlock's might,
And your sweet maidhood, soured and wizened,
Condemned to wilt in dungeon night?
Or will a rival, bold and lusty,
Outride me? No, love—never fret:
My shoulders wield a sabre trusty,
And there's a head upon them yet."

One day at dusk Ruslan was riding
A bank that, steep like an abyss,
Plunged to a river darkly gliding
Deep down. All of a sudden, hiss!
An arrow hard beside him wailing,
The clink of mail, a whinny, hailing,
Withal a hollow thud and clout,
Then "Halt!" a challenge thunders out.

He looks around and sees downfield,
Raised to-the-ready spear and shield,
A horseman storming up—and grim,
He wheels to match him stride for stride.
"Stand still! Aha! caught up with him!"
Exults the fierce assailant, flashing
His teeth—"now for a mortal slashing;
Here you lay down both life and pride;
Right here go questing for your bride."
Ruslan, outraged at his upbraiding—
He knew that blustering voice at once—

But reader! What about our maiden?
Let's leave the horsemen for the nonce;
We'll soon be back there, but before,
It's more than time now to be turning
To the fair prisoner and learning
Her fate with dreaded Chernomor.

Indecorous comrade-in-arms
Of my disorderly invention,
I took the liberty to mention
How one dark night Liudmila's charms
Were whisked away at one fell stroke
From eager hands in swathes of smoke.
Now, at the time—distressful plight!—
The fiend's inexorable might
Had swept you off the bridal pillows,
Spun like the whirlwind up and out,
And through black air and foggy billows,
Sped to his mountainous redoubt—
You, reft by the revolving vastness
Of nerve and sense, revived—in dread,

Still speechless, tremulous, half dead—
In the enchanter's fearsome fastness.

Thus, standing by my cabin door
Once in the summer time, I saw
The chicken-run's majestic pasha
Pursue one of his harem, rush her
About the yard, with outspread wings
In sensuous ecstasy already
Embrace his love; but aerial rings
Are drawn above him, shrewd and steady;
Pernicious stratagem in train,
The village poultry's ancient bane,
The gray kite hovered—veered to lunge,
And struck the yard with lightning plunge.
He soars up, spirals high, and passes
To far-off shades of safe crevasses,
Grim talons in his luckless prey.
Grieved at the murderous foray,
No less by chilling terror shattered,
The rooster vainly calls his love...
All that he sees is drifting fluff,
On drifting breezes slowly scattered..

The princess labored until morn
In throes of dreamlike indecision,
As one who in a nightmare vision
Lies paralyzed—until at dawn
She rose; her waking mind unsealing
Excitement mixed with nameless fear;
Her soul seeks flaming heights of feeling
Gropes for a someone, senses reeling:
"Where is my spouse," she lisps, "my dear?"

She calls—and would recall the sound,
And gazes fearfully around.
Where is her chamber gone? Instead
The captive maiden's limbs are spread
On swells of down; above her hovers
A splendid silken canopy;
The tapestries, the quilted covers
Are patterned, tasseled broidery;
Brocaded tapestries abounding;
In clusters rubies wink and blaze;
And golden censers, all surrounding,
Diffuse an aromatic haze;
Enough, though...luckily I needn't
Describe this realm of magic thrall:
Scheherezade, my antecedent
To those purlieus, has done it all.
But rich appointments go unheeded
If our true love is not on call.

  Three girls, of comeliness entrancing,
In charming light attire advancing
Upon the princess, with profound
Obeisance curtsied to the ground.
Then, all inaudibly, one darted
Up to Liudmila, light as air,
And with ethereal fingers started
To braid our maiden's golden hair,
(An art spent nowadays on curls),
Then pressed on her pale brow and parted
Fair hair a diadem of pearls.
With modestly averted glances
The second maiden now advances;
A saraphan of azure dims

The splendor of Liudmila's limbs;
A filmy veil descends, enfolding
Her shoulders, breast, and tresses golden,
Like mist at dawn in gauziness.
Begrudging covers now caress
Enchantments fit for Eden's dwellers,
And flimsy slippers lightly press
Those feet of which the gods are jealous.
The third girl hands her, last to linger,
A belt of pearl-encrusted skeins,
The while, invisibly, a singer
Diverts her with her merry strains.
Alas—her heart derives no easing
From saraphans or pearly bands,
From songs or entertainments pleasing,
Or jeweled clasps for golden strands.
Unseen, the looking glass might borrow
The glory of her form, her dress;
She, eyes cast down and motionless,
Persists in silence and in sorrow.

(Those who have gleaned the truth of ages
From heart's most dark and private pages,
Emerge confirmed in the belief
That if a lady, deep in grief,
Through tears, by stealth, in spite of reason,
Decorum, common sense, or season,
Does not still look into the glass—
She must be in a hopeless pass.)

Liudmila, lonesome and forlorn,
Not knowing what to do, is drawn
Up to the latticed window yonder,

And lets her glances sadly wander
Across that vastness far and drear.
All speaks of death. The snowy highlands
For glaring carpets glitter near,
Whence, like immense and changeless islands
Of craggy white, the peaks protrude
And in eternal stillness brood.
No smoke from cottage chimneys stealing,
No snowy path a wanderer gropes,
No hunting pack's melodious pealing,
No horn-notes thrill these desert slopes.
At most you see a whirlwind sailing
That emptiness with dismal wailing,
And on the skyline's sallow gray
Denuded forests sadly sway.

In helpless tears, Liudmila stands
And thinks, face buried in her hands:
God—what awaits me, wretched mortal?..
She pushed against a silver portal;
It opened with a tuneful sound,
And the astonished maiden found
A park: far more enchanted ground
Than all the pleasances, we read,
Were roamed by pastoral Armide,
Than terraces King Solomon
Or dukes of Tauris sported on.
The world of green about her harbors
Palm avenues, and laurel banks,
And myrtle trees in fragrant ranks,
A wealth of swaying, rustling arbors,
With cedar spires superbly towering,
And orange groves, part gold, part flowering.

Their shapes in tranquil pools revive;
Hills, glades, and valleys all around
In fervent spring's renewal thrive;
The cooling airs of May run throbbing
Along the wonderstricken ground,
In shades of trembling foliage sobbing
The Chinese nightingale is found.
Slim adamantine founts aspire
With merry splashing to the sky:
Beneath are statues to admire
That seem alive...if Phidias' eye,
Whom Pallas and Apollo taught,
Had seen them gleam there in the drizzle,
He would have dropped his magic chisel,
At first enchanted, then distraught.
On marble barriers led to shatter
In winking arcs of nacreous flash,
Plunge waterfalls, foam up, and scatter;
While brooks in shade of birch and ash
With lazy ripples barely plash.
Like shelters from the verdant brilliance
For cool and quiet here and there,
There wink ethereal pavilions,
And eager roses everywhere
Lend flush and fragrance to the air.
Yet my Liudmila, feeling tragic,
Walks by it all but does not see;
The gloss and luxury of magic
Have lost the charm of novelty.
She strolls, not caring whither bound,
And walks the garden all around,
And has her fill of bitter weeping,
At times with stricken glances sweeping

The sky's impenetrable vaults.
The lovely eyes abruptly brighten:
A finger on her lip, she halts;
It seems, a thought to tempt and frighten
Has struck her... An escape she fears
Lies open: high above her, clinging
To facing boulders, there appears
A bridge across the fall—and wringing
Her hands, disconsolate, she nears
And stares into the foaming eddy
In tears, resolved to end it all;
Brow clutched, breast beaten, she is ready—
But does not jump into the fall
And goes on walking after all.

   But tiring soon, our charming captive
(So long outdoors and on her feet),
Stopped, dried her tears, and grew receptive
When something in her murmured "eat?"
She sat and looked about—how easy!
For whoosh! an awning rustles down
To shelter her, all dim and breezy;
An exquisite repast is laid,
The setting sparks with crystal glitter;
From quiet depths of leafy shade
Clear runs of harp-notes trill and titter.
The princess marveled much at this,
In private though, took it amiss:
"Torn from my love, imprisoned, friendless—
Why should my stay on earth be endless?
Ah, jailer, whose pernicious lust
Would now indulge me, now torment me—
Your evil might cannot prevent me

From choosing death: I can! I must...
I have no stomach for your tents,
Your tedious songs, your blandishments—
I want no meals, no tunes, no meeting,
I'll die amidst your opulence!"
The princess thought, and—started eating.

Liudmila rose; which action banished
From sight the sumptuous repast,
The awning next, the music last,
Till all the sorcery had vanished.
Alone again, she roams the gardens,
From grove to glade she strays, forlorn,
Serenely through her sapphire stardoms
Selene, queen of night, is borne.
On every side the vapors thicken,
With streamers weaving hill to hill;
And she, abruptly slumber-stricken,
Feels lifted by an unknown will,
Which wafts her through the air and eases
More airily than vernal breezes
Through vesper incense of the rose
Her form across the chamber sill
Back on her couch, more gently still—
Her couch of mourning, bed of woes.
In come, once more, the three young girls
And, bustling, set about their service
Unrobing her of gown and pearls;
But their expressions, sad and nervous,
Their downcast, taciturn constraint,
Speak unavailing reprimands
To Fate, a wordless shared complaint.
We hasten on: by tender hands

The slumbrous princess is undressed;
Sweet with the charm of careless ease,
In but a snowy-white chemise,
She beds herself at length for rest.
Obeisance rendered, heavy-hearted,
The maidens hastily departed
And gently pressed the portals to.
And now—how does our prisoner do?
Shakes like a leaf, her breathing stilled,
Eyes black with fear, her bosom chilled;
A fitful slumber leaves her troubled;
She strains to penetrate the gloom,
Unstirring, watchfulness redoubled:
Her heartbeat in the pitch-black room
Thrums in that silence of a tomb.
The darkness whispers...now she hears
A creeping sound behind her curtain;
And now... oh horror! steps, for certain—
She hides in pillows to her ears...
A noise outside her door. The night
Was rent apart by sudden beaming,
The door became a shaft of light,
And wordlessly, majestic-seeming,
With scimitars unsheathed and gleaming,
A long twin file of moors appeared,
Most solemn of expressions wearing,
On pillows sedulously bearing
An equal length of silver beard.
And chin in air, there stalks behind it,
With measured gravity highminded,
A hunchbacked dwarf of haughty mien;
A tall tarboosh protects the sheen
Upon his skull, completely shaven—

Those whiskers' launching place and haven.
He is quite near now! Like a streak
Liudmila hurtles through the curtain
And flies to clutch the grizzled freak
With nimble fingers by the turban;
With shaking fist she gives a tweak,
And, terrified, lets out a shriek
That all the moors are deafened quite.
The startled hunchback cringes, winces,
Turns paler than the frantic princess,
His hands clapped on his ears in fright;
He tried to run away, but tangled
In his own beard, fell down, half strangled
Got up, fell down; he lurched and swerved,
The dusky train of thralls, unnerved,
Broke up and buzzed and whirled and wrangled,
Then picked the wizard off the mat
And whisked him off to be untangled,
Leaving Liudmila with his hat.

But what about our hero bright?
Recall that startling clash of gallants!
Orlovsky,[4] lend your pencil's talents
To limn the slaughter and the night!
Upon that lurid moonlit stage
The heroes' fight to death advances,
Their hearts are choked with silent rage,
Far off already hurled their lances,
The sabres shivered to the cage,
Blood from their iron tunics leaking,
Their bucklers chopped to chips and creaking...
They wrestle, matching wrench and thrust,
And, raising clouds of inky dust,

The blooded steeds beneath them battle;
With armors locked, the fighters bold,
Each as if welded to the saddle,
Maintain their double stranglehold.
Their limbs with hatred intergrow
And stiffen, as if fused forever;
Their veins abrim with fiery glow,
Each chest agasp on chest of foe—
But now they weaken, seem to sever—
One must go down...there! still astraddle,
My knight with arms of iron clasps
And wrests his foeman from the saddle;
He lifts him high above his head,
And—hurls him to the riverbed.
"Go under!" vengefully he rasps.
"One faithless grudging foe is dead."

You guess, my friends, who shared the glory
Of that affray Ruslan has fought.
It was that battle-seeker gory,
Rogdai, the pride of Kiev's court,
The bright Liudmila's sombre slave.
Along the Dnieper, northward bound,
He'd sought his rival's trail; had found,
Caught up; albeit the strength of yore
Forsook the fosterling of war;
And Kiev's champion, ever brave,
Found in the wilderness his grave.
They say, one of the river daughters,
A young rusalka of those waters,
Received him to her chilly breast,
And kissing him with laughing zest,
Drew him to share her moisty quarters.

And in the deep of night since then,
There stalks the quiet banks at random
The captive hero's mighty phantom,
The scare of lonely fishermen.

CHANT THE THIRD

In vain you lingered in seclusion,
My verse, for happy friends to see!
You still must suffer the intrusion
Of evil-minded scrutiny.
Has not a sallow carper tried
To floor me with the fateful question:
Why do I call my hero's bride,
As if to wound her husband's pride,
"Princess" and "maid?" A fine suggestion!
You recognize, my gentle reader,
Aspersion's spiteful Judas-kiss!
Come, Zoilus,[5] come, mischief-breeder,
How am I to reply to this?
For shame! But I refuse to quarrel;
Blush, graceless wretch, and hie thee hence!
I know myself profoundly moral,
My lips are sealed by innocence.
You, though, will feel for me, Climène,[6]
With sultry languor downward gazing,
Slave to an irksome Hymen's ban...
I see a fallen tear is hazing
My page, which to the heart is clear;
You flush, your eyes grow darker, glower;
A sigh unspoken...speaks! Ah, fear,
Sir Jealousy, here comes the hour;
Beware—for Love and Anger flouted
Have entered an audacious pact,

Your graceless brow will soon have sprouted
The mark of the avenging act.

   A frigid dawn by now is gilding
The Borean summits' rugged hulks;
Still silent stands the magic building.
But Chernomor, in moody sulks,
Tarboosh-less, dressing-gowned, sits yawning
Upon his bed and chides the morning.
His flowing silver beard alone
A score of silent moors are serving;
And tenderly a comb of bone
Meanders down its every curving.
On his interminable whiskers
Are sprayed, for lure and benefit,
Sweet balm of musk and brisk hibiscus,
And cunning waves are crimped in it.
Abruptly through the window flashing
A dragon sailed on horny wings;
It set its scaly armor clashing,
And coiling up in glistening rings,
Changed to Naina—yes, none other,
Before the wonderstricken throng.
"Salute to you," she hailed, "Sir Brother,
Confrère I have esteemed so long!
By clamorous report alone
Great Chernomor to me was known;
Now secret fate has joined us strangers
In common enmity and dread;
You are beset by certain dangers,
Black clouds have gathered overhead;
To me, the voice of honor slighted
Is retribution's goad and spur."

The dwarf extends his hand to her,
His smile is crafty and delighted,
"August Naina," he exclaims,
"I truly cherish your alliance.
We'll set at naught the Finn's defiance,
I do not fear his knavish games.
A feeble adversary he;
For learn my power's mysterious essence,
How Chernomor not randomly
Displays his hirsute efflorescence:
As long as these my whiskers white
A hostile sabre does not sever,
So long no mortal man, no knight,
No, not the boldest champion ever,
Can tamper with my least endeavor.
Liudmila stays my captive darling
Forever, and Ruslan is doomed."
The witch malignly echoed, snarling:
"To be entombed! To be entombed!"
With this, three times she stamped the ground,
Let out three hisses, shook her ruff,
And dragon-shaped again, flew off.

Resplendent in brocaded gown,
The magus, cheered by reinforcement,
Once more decided to show off
For the fair prisoner's endorsement
His beard, his homage, and his love.
He follows, then, his fragrant skein
Into Liudmila's room again;
He paces down the whole long floor—
No princess there. He tries the door
Out to the park; past cedars tall

Along the lake, around the fall,
In groves, in arbors tries to find her:
In vain! she left no trace behind her.
Who can describe his palsied quaking,
His bridling outrage, frenzied shaking?
The midget's strident bellow sounded;
Beside himself with rage, he rounded
Upon his thralls: "Here, at a run,
Look for Liudmila every one!
Off, I rely on you! At once!
Mark me—at once! I will be feared!
Just try to take me for a dunce,
And you'll be strangled in my beard!"

Well, reader mine, shall I relate
Just where our lovely one had skittered?
All night she had bethought her fate
In moist-eyed wonderment and—tittered.
The beard still awed her, but the dwarf
No longer was a dreadful rumor;
She knew him, and he was a laugh—
And terror sits but ill with humor.
The rays of morning slanting nearer,
Liudmila, rising to the dawn,
Had her regard obliquely drawn
Into a lofty limpid mirror.
From lily shoulders golden strands
Unthinkingly she culled and parted,
Unconsciously by careless hands
A glossy braid was somehow started.
Then, in a corner, unawares
She came upon her first day's clothing;
She sighed, and dressed, and, struck with
                                    loathing,

Gave way again to quiet tears.
Her eyes, however, did not leave
The faithful glass in her emotion;
And then she happened to conceive
A frivolously girlish notion:
To try for size the wizard's hat.
All private in her habitat,
No prying eyes—what could it matter?
What sort of headgear does not flatter
A girl of seventeen, at that?
And trying on is always fun!
She turned the hat: now backward slanted—
Down on one eyebrow—level—canted—
And front-to-back she put it on.
Just then—oh miracles of yore!
Liudmila vanished from the mirror;
She turned the hat back, ventured nearer,
Her image met her as before;
She turned it back—a void once more—
She took it off—back in somehow!
"Too bad, my spellster friend, too bad!
What price the great magician now?
This should dispose of you, my lad!"
The maiden, flushed with wicked pleasure,
Put on the hat of the old lecher
And turned it backward as she had.

Back to our hero, though. I blush
To have dilated long and late
On moors and whiskers and tarboosh,
Abandoning Ruslan to fate!
Fought off the onslaught of Rogdai,
He slowly rides through drowsing forest

Down to a valley broadly terraced
Beneath a lustrous morning sky.
He cannot help a shudder, sighting
A grim tableau of ancient fighting.
Bleak desolation: everywhere
Shine bleaching bones—now here, now there
Stray armor rusting in the field,
A broadsword, clutched in bony fingers,
A gorget, a corroded shield;
Weed-grown, a shaggy helmet lingers,
Within, a shrunken deathshead fraying;
A knight's entire skeleton
Lies where he fell, still mounted on
A steed unfleshed; spent lances, graying,
Rise slanted from the softened site,
In peaceful ivy garlands swaying.
No sound appears about to alter
This spectacle of torpid blight;
The sun from his empyreal height
Illuminates the vale of slaughter.

   The prince looks all about with groans,
And murmurs, heavy-eyed and sighing:
"Oh field of battle, field of dying,
Who planted you to brittle bones?
What host in bloody battle-gear
Last stamped on you, whose noble prancer?
Who sank on you with glory here?
Whose prayers did the heavens answer?
Why have you fallen mute and yield
To rank oblivion's choking grasses?...
What if from time's black grip, oh field,
Not I, not anybody passes?

What if some hillock mute and grim
Becomes the grave of Prince Ruslan,
And bardic music of Bayan
Strikes up no memory of him?"

But a knight-errant needs a sword,
And armor-plating never harmed him;
So presently Ruslan recalled
That combat had of late disarmed him.
He strides about the battlefield;
'Mid bones with creepers interwoven,
In rustling piles of cuisse and shield,
Of sword and helmet bent and cloven,
He seeks a suit of mail or chain.
Then woke the steppe from numb abandon,
With clash and clatter shrilled the plain,
He picked a buckler, half at random,
A ringing horn, a helmet trim—
Alone a sword eluded him.
All kinds of carvers leaned and lay,
But all were flimsy or too short;
He was a fine substantial sort,
Not like the knights of latter-day.
In want of exercise and fun,
He picked a lance of steel for play,
Then pulled an iron tunic on
And thus continued on his way.

The ruddy western flares are paling
Above an earth to slumber soon;
From bluish swathes of vapor sailing
There now ascends a golden moon.
The steppe is shadowed, dark the track,

From it across nocturnal gloom
Ruslan, bemused, sees, deeper black,
Far off a massive hillock loom;
There something fearsome seems to snore.
He rides up closer, close—and hears:
The mound is breathing, it appears.
He looks and listens as before,
In perfect calm, his heart unflagging;
But, nervous ears erect and wagging,
The horse digs in his heels and quakes;
His stubborn head flung high, he shakes,
His bristling mane on end with fright.
Beneath the moon, no longer clouded,
The mound, in gauzy vapor shrouded,
Before the prince's eyes turns bright,
Revealing a portentous sight...
How bring it home to mind or sense?
It is a living head—immense,
Its massive eyelids closed in slumber;
It snores; from the prodigious rumble
The helmet rocks, its windblown plume
Fades out aloft in shadowy gloom.
In frightful comeliness, inert
Above the darkened prairie towering,
With overwhelming silence girt,
This desolation's guardian louring
Looms awesomely in front of him,
A misty hulk with menace grim.
Ruslan, incredulous, would close
With this gargantuan repose
And break it, if he might with profit.
He rode a watchful circuit of it
And, speechless, stopped before the nose.

Its nostrils with a spear-tip teased,
The head raised up its lids and shivered,
Then quickly puckered up and sneezed...
A whirlwind rose, the prairie quivered,
Dust swirled; from whisker, brow, and lash
A tumbling swarm of barn-owls crash;
From slumber waken brush and weed,
An echo-sneeze—the dauntless steed
Rears, neighs, speeds off on flying feet;
The rider barely keeps his seat.
And then a voice behind them thundered:
"Hoy, foolish knight, where have you blundered?
Come, let's enjoy our rendezvous!
I gobble cheeky boys like you!"
Ruslan looked back, by proud if painful
Exertion reined his steed about,
And gave a laugh, his voice disdainful.
"What do you want?" the head cried out.
"What kind of visitor, God rest me,
Fate sends on purpose to molest me!
Run, while you can without a fight!
I'm going back to sleep, it's night,.
Good-bye!" The knight, with indignation
Responding to this rude address,
Exclaimed in angry reprobation:
"Subside, you boom of hollowness!
Have you not heard the true refrain:
A giant skull, a midget brain?
I ride and ride, straight down the middle,
And when I strike, I do not fiddle!"
At this, dumbfounded by his daring,
The head, with pent-up fury glaring,
Swelled up; the bloodshot eyes resembled

Live embers with their scarlet gleam;
The lips, all flecked with lather, trembled,
While ears and mouth were wreathed in steam—
And suddenly, its cheeks dilated,
It fell to blowing at our knight;
In vain his steed, its chest inflated,
Head straining sideways, eyes closed tight,
Tried to press forward unabated
Through all this whirlwind, rain, and night;
Exhausted, terrified, half-blinded,
Once more it flings its legs behind it
And flies for cover out of sight.
Once more the hero, stoutly tackling
The head, is blown away, alack!
That monster, for its part, is cackling
Behind him like a maniac
And shouts: "Prince Charming! Hero! Clown!
You are not off?? Don't let me down!!
Tut, tut, he's running like a stag!
And you a champion fighter! Hear me,
Give me one teensy slap to cheer me,
Before you've ruined your poor nag!"
With this the thing, for illustration,
Struck out its tongue and gave a leer;
Ruslan, concealing his frustration,
With silent menace weighed his spear.
His arm propelled it, sinews pliant,
The chilly iron hissed, defiant,
And quivered in the shameless tongue;
And blood came weltering in torrents
Where from the frantic maw it hung.
The head, from pain, surprise, abhorrence
In a profoundly chastened mood,

Its crimson color fading, chewed
On steel; still seething, but subdued.
Thus on our stage you see at times
One of the Muse's lesser mimes,
From unexpected hissing deaf,
No longer know stage-right from left;
He pales, forgets his lines, sweats rivers,
His head droops to his chest, he shivers,
And with a gulp comes quite unglued
Before the hooting multitude.
To profit by the state of nerves
Which grips the head, our gallant swerves
And, hawklike, swoops to the attack.
His doughty right hand, raised above,
Deals with its heavy armored glove
The giant cheek a frightful thwack;
The steppe reechoed with the crack,
Which carnadined its dewy heather
Both far and wide with bloody lather.
The head was rocking—teetered back,
Half wheeled, fell down, and started rolling,
Its iron helmet loudly tolling.
Look! on its recent base or source
A sword of chivalry lay glinting.
The joyful prince with quick resource
Took hold of it, and followed, sprinting,
The head along its blood-daubed course,
Intent (of all uncouth ideas)
On lopping off its nose and ears.
The falchion is already raised,
Already starting down and swishing—
When suddenly he hears, amazed,
A plaintive moan of meek petition...

He drops the sword-arm, harks intently,
His wolfish wrath subsiding gently;
The vengeful soul is given pause,
Is mollified by mild entreating;
So in the vale the snow-bank thaws
Beneath the blazing noon-sun's beating.

"You have returned me to my senses,"
Confessed the head in contrite tone;
"I offered you unjust offences,
As your right hand has amply shown.
To your command I am obedient;
But you, oh noble knight, be lenient!
Worth your compassion is my plight.
I too was once a gallant knight!
In bloody fray I met no other
To equal me in pluck and brawn;
And happy me—had I not drawn
The rivalry of my young brother!
You, Chernomor, with craft and spite
Did all my dire misfortunes wreak!
The family escutcheon's blight,
A dwarf from birth, a bearded freak,
From early childhood he had smarted
To look at me, so tall and whole,
And in his wickedness had started
To hate me for it in his soul.
I had been always somewhat simple,
Though tall of stature; and that wretch,
While not much bigger than a pimple,
Is devilish smart—and vile to match.
To my discomfiture, besides,
In his outlandish beard resides

Of sorceries some fateful junction;
Dismissing a⁞l humane compunction,
While yet the beard remains intact,
He shrinks from no unholy act..
Thus in fraternal accents warm—
"A word with you," one day he pleaded,
"Do not refuse—your gifts are needed
A weighty service to perform.
Beyond the mountains (say my parchments)
Upon a placid ocean beach,
Sequestered under dungeon archments,
A sword is kept—of fearful reach!
I am apprised by magic sources
That through the will of hostile forces
This sword shall know both you and me;
It would undo us both forever;
From me it is ordained to sever
My beard, from you—your head. You see
That it is vital we acquire
This tool of injury and shame!"
"Well, on with it—who's hanging fire?"
I told the midget, "I am game,
To the four corners of creation,"
On my right shoulder flung a pine,
And on my left, for consultation,
I set that viper kin of mine
And started on the long, long road.
Good luck would have it, as I strode,
That all, as if to spite the curse,
Went prosperously just at first;
Beyond far heights of orient sloping
To sea, we found the fateful crypt;
With my bare hands I tore it open,

And the sequestered sword I gripped:
But not secured! Fate willed it, rather,
That we fell out with one another—
Nor was it over small reward!
But over who would own the sword.
I argued, he flared up, we gave
As good as got—till he invented
An underhanded trick, the knave,
Grew calm and outwardly relented.
"Let us break off this painful scene,"
Said Chernomor with pious mien,
'Which but dishonors our accord;
Both sense and heart to peace impel us;
Let us appeal to Fate to tell us
Who is the owner of this sword.
Let's hug the earth, start listening;
(How truly malice makes you clever!)
And which is first to hear a ring,
Let him possess the sword forever.'
With this he crouches, ear to ground,
And I, fool that I am, believe him;
I lie there, hearing not a sound
And gloating how I will deceive him—
But foully was myself undone!
The villain, when I could not see,
Rose soundlessly, stole up to me
Upon my blind side, straightened, spun,
And like a gale the blade hissed to it—
Ere I could look to my defense,
I had no head with which to do it.
Some supernatural influence
Preserved the head both life and sense.
In briars lies my ribwork rigid,

My bulk is rotting uninterred
In distant land by man unheard;
This part of me the evil midget
Transferred to this forsaken land,
Where ceaseless watch I was to stand
Upon the sword you took today.
Oh knight! I see the fates preserve you:
Take it, and stoutly may it serve you!
Should chance decree that on your way
You meet this feeblebodied charmer,
And feel in best of form and armor,
Avenge his treason and foul play!
This will rejoice my soul and save me,
Then I shall leave the earth content—
Nor in my gratitude resent
The unforgotten slap you gave me."

CHANT THE FOURTH

Each morning as I test conditions,
I render thanks to *le bon Dieu*
For making sure that our milieu
No longer buzzes with magicians.
And further, that—God bless this roof!—
Our marriages are burglar-proof...
Hence evil spells leave unaffected
Young men and maidens so protected.
There's witchcraft otherwise beguiling
Which I avoid like pestilence:
It's worked by eyes of blue, by smiling,
By velvet voices—oh my friends!
Do not believe them: they delude!
Eschew, observing my estrangement,
Their sweet, insidious derangement
And walk in sober quietude.

Most wondrous genius of verse,
Oh bard of reveries and revels,
Of love, of mysteries and devils,
Oh faithful mate of hearth and hearse,
And to my Muse (no stuffy matron)
Preserver, intimate, and patron!
Forgive me, Orpheus of the north,
If in my rambling back and forth
I briefly touch your lofty levels
And tilt your upright lyre awry
To trap it in a charming lie.

My friends, you all remember hearing[7]
In days of old a sinner sell
His soul to the foul Fiend, despairing,
And then his daughters' souls as well;
How after charitable giving,
Strict fasting, telling bead on bead,
And exemplary contrite living
He moved a saint to intercede;
How then he died, and how his dozen
Fair filial forfeits fell asleep—
And we sat gibbering and buzzing,
Rapt by the tale's mysterious sweep,
Those wonderfully vivid touches,
That wrath Divine, the devil's anger,
The sinner's writhing in his clutches,
Those blameless maidens' lovely languor.
We wrung our hands with them and wandered
Within that crenelated wall,
With floods of fulsome feeling pondered
Their silent sleep, their tranquil thrall;
We tried to haste Vadim's arrival,
And holy hermit women led,
Upon the daughters' glad revival,
To their poor father's burial-stead.
And all this time—we were misled!
But dare I let this out? I blush...

Ratmir, the hothead, southward guiding
His thoroughbred's impetuous rush,
Had thought before the vesper hush
To track Liudmila's place of hiding.
But day burnt out in crimson tapers;
The champion vainly peered ahead

To pierce the veil of distant vapors:
The river banks were bare and dead.
The setting sun was blazing brightly
Across the forest's gilded space,
And our contender, trotting lightly
Past shaded boulders, slowed his pace
To pick a sheltered sleeping-place.
But now he saw the woodland clearing,
A castle on a granite mound
Its crenelated bastions rearing;
Black keeps at every corner frowned.
Down by a parapeted stair,
Lone as a swan at sea and fair,
In vesper glow a maiden glides,
And faint across the distance rides
Her song upon the drowsing air.

"Now darkness shades the meadows over,
A chill is wafted from the sea.
Late is the hour, oh fair young rover,
Come, join our pleasant company.

Here days are gay with wine and song,
And nights enlanguored bliss engender;
To friendship's soft appeal surrender,
Come here, oh rover fair and young!

Of beauties you will find a swarm,
Their words, their blandishments are tender.
To ardor's mystic lure surrender,
Come here, young rover fair of form!

Tomorrow at the break of day
Your stirrup-cup we shall be speeding.
Surrender to the gentle pleading,
Come, fair young rover, turn our way!

Now darkness shades the meadows over,
A chill is wafted from the sea.
Late is the hour, oh fair young rover,
Come, join our pleasant company."

She pleads with him, she sings to him,
By now the Khan is at her feet;
More maidens, fair as seraphim,
Throng up and make his welcome sweet;
Endearing speeches overbrim,
He is besieged; they seem unable
To take their melting eyes off him;
Two lead his charger off to stable;
Thus makes the Khan his entry here,
Fair hermits bringing up the rear.
One eases off his wingèd casque,
Another his embossed cuirass,
A third his sword, his dusty shield;
All armored panoply must yield
To raiment pliable and tender.
But first the noble youth is led
Into a bath of Russian splendor.
Already steaming floods are fed
Into the silver vats with splashing;
Cool founts, in turn, come hissing, plashing.
They spread rich fabrics of Iran,
Whereon reclines the weary Khan;
Fine wisps of steam about him loop;

Fond eyes cast down, the lovely troupe,
All eagerness to serve him, press
Their charming all-but-nakedness
About his couch, a playful group.
Above him, one of them is waving
The supple birch-twigs's tender points,
His frame with fervent freshness laving;
Another cossets, silky palms
Perfumed with rose, his stiffened joints
As she most winsomely anoints
His dusky curls with fragrant balms.
'Mid such delights, Ratmir, enraptured,
Has lost all memory of captured
Liudmila's lately dreamed-of charms;
What roving eyes light up to see
He craves with pangs of sweet desire,
His heart is molten, caught on fire
With passionate expectancy.

Here from the fountain-house he issues,
Is gently swathed in velvet tissues,
And by these lovely hands released
But to be seated to a feast.
No Homer I: who else is able
In lofty cadences to sing
The joys of Grecian youth at table,
The bellied goblets' swirl and ring;
No—following Parny, I might
More fitly bid my careless lyre
Adore dim nakedness at night,
And love's not unassuaged desire!
The castle dreams beneath the moon;
I see where in secluded chamber

Our champion, drugged by amorous languor,
Drifts into lonely slumber soon;
I see, too, that his brow, his cheek,
Now glow, now fade with ambient flushing,
And lips half-open seem to seek
Another pair's complaisant brushing!
His breathing hastens, fever-fashion,
In live illusion of their sight
He clasps the quilt in token passion...
There gapes the door, in deep of night—
And through the eery lunar light
A maiden glides. Dream visions feckless,
Wing back your way, to realms unknown!
Wake up—now is the night your own!
Wake up—each moment's loss is reckless!..
She comes towards him, sees him spread
In charming sensuous abandon;
His coverlet slides off the bed,
Quick flushes paint his brow at random.
A moment there the maiden waits
Before him, motionless and panting,
As Artemis dissimulates
Before a shepherd lad enchanting;
Then lifts a dimpled knee to crouch
Across the restless lover's couch;
All languishing, she leans down deeper,
And with a sigh, a quivering reach,
Draws from his dream the lucky sleeper
With lips that know but passion's speech...

But stay, the maiden lyre, oh friends,
Has fallen mute beneath my finger,
My bashful music fails and ends,

No more with young Ratmir to linger.
I dare not warble in this vein:
Ruslan should claim our mind again,
Ruslan, the bravest of the brave,
Fair knight, true lover to the grave.
Exhausted by the evening's fighting,
He found a restful sleeping-place
At the disbodied titan's base.
But now the flush of dawn is lighting
The quiet heaven's eastern face;
Soon playful sunbeams, winking, peering,
Across the shaggy forehead drift.
Ruslan springs up—his charger, rearing,
Propels him onward arrow-swift.

    The grain turns gold; the foliage lingers,
Then sadly slips from crown and bough.
The autumn gusts outwhistle now
In plundered woods the feathered singers.
November fogs on fell and tarn
Have settled, pendulous and dreary;
It's winter striding up—Ruslan
Rode north, undaunted and unweary.
Each day some agency unknown
Would make a nuisance of itself:
A chap in arms, a witching crone,
Some clod absurdly overgrown,
A clearly deleterious elf,
Some wizard wallah—oh, you name it,
Our hero fought and overcame it.
He even saw, one moonlit night,
As through a dream or second sight,
Rusalkas, wreathed in silver vapor,

'Mid shady branches slimly taper,
And cradled so, they would beguile
The youth with deeply knowing smile
And say no word... But he, protected
By secret craft, is not deflected;
Of idle lust his soul is pure,
He never felt the nixies' lure;
In him Liudmila reigns secure.

Meanwhile unseen, from nameless ruin
(Through lechery-cum-magic) shielded
By that tarboosh, adroitly wielded—
What's my elusive princess doing,
The arch-delectable Liudmila?
She, tuneless, cheerless Philomela,
At random strays through the plantation,
Thinks of her friend with desolation
Or lets imagination wander
Back to her native Kiev yonder,
And gives her heedless heart free play:
Embraces father, brothers, cheers
Her girlhood playmates' fond array,
Frail nannies of her infant years—
Forgotten bondage, separation!
But soon the luckless maiden's mind,
Recalled from happy aberration,
Once more is dismal and confined.
The minions of the love-struck midget,
Afraid to take a nap or fidget,
Both late and early pad about,
Patrolling gardens, keeps, and castle
In search of the delicious morsel
Mislaid; they beat the bushes, shout—

But all in vain as it turns out.
Liudmila had her sport with them:
Would in a clearly girl-less vista
Rise capless from some aspidistra
And call: Yoo-hoo, there! Here I am!
They'd all come charging over then,
While she, invisible again,
On feet unlike their clumsy paws
Would nimbly foil their grabbing claws.
There was no doubt of their beholding
Her passing's transitory signs:
It might be fruit that, ripe and golden,
Would vanish from the quivering vines,
Or they would gather with content
From freshly sprinkled water beads
Beside a rumpled shock of weeds
That she was taking nourishment.
In birch or cedar she would nestle
At fall of dark and seek relief
In slumber, were it but so brief—
But through the weary hours would wrestle
With anguish, call Ruslan, would weep,
Worn out between despair and yawning,
Her face against the rugged bark,
And seldom, seldom by the dawning
Have drifted into shallow sleep.
When early purple flushed the dark,
She wandered to the cataract
To wash beneath its chilly arc.
The dwarf would know her in the act
Some mornings, seeing from the palace
Cupped hands like a transparent chalice
Trace in the jet their fleeting mark.

Then as before, in agitation
And grief until another dark,
She'd roam the ever gay plantation.
At times, before the sunset faded,
Her purling voice came to their ears,
Or in a bower, or by the fall,
They'd find a wreath which she had braided,
A tuftlet off her Persian shawl,
A handkerchief still moist with tears.

No less by passion racked and saddened,
Than by defiance stung and maddened,
The magus vowed to have his way
And catch Liudmila, come what may.
Just so did Lemnos' crippled smith,
Endowed with the connubial wreath
By mind-disturbing Cyprid's arms,
Lay out a net to guard her charms,
And trap them, tenderly misspent,
To quenchless godly merriment...

Cool in a marble summer-house,
The princess, sunk in sad inaction,
Gazed through the window in abstraction
Across the softly swaying boughs
Upon a flowery meadow nearest
Her perch. All of a sudden, "Dearest!"
She hears, and sees—Ruslan, her spouse.
His frame, his face, his every trait,
But blur-eyed, drained, with broken gait,
A gaping wound across his flank —
"Ruslan!" The heart within her shrank,
"Ruslan! By heaven!.." All unheeding,

The captive flies across to him,
Distraught, unstrung in soul and limb,
"You here!.. what happened?.. you are bleeding!.."
She is upon him, arms outspread...
God! vanished is the phantom lover,
A net enmeshes her all over,
The magic cap slips from her head.
"Now she is mine!" With this dread word
Before her eyes the magus rises,
The maiden's piteous moan is heard—
A grateful magic swoon disguises
The infamy that has occurred.

Poor hapless lamb! Who but abhors
The sight: the wizened maiden-stealer
Lays insolent (if brittle) claws
Upon the charms of young Liudmila!
Will his vile stratagem reward him?
Hark! horn-notes view-halloo toward him,
Sharp challenge to the dwarf they bear;
He straightens, ashen-faced and drawn,
Puts back the magic cap on her—
Still nearer, louder blares the horn—
And flies to guard his priceless stake,
His whiskers streaming in his wake.

CHANT THE FIFTH

A darling girl, my princess! Royal
Or not, I hold her kind most dear:
She's sensitive and modest, loyal
To married duties less than clear,
A trifle flighty, if you will?..
That merely makes her sweeter still.
Her ways and whims incessantly
Contrive to charm our minds anew;
Now take Delphire's austerity—
You simply can't compare the two.
Upon the first her fate has lavished
Whatever heart and eye beguiles;
The way she speaks, the way she smiles
Leave me inspirited and ravished.
But that—hussar in petticoats?
Add spurs and whiskers and be done!
No—of an evening, blessed the one
On whom in blithe seclusion dotes
Liudmila's charming counterpart,
And calls him ruler of her heart!
And blithe no less is his career
Who breaks away from a Delphire,
Or never lets her get a start.
But we have wandered far astray!
Who blew that challenge then, compelling
The magus into mortal fray?
Who caused the sorcerer's dismay?

Ruslan—his heart with vengeance swelling,
Had reached the malefactor's dwelling.
Right to the bluff the knight progresses,
The trumpet keening like a storm;
The steed's impatient hoofbeat presses
Into the snow its mighty form.
The prince is waiting. Of a sudden
From nowhere falls with crash and thudding
A blow upon his helm of steel,
As stunning as a thunder-peal.
Ruslan looks up, his sight grown dim
And sees, directly over him,
The bearded magus hovers winging,
A fearful bludgeon raised and swinging.
Ruslan bent low, his shield for ward,
Slashed, flourished upward with his sword;
But he soared up, past human ken
For some short while—then from his towering
Cloud eyrie hurtled down again.
Our champion sprang aside, unstruck,
And he, with impact overpowering,
Crashed to the snow—and there he stuck.
Dismounting in a flash, refraining
From speech, Ruslan rushed over, neared,
Caught up the dwarf and gripped his beard;
The trapped magician, groaning, straining—
Loops up with him into the air!
Well might the fiery charger stare—
They're up amid the clouds' dim scope;
Ruslan suspended by this rope.
They cross the wildwood's sullen verges,
They cross the frowning mountain gorges,
They fly above the plumbless deep;

Though stiffened from the strain and blistered,
Ruslan maintains upon the whiskered
Hellhound his unrelenting grip.
His buoyant magic draining, failing,
In awe by now of Russian strength,
The sorcerer, more slowly sailing,
Says slyly to Ruslan at length:
"I prize young valor—I feel guided
To cease from hurting you at last;
I pardon you, forget the past,
And start descending now—provided..."
"No! there is nothing to provide!"
The Prince flared up, "with Chernomor,
With the tormentor of his bride,
Ruslan knows neither truce nor law!
This ruthless sword shall pay your score.
Fly to the polar star, and still
Your beard is forfeit to my will!"
The tiring warlock, struck with panic,
Still loath to credit what he feared,
In mute chagrin, in wrath satanic
Jerked vainly at his captive beard;
Ruslan would not release it, and
From time to time would tweak a strand.
Two days the wizard bore the prince,
The third, he begged deliverance:
"Oh knight, have mercy on me, pray,
This plight is more than I can stand;
Spare me—I am at your command:
I'll land us anywhere you say."
"Ha! Worn and shaking at my hand!
Surrender, bow to Russian valor!
Conduct me, then, to my Liudmila."

The sorcerer listened, meek and weary,
And bearing homeward with our knight,
Descended—shortly to alight
Within his awesome mountain eyrie.
Then with his right the champion leveled
His sword—the lop-head giant's prey—
Seized with his left the beard and severed
The whiskers like a tuft of hay.
"Thus know my race!" he shouted grimly,
"Where is your famous furpiece, thief?
Where is your might?" and fastened trimly
About his helm the silvery sheaf.
He whistled for his mettled horse,
It cantered up with cheerful neighing;
The dwarf, a negligible force,
Into his saddle-pocket laying,
He faced, with not a minute's waste,
The crag, his riding wild and callous;
Atop, he broke with joyous haste
Into the necromancer's palace.
Seeing his helm with whiskers graced,
Pledge of the fated fall of wrong,
The moorish servants' wondrous throng,
The timid corps of captive virgins,
Dissolve away at his emergence
Like wraiths, and vanish on all sides.
Down stately halls alone he strides
And calls for his beloved spouse;
His voice alone from vaulted ceilings
Re-echoes in the magic house;
In access of impatient feelings
He thrusts the park-door open, roves
The grounds—endeavor unavailing;

He scans the pleasance, spirit quailing,
Both nothing stirs there: silent groves,
Deserted bowers; up sloping alleys,
Along a stream-bed, down the valleys,
He nowhere sees Liudmila's trace,
And the acutest hearing fails him.
At this an inner chill assails him,
The world turns dark before his face
With thoughts from nights of fancy risen...
"Perhaps her grief...the gloom of prison...
There comes a time...the brook..." he borrows
This scene and others; numb with dread,
The shaken champion hangs his head;
He stands engrossed in forecast sorrows,
Oblivious like a cliff at flood.
His reason clouds; the savage daring,
The poison drug of love despairing
Have started coursing in his blood.
Liudmila's presence, close, delightful,
Had brushed his trembling lips, he felt,
And of a sudden, frantic, frightful,
He strode about the park and dealt
Destruction: called her name with roaring,
The slopes with wrenched-off boulders scoring,
All slashing, crushing with his sword—
Pavilions, pleasances are tumbling,
Trees, bridges, all awash and crumbling,
The park reduced to barren sward!
The distant hills re-echo, rumbling,
The rush and uproar, thud and crash;
His saber-passes ring and flash—
Despoiled the exquisite oasis!
For victims thirsts the maddened knight,

And with his saber-strokes crosslaces
The empty air on left and right...
There now! a random flourish carried
From the bewitched Liudmila's forehead
Foul Chernomor's departing gift...
At once, the spell was seen to lift,
The princess and the net revealing!
Then, slow to trust the happy shift
Of fortune, her redeemer, reeling
Beneath the shock of joy, was kneeling
Before his love, his faithful one,
Kissed her dear hands, tore up the net,
And shed glad tears of love rewon.
He called to her—but she was sunken
In slumber, lids and lips were closed;
With sensuous fancies sweetly drunken,
The youthful bosom sank and rose.
New devilment profoundly fearing,
He never lets her from his sight...
But then familiar accents cheer him—
The saintly Finnish anchorite:
"Take courage, Prince! Arise, make ready
For home now with your slumbering bride;
Keep love and honor for your guide!
Your strength of soul renew and steady.
God's thunderbolt will shatter malice,
And sweet tranquility provide—
In shining Kiev, in the palace,
Before Vladimir as you bend,
Liudmila's magic sleep will end."

Ruslan, much heartened by his mentor,
Now gathers up his precious find;

The eyrie of her late tormentor
Is gently, swiftly left behind,
As down a lonely glen they canter.

Ruslan rode silently along,
The dwarf behind his saddle slung;
In his bent arm Liudmila nested,
Fresh as the vernal dawn, and rested
Her peaceful rosy countenance
Against the shoulder of her prince.
The winds of wildernesses flutter
Her tresses in their ring-shaped braid;
How often, drowsy, she will utter
A sigh, her quiet profile show
A flush of roses come and go!
Love and the sway of slumber bring
Ruslan before the secret dreamer,
Her lips with fervent whispering
Pronounce the name of her redeemer...
Ruslan, in turn, has ear and eye
But for the wonder of her breathing,
Her smile, her tears, her tender sigh,
The slumbrous bosom's gentle heaving.
Through hills and dales, along, away,
In black of night, in white of day,
Course steed and knight, and never tire.
Still far the land of heart's desire—
The maiden sleeps... Did our young blade,
By fangs of fruitless ardor flayed,
Forewidowed for it felt like years,
Check all indecorous ideas?
Stand chastely at his guardian's station,
And from abstemious contemplation

Derive his frugal sustenance?
The monk who made my storied prince
The subject of his faithful annal,
Posterity's unrivalled channel,
Assures us that he did no less.
And I believe him! Stripped of sharing,
Delights of love are coarse and wearing,
It does take two for happiness.
Liudmila, nymphets of the meadow,
Did not sleep in the least like you,
As in the pandering spring you do
Upon the mead, in sylvan shadow.
I well recall a grassy glade
Amidst a twilit grove of birches,
I well recall a deeper shade,
Where Lida's cunning slumber perches...
My kiss, a maiden lover's gift,
Too light, too shy, too unarousing,
Was not enough, alas, to lift
Her patient and determined drowsing...
But there! what nonsense I am prating!
Who needs these memories of love?
His ravages, their sweet abating,
I have been long oblivious of.
Back to the topic I was on:
Liudmila, Chernomor, Ruslan.

Before them lay a spreading prairie
Where here and yonder spruces grew;
Then in the distance hove in view
A looming mound whose topmost aerie
Showed black against the radiant blue.
Our hero guessed as it grew larger

It was the giant head he knew;
More swiftly speeds his dashing charger;
The prodigy becomes distinct:
His gaze is fixed, the hair resembles
A gloomy forest-border inked
Across the towering brow and temples;
Down cheeks of life and color drenched
A wave of livid pallor darted,
The Brobdignagian lips were parted,
The rows of monstrous grinders clenched...
His day of final doom, none other,
Now overhung the failing head.
To him the valiant hero sped
Liudmila and the craven brother.
"We meet again, great head," he cried,
"I have brought back the chastened slayer,
Look! Here, in bonds, is your betrayer!"
Behold—the prince's words of pride
As if revivified the creature,
New feeling stirred each massive feature,
It rose from slumber as it were,
It gazed, and made a dreadful moaning...
Straightway it knew its conqueror,
And marked its kin with hate and groaning.
The nostrils swelled; with parting glare
Of crimson stains the cheeks were brindled,
The eyeballs, glazing as they were,
To final flames of fury kindled.
In throes of outrage, speechless wrath,
The titan grinders fell to gnashing,
The chilling tongue reviled the dwarf
With half-articulated passion...
But now the long-drawn pain was soothed,

The momentary furor faded,
The heaving breath was gently smoothed,
That superhuman vision shaded
And broke; prince and magician saw
Life shiver briefly, and withdraw...
Eternal slumber now it slept.
In sober mood the knight departed;
Shrunk in the bag where he was kept,
The kobold never stirred nor started,
But in black wizardry's argot
Sent fervent prayers to fiends below.

Upon the darkly sloping bank
Of a clear rivulet uncharted,
In forest twilight green and rank,
Half sunken in, a cabin shrank,
Where firs the densest shade imparted.
The water, somnolent and glassy,
In lazy ripples lapped in passing
A fence nearby of plaited reeds,
And barely chuckled in its sally
Above the soughing of the breeze.
Here ambled a sequestered valley
Its dim and solitary way,
Where sylvan silence, one would say,
Had reigned since Time began his tally.
Ruslan reined in and stopped his bay.
In stirless silence lay the cove;
Beneath the efflorescent day
The valley and the brookside grove
Broke glinting through the morning haze.
Ruslan sank on the grass, and setting
His bride beside him, fell to fretting

His mind in sweet and rueful daze.
Then, straight ahead, he saw them furling
The canvas of a modest boat,
And heard a fisher's chanty float
Above the current's tranquil purling.
Cast far astream the heavy webbing,
The fisherman, bent to the oar,
Stood straight in for the leafy shore,
The threshold of the humble cabin.
Good Prince Ruslan sat up and watched;
The vessel reached the bank and lodged
Alongside; from the swarthy cabin
A maiden runs; her graceful habit,
Her tresses, loosely downward streaming,
Her quiet, steady gaze, her smile,
The breasts, the naked shoulders gleaming,
At once endear her, and beguile.
Not seated yet, they take their pleasure
Embracing by the water's cool,
Affection ushering in the rule
Of surcease and untroubled leisure.
To his incredulous surprise,
Whom does our hero recognize
In this young netter of great treasure?
The Khazar khan, for glory fated,
Who had in love and war been rated
His young competitor—the same!
Ratmir in lone and blissful places
Had spurned Liudmila, cast off fame,
And waived forever quest and name
In this dear maiden's sweet embraces.

The prince approached, and with a start

The recluse knew Ruslan; he bounded
Across to him, a cry resounded...
Each pressed the other to his heart.
"What do I see?" the hero queried,
"Why are you here? Can you have wearied
Of knightly life and its alarms,
Of laurels wound on bloodied arms?"
Replied the fisherman: "In faith,
War's glory can no more deceive me,
That vacuous and baneful wraith!
Pastimes of innocence, believe me,
The green and peaceful wildwood, love,
My heart is tenfold fonder of.
Renounced the lust for blood and booty,
I pay that myth no further duty,
And, rich in bliss not soon to end,
I have forgotten all, dear friend,
All—even, yes, Liudmila's beauty."
"This is good tidings, my dear Khan,"
Remarked Ruslan, "she is with me."
"Here? By what miracle, Ruslan?
The Russian princess? Could it be?
Where, if with you, then? May one see,
Allow... but no, this gives me pause;
I hold my lovely friend too dear;
The happy change which brought me here
Has her for authoress and cause;
In her is all my life, my laughter,
She has revived for me the lure,
The bloom of youth I hankered after,
And peace, and love when it is pure.
In vain young sirens have caressed me
With whispered prophecies of bliss;

A dozen maidens have possessed me—
I left the lot of them for this;
I left behind their merry bower
There in the wildwood-sheltered realm,
Laid down my sword, the weighty helm,
Forswore renown and martial power.
Peace and obscurity in mind,
I chose this happy hermit's part,
With you, enchanting, ever kind,
With you, bright beacon of my heart!"

The charming shepherdess the while
Took in their converse unconstrained;
Her gaze upon her lover trained,
She offered him now sigh, now smile.

Thus knight and hermit by the landing
Sat talking all the evening long
All heart and soul upon the tongue—
Fleet hours departed undemanding.
Now wood and hill were shaded over,
The world in moonlit silence lay;
Our knight should long be on his way.
So, having gently thrown a cover
About the sleeping maid, Ruslan
Goes off to loose and mount his stallion;
While, silent and bemused, the khan
In spirit follows the young valiant
To wish him victories, fresh thriving
Of love's green garland, honor's bays;
Himself half-ruefully reviving
The dreams of youthful, prideful days.
Alack! why did the misanthropic

Fates disallow my fickle strings
To cling to the heroic topic,
And charming, quaint, historic things
Like love and friendship, long outdated?
Slave to sad fact, why am I fated
To bare for readers yet unborn
Disgrace and outrage contumacious,
And be melodiously veracious
To plots of villainy forsworn?

The princess' unworthy courter,
Farlaf, all thirst for glory gone,
Skulked in seclusion, known to none,
In some remote and lonely quarter.
Here was Naina to appear;
And now the solemn hour was here.
The witch appeared; in accents hollow
She spoke: "You know me well enough!
Mount; where I lead, you are to follow."
The charger saddled, she was off,
Transformed into a cat instanter;
And after her began to canter,
Down gloomy forest paths, Farlaf.

The tranquil valley had subsided
In misty coverings of night;
The moon in veils of vapor glided
From cloud to cloud and shed its light
But fitfully upon the barrow
At which, upon the day's long ride,
Ruslan, engrossed in his old sorrow,
Was seated by his slumbering bride.
Bemused he sat, new fancies covered
The old in swift imaginings,

Till slumber nebulously hovered
Above on cool-dispensing wings.
He watched her, drowsy eyelids blinking,
In torpor languorous and deep,
And, head and shoulders slowly sinking,
Against her feet, he fell asleep.

He dreams a dream of bodefulness,
In which it seems as if Liudmila
Hard on the brink of an abyss
Were standing pale and motionless...
Then of a sudden mists conceal her,
He stands atop the gulf alone...
The voice he knows, a call or moan
Re-echoes up the precipice...
Ruslan strains forth to reach his spouse,
Flies headlong in the plumbless gloom;
But next, he sees before him loom
The state-room of the ducal house,
Vladimir, gray-haired echelons
Of hero-knights, his dozen sons,
Of noted guests a goodly throng
The richly covered tables long.
The Duke, it seems, is just as wroth
As on the dreadful day of parting,
And all sit staring at the cloth,
No table talk or banter starting.
Gay shouts have yielded to unease,
The bowl and ladle stilled their rattle;
And now among the guests he sees
Rogdai, whom he has slain in battle:
The dead man raises, as if living,
A foaming beaker, unaware

Of Prince Ruslan, and drains it, giving
No heed to his astonished stare.
There, too, he sees the youthful khan,
And others, friend and foe... again
Resounds the nimble gusli's strain,
The chanting of the bard Bayan,
Of valiant deeds and feasts the singer.
Farlaf steps in the chamber, and—
Draws in Liudmila by the hand.
The Duke, however, lifts no finger,
In mourning droops his diadem.
Boyars and princes, all are grim
And quell emotions without number.
Then all is gone—a deadly chill
Engulfs the hero in his slumber.
Too deeply snarled in coils unreal,
He sheds hot tears of fury thwarted;
It is a dream, his senses feel;
And yet he fails, all strength aborted,
To break the dreadful nightmare's seal.

The moon hangs low above the hills,
The night has hushed the dale and fills
The forest with a mortal gloom...
Here rides Naina's knavish groom.

Before his eyes a glade discloses
A mound; Liudmila on a mead,
Stretched at her feet, Ruslan reposes;
Around the barrow walks the steed.
Farlaf in quick alarm stands idle;
The witch becomes a wisp of mist;
As, quavering, he drops his wrist,

From clammy hands rein and bridle fall.
Advancing stealthily and drawing,
He hopes to cut in two our knight
By one fell stroke, without a fight...
In vain the hero's stallion, pawing
In anger as he sees him creep,
Lets out a whinny. Useless token!
It seems that nothing would have woken
Ruslan from his oppressive sleep...
Spurred by the witch, the traitor lunges—
Into the sleeper's breast he plunges
Three times the steel with impious hand...
Then rides in panic overland,
Propped on his mount his priceless prey.

   Throughout the night the champion lay
Insensible beside the barrow.
The hours flew past. The blood in narrow,
Pulsating fountains gushed away.
At dawn he lifted turbid eyes,
Gave out a feeble groan and, spurring
His utmost strength, made as to rise,
Peered, helmet-bowed, in dim surmise,
And sank, unbreathing and unstirring.

CHANT THE SIXTH

You order me, my heart's desire,
To keep the light and careless lyre
Resounding to the tales of old,
And for the Muse forbear to savor
The boon of leisure hours untold...
But drunken with your blessed favor,
Dear lady love, I shun those pains:
Your friend abhors the lonesome toil,
Estranged by now from midnight oil
Spent on ephemeral refrains.
Yes—from melodious allegories
I turned to vivid ecstasy...
I breathe by you, and other glories
Have lost their sorcery for me!
The knack of being fresh and clever
Eludes me, weaned from cool conceits;
My fancy's stage is haunted ever
By love and his celestial treats...
But you command, but you applauded
The tales related heretofore,
Accounts of glory and of love—
Of my Ruslan, his gentle dove,
The witch, Vladimir, Chernomor,
The Finn's true sorrow—were accorded
Your kindly reverie, and lauded;
As I meandered, you would linger,
A pensively indulgent guest;
At times your tender eye would rest

More tenderly upon the singer...
This stirs the mind and lends it wings:
Enamored prattler as before,
Back at your feet I twang once more
For knight and maid these lazy strings.

Where is Ruslan? Betrayal craven
Has stretched him on the level field,
His lifeblood horridly congealed;
Above him swoops a greedy raven;
His armor sprawls, the horn is muted,
The helmbush splayed as if uprooted.

Around Ruslan the charger plies,
His noble head now lowered sadly;
His eyes are dimmed, no longer flies
The golden mane he tossed so madly.
He neither frolics now nor leaps,
Entreating dumbly to be saddled...
But, cold and stark, his master sleeps;
It's long since spear and shield have rattled.

And Chernomor? Still saddlebagged,
He has not been in any state
To keep himself abreast of late;
Disgruntled, somnolent, and fagged,
His magic sway reduced to zero,
He damns the princess and my hero
Above his breath as well as under;
Hears nothing; peeps outside—oh wonder!
He sees the champion is no more—
Lies rigid in a pool of gore;
Liudmila gone, the place forsaken!

The dwarf, by evil chuckles shaken,
Crows: All is over, I am free!
But wrongly—it is not to be.

Meanwhile, watched over by Naina,
With calmly slumbering Liudmila
To Kiev hies himself Farlaf,
His mood both tremulous and heady;
Before him Dnieper's flow already
Meanders through familiar leas;
He sees the gold-topped city, sees
The streets and markets wheel about him;
There starts a running, swirling, shouting,
A crowd, in gladness long deferred,
Cheers in his wake, grows ever greater;
They run to bring the father word:
The Palace gate admits the traitor.

While this procession presses on,
In his high hall above the borough
There brooded Vladimir the Sun,
Weighed down by unrelenting sorrow;
And, steeped in gravity profound,
The knights and heroes sat around.
About the gate a sudden sound
Of hubbub, shouting, shuffling centered,
The heavy portals swung apart,
An unknown knight-in-armor entered.
All present rise, dull mutters start,
They marvel, gloomily enough:
"Liudmila back! And... What? Farlaf?"
Roused from his sorrow-stricken air,
The Great Duke rises from his chair,

With ponderous despatch advances
To his afflicted daughter's side
To reassure his doubting glances
By father's touch; but stupified
In magic slumber lies the bride
In the assassin's arms, attending
To no one, nothing... All are bending
Shy gazes on the aged prince,
Whose anxious wondering countenance
In silent query probes the knight.
A crafty finger at his lips,
Farlaf proclaims: "Liudmila sleeps;
In a forsaken forest site
I came on her in this condition,
The captive of an evil sprite;
There valor came to fine fruition:
Three days I fought with sword and lance,
Thrice rose the moon above the battle;
And when it set, the royal chattel
Fell in my hands, still in a trance.
And who can break this wondrous sleep?
What might effect her resurrection?
Who knows—the ways of fate are deep!
From hope and patience we must reap
The balm of comforting reflection."

All through the capital ere long
There flew the word of gloom and pity;
From palace square a seething throng
Filled up the center of the city;
The house of grief throws wide its doors;
The concourse surges forward, pours
Where on an elevated trestle
Upon a cloth of silk brocade

The sleeping princess seems to nestle;
The knights and boyars stand arrayed
In sad observance; tympans thrumming,
Horns, gusli, muted trumpets, drumming
Swirl up about the kneeling prince,
Whose silver temples have been pressing
Liudmila's feet forever since
With tearful, prayerful caressing.
An ashen-faced Farlaf looks on
In mute remorse and angry pity;
He trembles, glib assurance gone.

Dark fell, but no one in the city
That night of wonders closed an eye,
Men argued, huddled close together,
What such a bane might signify;
Too late, young husbands wondered whether
They even told their brides good-bye.
But hardly had the twin-horned crescent
At break of morning paled and lessened,
When Kiev shook to new alarms!
Harsh clamor, wailing, clink of arms
Sprang up; the men of Kiev all
Came swarming up the city wall;
And through the mist they see, and shiver:
White tents have bloomed beyond the river;
Like surf aglitter shine their shields;
The mounted raiders churn the fields,
Black puffs of dust ascending, sinking;
One sees their carts crawl up and halt,
Along the hillside campfires winking...
Alarm! A Pecheneg assault!

All through this time the vatic Finn,
The spirits' mighty sovereign,
Had imperturbably awaited
In his retreat the imminent,
Clairvoyantly anticipated,
The ineluctable event.

Beyond the steppelands' torrid reaches,
Beyond a chain of savage mountains,
The home of winds, of thundering gales,
A realm which even brazen witches
Are loath to tread when daylight fails,
Deep in a dale two magic fountains
Have broken from the valley bed:
The one with *living* water gushing,
And down the boulders gaily rushing,
The other charged with waters *dead.*
There all is silent, nothing stirs,
With cooling breath, a stillness hushing
The sough of hundred-year-old firs
Undwelled by birds. No roe-fawn dares
To drink here; for twin spirit forces,
Mute in the very womb of calm,
Since earth spun off the Father's palm
Have stood on guard above these sources...
Two empty flagons in his hands,
The hermit came; the guardians started,
They broke their immemorial stance
And, filled with holy fear, departed.
The hermit, bending over, hung
The jars into the virgin waters;
He filled them full, and straightway swung
By sightless airways to those quarters

Where by a barrow, stark and cool,
Ruslan lay in a crimson pool.
The sage bent over him and sprinkled
Upon the corpse the drops of death:
Which made its gashes, raw and wrinkled,
Close up, and spread a rosy breath
Of comeliness; and next he sprinkled
The drops of life upon the form;
And resurrected, vital, warm,
Athrob with eagerness and vigor,
Ruslan stands up again, a figure
Of dazzling youth, who keenly eyes
The clear of day, while bygone rigor
Fades like a dream, a dim surmise...
He is alone, though! Where's his bride?
Fears freshly banned return to hound him;
He starts: the sage is by his side
And gently lays his arm around him:
"Foiled, son, is infamy accursed,
And bliss awaits—fulfilled your mission;
A bloody banquet calls you first;
Your sword is bid to spread perdition.
When gentle peace restores the land,
You take this ring before Liudmila;
The spell of evil will be banned,   '
Its touch against her brow will heal her.
Your countenance will rout the foe,
Peace will descend, and malice perish.
Prove worthy of your bliss, and cherish
Our friendship, knight! Your hand... for lo!
It is beyond the grave we twain,
Not sooner, are to meet again."
He spoke—and vanished as he told him.

Our hero, speechless with delight
To be restored to sound and sight,
Threw out his arms as if to hold him,
But did not hear a further sound;
Deserted are both air and ground.
Alert, the dwarf still bagged astraddle,
Ruslan's proud steed, in fighting vein,
Rears up and neighs and shakes his mane;
Now mounts the prince, now grips the saddle,
Now charges forward hale and bold
Across the fields, across the wold.

What aspect offers, while he speeds,
Beleaguered Kiev? Battle-tense
The people on its eminence
With horror scan their crops and seeds,
On battlement and turret station
In tremors bide the visitation.
The houses keen with mournful airs;
Pale fear has hushed the thoroughfares.
Next to his daughter, bowed and gray,
Vladimir stayed behind to pray;
His stalwart army, knights and yeomen
And paladins, prepares the foemen
A deadly, decimating fray.

The day had come. The raiders swarmed
Down from the hills in waves unformed;
The teeming plains, like seething caldrons,
Rolled forth indomitable squadrons
To lash the walls like surf the coast.
In Kiev, trumpets, banners flurried,
Defenders formed in ranks and hurried

To meet the reckless surging host.
They clashed—and slaughter raged unbridled.
Forescenting death, the war-steeds sidled
As sword and armor clashed head-on;
A cloud of arrows whirred and spun;
With blood the fields began to run.
The hordes plunged forward hell for leather,
Now mounted squadrons crashed together,
Each tightly locked fraternal rank
Hacks at the foemen, bank by bank.
Here's pawn and horseman, slashing, jolting,
There frightened chargers wildly bolting,
There's carnage, close-in, leg to leg,
A Russian falls, a Pecheneg,
The second maced, the first upended
By feathered death swift as a bird;
A heavy shield has crushed a third,
And maddened horses' hoofbeats end it...
Both sides outfought the light to gain
The battle-day, but neither could;
Behind the bleeding mounds of slain
The fighters tumbled where they stood.
And firm the armored sleep they slept;
But seldom from the field of horrors
The groan of fallen men was swept,
Or prayers of the Russian warriors.

There paled at length the shade of morn,
The ripples silvered in the water;
The day of destiny was born
On heaven's misty eastern quarter.
The skies unveiled themselves of night,
And hills and forest flushed with light.

But still in bonds of slumber sealed,
Inertly lay the battlefield.
Abruptly, loud alarums shattered
The silence in the hostile part,
Outcry and challenge, weapons clattered,
Unnerving to the Kiev heart.
The throngs crowd forward helter-skelter
And see amongst the foe, afar,
Steel-clad and flashing like a star,
A mounted warrior, in a welter
Of carnage, stabbing, slashing, keening
The strident horn in his careening...
It was Ruslan. He raked the raiders
Like bolts of God the infidel;
The dwarf behind him still, he fell
Upon the terror-struck invaders.
Whereso his saber flashed, where steed
Had borne him in its angry darting,
There heads and shoulders started parting,
Ranks shrieked and sank like swathes of weed.
At once the martial sward appears
Bestrewn with bodies maimed and redded,
Still breathing, trampled down, beheaded,
And piles of armor, arrows, spears.
The battle sounds, the trumpet's wail
Sent armored Slav platoons with thunder
Of hooves upon the hero's trail
To slaughter... Infidel, go under!
Wild fosterlings of fell incursion,
The Pechenegs, in panic, wheel;
They call their scattered cobs to heel;
Averse to further armed exertion,
Down dusty fields in shrieking hordes

They flee the flash of Kiev swords,
But all are sentenced to perdition,
A sacrifice to Slav renown;
Kiev exults... But on to town
The mighty prince pursues his mission.
The sword of vengeance in his right,
His brazen armor running gore,
His lance-tip like a streak of light,
His crest the pelt of Chernomor,
He seeks, all hope re-animated,
The ducal house through roar and shouting;
The populace, intoxicated,
With chants of homage crowds about him.
Now high in hope, he penetrated
Where wrapt within her wondrous spell
The sleeping maid was said to dwell.
The Duke sat at her feet, his head
Bowed low in sorrow and suspense.
He was alone; his friends had sped
To battle in the town's defense.
Alone Farlaf, averse to war,
Despising bellicose alarms,
Was standing vigil at the door,
Aloof from adversary arms.
The instant that he knew the prince
His blood ran cold, his stare grew senseless,
Pale terror froze his countenance,
He crumpled to his knees, defenseless...
The wage of treason, earned long since,
Was due! Ruslan remembers, clutches
The gift ring, takes a rapid pace
And with a trembling movement touches
The placid slumber-cradled face...

And lo! the petals drew asunder,
The flower-eyes opened, shining bright;
She sighed, as if in musing wonder
About so lingering a night.
It was as if she felt the trace
Of some dim nightmare—then she knew him,
And gave a gasp, cried out, and drew him
Into the bliss of her embrace.
His soul in fiery transports throbbing,
Ruslan stands deaf and blind and numb;
The noble ancient, overcome,
Caressed his long-lost children, sobbing.

How shall I end my endless drone?
Of course, my dearest, you have guessed it!
The ancient's groundless wrath was flown;
At Ruslan's feet and at his own
Farlaf in abject shame confessed it,
His foul and murderous stratagem;
The happy bridegroom pardoned him;
The dwarf, his magic mischief ended,
Was added to the Court supply;
Vladimir, toasting evils mended,
Sat in his wassail-chamber high,
By all his dearest ones surrounded.

The lore of ages long gone by,
In deep antiquity compounded.

EPILOGUE

And thus, a tranquil worldling, dwelling
Where idleness and quiet last,
I set my docile lyre retelling
Traditions of a trackless past.
I sang—and healed the harsh excesses
Of human spite and bumbling luck,
Deceits of flighty shepherdesses,
And idiot chatter run amuck.
On wings of inspiration lifted,
The mind outreached our earthen stead—
While unbeknownst a tempest drifted
With thunderclouds above my head!..
And I went down... August defender,
Who took my brash young manhood's part,
O friendship, bourne of solace tender
Unto my lacerated heart!
You tempered then the tempest's rigor;
You pacified the spirit's ruth;
You saved my freedom—graven figure
Of worship to ebullient youth!
Far from the social swim that bore me
By the Neva's embabbled banks,
I now see looming up before me
Caucasian peaks in haughty ranks.
Upon their scarpments sheer and broken,
Atop their steep and craggy heights,
I feed on sentiments unspoken
And on the ever fresh delights

Of nature savage yet and bruising;
The spirit, as before, is bent
Each hour on melancholy musing—
But the poetic blaze is spent.
In vain I grope for stimulation:
The time of verse is gone, it seems,
The time of love, of merry dreams,
The time of spirit's evocation!
The span of ecstasy has sped—
Forever from my ken has fled
She of the whispering incantation...

1820

THE GABRILIAD: INTRODUCTION

A parody, like *Aucassin et Nicolette*, ridicules the style and manner of an author or a genre by exaggeration of its own conventions and terms. A mock epic makes fun of a genre that has had its day by slipping into it grossly unfit subject matter like a cuckoo's egg. The Gabriliad is a mock-epic poem written in 1821, during the second year of Pushkin's southern exile at Kishinev, in lately and incompletely russianized Bessarabia. Comically reinterpreting in the Aristophanic manner the sacred story of the Annunciation, it fits far better into the poet's earlier output of the first St. Petersburg period, 1817-20, than into the brief but intense spell of Byronic romanticism which followed it. As for its kinship with antecedents in its genre, it is closer in its disarming impudence and youthful gusto to *Ruslan and Liudmila* than to the didactic sneering of Voltaire's *La Pucelle d'Orléans* or the feeble Boucheresque eroticism of Parny's *La Guerre des Dieux*, the two French mock-epics in Pushkin's library with which it has often been linked. No note of iconoclasm or sacrilegious fervor can possibly be read into Pushkin's saucy conversion of the Judaeo-Christian Jehovah into a philandering Zeus, the archangel Gabriel into his panderer, Satan into an eloquent advocate and deft instructor of sexual liberation, and virginal Mary into an increasingly complacent recipient, all in one day, of three ever higher-ranking favors. On the other hand, for all the poem's ribald fable, Pushkin neither leers nor blasphemes, nor does he pontificate. Worldly prelates of the ancien régime would have read this brilliant squib with pleasure, and Rubens or Tintoretto might have gladly done justice to the wrestling match between Satan and Gabriel and its startling climax. Moreover, the buoyant geniality of the poem's narrative mood in several places rises to a purity of lyric power which dissolves the frivolous associations of the genre. One such passage early in the poem relates the consummation of Adam and Eve's young love; another pictures Mary's amorous vigil between Gabriel's visit and the miniature ecstasies of the dove-shaped Lord.

As far as is known, Pushkin never voluntarily admitted his authorship of this poem, which was of course unprintable but gained a wide clandestine circulation. In 1828 it returned to haunt him when the police confiscated a vagrant copy, and persistent repudiation of it by himself and his friends at court was unavailing. He finally admitted the truth in a confidential letter to his personal censor, Tsar Nicholas I, and received absolution, whereupon the perilous enquiry was quashed.

This translation appears here in its original 1974 shape. The editors of *Playboy* for the Christmas issue of 1975 made sweeping excisions and changes.

THE GABRILIAD

A Tale in Verse

The Hebrew girl's spiritual salvation
Is my sincere concern, I do avow;
Come here to me, my lovely angel, now
And listen to a pastoral laudation.
I want to see earth's beauty prospering!
Content with smiling lips' delicious rounding,
Glad lines to Jesus and to Heaven's King
I chant, my reverential lyre resounding.
Who knows but that my lowly strings will find
Her ear with cadences of pious merit,
And send my maiden's soul the Holy Spirit,
Who is the regent both of heart and mind.

Sixteen of age, obedient and modest,
Raven her brow, the maiden mounds below
Swaying against the pendent linen bodice,
A lovesome foot, her teeth a pearly row . . .
Why did you smile, my little Jewess, making
Your cheeks' pale ivory petals flush anew?
Oh! No, my love, I fear you are mistaken—
My words referred to Mary, not to you.

Withdrawn, far from Jerusalem, there dwelled,
Remote from gaieties and young pursuers
(Such as the Tempter fosters to undo us)
A lovely girl, by no one yet beheld,
Whose tranquil life flowed passionless and mellow.
Her husband was an honorable fellow,

A greybeard, no great shakes at drill and brace,
But still the only joiner in the place;
And night and day (what with the time he took
With axe and plane, the tools of his profession,
And faithful saw) he was not apt to look
Upon the maiden charms in his possession,
And the secluded little floral gem,
Whom fate had groomed for sacred indiscretion,
Had never dared to open on its stem.
The feeble spouse's crumpled watering-kit
Did not bedew her of a morning—rather
He lived with his dark blossom like a father:
He fed her—that was all there was to it.

My well-belovèd! The good Lord saw fit,
As from the upper world he spied the nether,
To eye his servant-maiden's supple waist
And virgin thighs, and, feeling in fine feather,
Resolved, in the high wisdom of good taste,
To spray this most deserving vineyard plot,
This arid, unplowed, never-watered lot,
With bursts of secret bounty, aptly placed . . .

The hush of night already numbs the world;
Maria lies in soothing slumber furled.
She dreams a dream—God willed it so—a wonder!
The heavenly vault abruptly draws asunder,
And, its unfathomed inner depths unsealed,
In dazzling bursts of glory are revealed
Great clouds of angels, here and thither pouring,
Uncounted seraphim above them soaring,
Massed cherubs strumming on those harps of theirs,
And grave archangels silent in their chairs,
Their heads in wings of azure pinion bowed;
Caparisoned in racks of shining cloud,
There stands before them the Eternal's throne—
And brightly now before all eyes He shone . . .
All fell prostrate . . . the twang of harps was frozen.
Maria, heart in throat, brow to the ground,
Shakes like a leaf to hear God's voice resound:

"Of all earth's graceful maids the loveliest found,
Young hope of Sion, prize of Israel's chosen,
I summon thee, with sacred love afire,
To share my glory and august desire:
Prepare thyself for destiny unknown,
The bridegroom comes to claim thee for His own."

Soon cirrhus wreathed the throne of God again . . .
The spirits' wingèd host disbanded then,
The cherub swarm resumed its harp rendition . . . .
Her mouth agape, arms crossed in sweet submission,
Maria lies, still gazing at the scene.
But what presents so exquisite, so keen
A cynosure within the heavenly choir?
What youth amid that glittering courtly stir
Can't seem to take his azure eyes off her?
The plume-surmounted helm, the choice attire,
The lustrous wings, the ringlets' golden bell,
The stately height, gaze modest yet appealing . . . .
Mary, although bemused, notes these with feeling.
He claims her eyes, her heart, she knows it well!
Exult, exult, archangel Gabriel!
The scene dissolved.—Thus, while the small fry moan,
Bright lantern pictures magically thrown
Upon a screen are suddenly withdrawn.

Our little beauty wakened at the dawn
And dallied for a lazy languid spell.
Her wondrous dream, though, graceful Gabriel,
Left images not easily resisted.
Her wish to meet her Maker still existed
(Of course), His words were pleasant to her ear . . . .
And awe of him (needless to say) persisted—
Yet Gabriel intrigued her more, I fear . . .
Thus may a general's spouse go addlepated
For some young beanpole of an adjutant:
There's nothing you can do, such things are fated—
As sage and ignoramus both must grant.

Let us consider love's arresting ways
(On other subjects I have little wisdom).
In that young season when a fiery gaze
Sets off a sore upheaval in our system,
And when the ache of wishful self-delusion
Envelops us and weighs upon the mind,
And we are everywhere oppressed, confined,
By one sore thought's importunate intrusion,
Is it not so? we cast about and make
A confidant amongst our young acquaintance,
To him we then translate the private ache
Of passion into hectic verbal paintings.
But once the fleeting instant has been captured
Upon the wing, the senses all enraptured,
And we have eased upon the couch of bliss
Our lovely, soon-no-longer-shrinking miss;
When we forget what love was, unrequited,
And we have nothing left to cavil at,
Then, to recall the turmoil it excited—
We seek our bosom friend for one more chat.

You came to know, o Lord, her agitation,
You caught on fire like us, God though You be.
The demiurge grew cool to all creation,
Bored with the prayers of His empyrean nation,
He worked on a romantic psalmody
And sang out loud: "I love, I love Maria,
Distractedly my deathless path I ply . . .
Ah, where are wings? To Mary will I fly,
At Mary's lovely breast to quench desire! . . . "
And more . . . all he could think of, in this vein—
He liked that florid oriental strain.
He then called Gabriel, His preferential
Consultant, and explained His love, in prose.
Their colloquy the Church keeps confidential,
The Gospel scribes just were not on their toes!
Armenian traditions, though, suggest
That Heaven's king, with words of praise unsparing,
Made Gabriel courier of his interest,
(Aware of sense in him, and proper bearing),

And sent him down at dusk to Mary's nest.
A different prize stung Gabriel's ambitions:
Not seldom he was lucky on the side
When on these note-or-message-bearing missions,
But though he profited, they hurt his pride.
The son of light, his thoughts kept dark, complied
And meekly turned God-Father's cupid's-imp,
Or as we call it here on earth—his pimp.

The ancient Fiend, though, Satan, slumbers not,
And roving all the world, has heard the newest,
That God has cast his eye upon a Jewess,
A beauty, destined by a sacred plot
To save our seed from Hell through a Redeemer.
This caused fierce anger to the cunning Schemer—
He bustled off. Our Lord meanwhile, impatient,
Oozed mooning through the cloudbanks, softly yearned,
Ruled not a thing, but daydreamed and vacationed,
And all took time off while his back was turned.

And what is Mary doing? Where is she,
The worthy Joseph's woebegone young consort?
She's in her garden, full of melancholy,
Spending an hour of harmless leisure, sponsored
By hopes of further dream-borne wizardry.
That angel's looks still challenge and unnerve her,
To him her heart goes out with longing fervor.

In palmy coolness, where a freshet purled,
She watched, distraught, the ripples' glassy vagrance;
She sat abstracted in her private world,
Unconscious of the wildflowers' balmy fragrance . . .
Then suddenly she spied a splendid boa,
His scaly coils hypnotic, iridescent,
In leaf-shade over her, a swaying crescent,
Which forthwith spoke: "The Lord's elect! . . . since Noah
The first! Fear not—I am your thrall eternal . . . ."
A perilous prodigy! Who flatters here
Our wondering innocent? The reptile's kernel
Was our old friend the fiend—Satan, I fear.

The serpent's varied harmony of hues,
His hail, the eyes' too-knowing lizard luster,
Were such as to intrigue as well as fluster
Young languor craving something to amuse.
She turned her melting gaze upon the Rogue
And thus commenced a parlous dialogue:
"Who are you, Serpent? By your coaxing smile,
Your elegant sheen, your sharp-eyed scrutiny,
I know the one who managed to beguile
Our mother Eve to that mysterious tree,
There but to plunge her in transgression vile.
You ruined the immaculate young lily,
Whence Adam's seed, down to this age, incur
Infinitude of evils, willy nilly.
For shame, indeed!"
                "The priests have blabbed you silly,
I never ruined Eve—I rescued her!"
"Rescued? From whom?"
                "From God."
                "Oh, shocking slander!"
"He was in love . . ."
                "Come, watch your tongue, beware!"
"He lusted after . . ."
                "Hush!"
                "No, in all candor,
She ran great risk of his impassioned grandeur . . . ."
"Serpent, you lie!"
                "Let God . . ."
                "You mustn't swear."
"Well, hear my side! . . . " Here Mary's conscience preaches:
"It can't be right, here in the trees alone,
To listen on the sly to serpent speeches
And, who knows how, become the Devil's own!
Yet the Almighty would not visit evil
Upon his servant . . . and for what? A chat!
The Lord is kind, He loves you and all that,
And would not wish you mischief with the Devil.
What's more, this boa's nothing if not civil . . .
Oh, pooh, there's nothing here to shiver at!"
Deciding to be cool but not unpleasant,

She shelved her love and Gabriel for the present
And listened. The sly Serpent spread his hood,
Uncoiled some yards of glistening self and shimmied
Out of the tree, to rear up where she stood.
He lit a sensual glow within her timid
Young inglenook and said: "I cannot square
My testimony with the tales of Moses;
His fancy conjured edifying poses
For God and Hebrew, and his servile air
Paid off, his bombast too, which was stentorian,
So his renown was bruited all about.
But I, believe me, am no court historian;
The rank of prophet I can do without.

　　　You, then: all other beauties, let me tell you,
Must envy you the splendor of your eyes;
Your fate, o modest Mary, will compel you
To trouble Adam's seed in wondrous wise,
To govern fickle hearts with slightest action,
With but a single smile dispense them bliss,
With casual phrases drive them to distraction,
At pleasure to accept, or to dismiss . . .
Such is your fate. Like you, young Eve in Eden
Roamed her green pleasance, modest, wise, and dear,
But loveless, wan—again like you, I fear.
Just man and maid, eyes linked with none impeding,
They wandered on by Eden's freshets clear,
Their life together pastoral and blameless.
But irksome grew each day's idyllic sameness.
Not youth, not health, not cozy nooks untold
Appeared to stir in them a sensuous thought;
They ate, they drank, and hand in hand they strolled,
Yawned in the daytime, and at night knew naught
Of tumbling sports, invigorating games . . .
Can one believe a tyranny so callous?
Desiring Adam's playmate for his own,
The God of Israel, crossgrained and jealous,
Had well-nigh tranquilized our Eden dwellers
And fenced them in a kind of sterile zone!
You know the role for which poor Eve was cast?

Some honor, that, a wild celestial blast!
A cell in Kingdom Come, and never a tantrum,
Pray at His feet, go into transports, fast,
Adore His works, extol the Great Panjandrum,
And never, ever, take a harmless break
To hobnob with a cherub, feel a snake,
Or arch with an Archangel! This awaits
The girl whom the Creator "elevates!"
And the reward? Compensatory joys
For all this crashing, soul-congealing boredom?
The prayers of superannuated whoredom,
Part-song by fuzzy, pimpled choir-boys,
The reek of incense, iconry inferior
Daubed by some frantic bungler in Siberia—
As gay as an embalmers' wake, I swear!

For pity of sweet Eve, I then and there
Made up my mind, his Lordship notwithstanding,
To stir the pair's repose. You are aware
Of how it came about, I think—by handing
Two apples to them from the Wisdom Tree
(A happy emblem, love's come-hither token):
She scents in them instinctual destiny,
The whisper of unconscious drives has spoken,
She sees and knows her state of sweet undress,
Feels inmost heat, a lovely stir and stress,
As well as her young husband's nakedness . . .
I witnessed it, I saw my science, love,
At its most young and touching, and least boring;
The two went off into a leafy grove . . . .
There swiftly eyes and hands began exploring . . .
Between Eve's gleaming limbs, all spread apart,
With earnest zeal, if awkward at the start,
Young Adam sought strange ecstasies, and urgent,
With swiftly kindling frenzy all alight,
He probed the fount of pleasure till, insurgent,
He breached it, and was reft of mind and sight.
And, scorning the Almighty's by-your-leave,
All kindled, raven hair fanned out, my Eve,
With lips but faintly moving in her bliss,

Clung fast to Adam in a lingering kiss,
In tears of love, blind waves of happiness
Beneath the palm fronds—and the youthful earth
With showers of petals greeted man's true birth.

    O blissful day! The bridegroom took his pleasure
With his resourceful bride from early dawn;
How richly strenuous was now their leisure!
They hardly closed an eye from dark to morn . . .
Till God, disrupting their devout endeavor,
Expelled my pair from Paradise forever.
I'd wrought them, though, that grove of sensuousness,
The gay, delightful pleasure-park of youth,
The sad, pure ecstasies of lust, of ruth,
Strange codes of tenderness, and tears of bliss.
Now say—am I deceitful? Vile? Abhorrent?
Was Adam stricken through me, you believe?
I would say not—in any case I warrant
I've ever since been best of friends with Eve . . . "

    The Fiend fell silent. Mary, thoughtful seeming,
Had listened closely to the shrewd old demon.
"Who knows, perhaps the Spirit's not to blame,"
She mused: "I've heard it said by others, mind you,
That it was not from worldly rank or fame,
Nor gold, that happiness most truly came,
Just love . . . but what, where, why—how will it find you?"
Meanwhile her maidenly imagination
Had drunk in Satan's tale, so free of strictures,
Its easy lilt, the forthright motivation,
The candid phrasing, memorable pictures—
Is novelty not every tyro's bait?
From time to time the mist about the gate
To perilous thoughts would thin, be almost banished;
Then, all at once, the snake, it seemed, had vanished—
Someone quite new was here, at any rate:
She saw a sleek young man, of dazzling looks,
Draped at her feet; without preliminaries
He throws bright eyes on her like glittering hooks,
He seems to plead with liquid courtliness;

One hand presents a flower, the other carries
Confusion to her simple linen dress,
Its nimble fingers steal beneath all robings
And frolic there with playful pats and probings
'Mid shyly puzzled privacies . . . all this
Seemed bold, uncalled-for, odd, but nonetheless
Absorbing . . . hard to stop . . . too hard to try . . .
Quick throes of . . . bashfulness? but not unmingled! . . .
Ran up, and down, and up, the maiden thigh;
Her breath grew short, delicious shudders tingled
The swelling nipples, seemed to lift them high . . .
She cannot speak . . . and soon she cannot stand,
Upon those radiant eyes there falls a shadow,
And drooping onto Satan's chest and hand,
She murmurs ah! and tumbles on the meadow . . .

O cherished friend! to whom my early dream
Of fame and hopes-fulfilled was first devoted,
Who held me precious, and on whom I doted,
Will you forgive these *souvenirs intimes*?
My sins . . . the games of fettered youth unbound . . .
Those reckless evenings in your family round
When in the presence of your bristling mother
I caused you clandestine alarm and bother
Developing what still was no man's land?
How I would teach the trusting, docile hand
To cheat apartness and its chafing pain,
Assuage lone hours that sorrow feeds upon,
And sleeplessness, the loveless maiden's bane.
By now your youth has lost its zestful power,
On pallid lips the smile is rare and wan;
Your loveliness was wasted in full flower—
Will you forgive me still, my cherished one?

You, Master of Deceit, must needs have relished
Seductive bliss as your poor dupe did there,
Still more perhaps: for you contrived to snare
The Lord's elect into your expert care—
A coup delicious in itself, and hellish.

Your triumph will be brief—enjoy it, Fiend!
The world grows dark, extinct the sun's last glimmer,
Behold! above the languid maiden shimmer
The Angel's pinions with a rush of wind—
Love's envoy's here, the Heavens' brilliant son.

Abruptly trapped in what might look like error,
Our lovely hid her face in artless terror;
In black-browed fury, though, the Evil One
Reared up and hissed: "You pie-faced paragon,
Who asked you down to take a snooty breather
With working folk? Back to your upper ether!
Your drafty featherworks and boorish stare
Disrupt a fragrant, gossamer affair! . . . "
But Gabriel's censorious intrusion
Cut short the Critic's insolent effusion:
"Benighted foe of Heaven's all-brotherhood,
Proud villain, hopeless exile from the Good,
You slithered through the wraps of guileless Mary
And dare to chide *me*, foul voluptuary?
Off, serf, and touch your forelock as you should,
Or watch me leave a grease-spot where you stood."
"No half-fledged hymningbirds shall make me tremble,
Court fowl that grovel, snivel, and dissemble,
And least of all, procurers for His Nibs!"
And Satan, raging now, with heaving ribs,
Fetched a one-two from left and well beneath
And bashed the Angel squarely in the teeth.
A cry was heard, and Gabriel lay up-ended,
In falling his left knee came half unshipped,
But soon he rose again, his spirit mended,
And there! quite unexpectedly he clipped
The Devil's cheek to make him rock and wail—
They fused into a clinch of fury, stamping,
They turned and churned, now thighs, now shoulders clamping,
But neither Fiend nor Angel could prevail,
Each, chin on enemy chest, would try, and fail,
To throw him or, by ruses fine or rough,
In a firm armlock drag him choking off.

Like me, my friends, you must recall the field
Where in the springtime, finished with reciting,
We used to revel, older scars unhealed,
And cultivate the noble art of fighting.
Just so, too winded now for chiding speech,
These spirits foundered in each other's clutches.
The Prince of Hell, of giant frame and reach,
Foiled by the lissom Angel's clever touches,
Resolves to deal a quick decisive blow.
He knocks the plume-topped helmet off his foe,
A golden helm bright with a diamond's glow,
He takes a grip of silky poll and ringlet
And pulls him from behind with mighty arms,
Bent backward; Mary sees beneath the singlet
The whole assortment of angelic charms
And mutely prays for their deliverance.
The Fiend prevails, ecstatic hell-folk dance;
But Gabriel has seized the moment's chance
And swiftly, brilliantly reversed the issue!
Has clamped his teeth upon that tenderest tissue
(Unusable in almost any fight),
The puffed-up limb wherewith the foe has sinned.
The Fiend surrendered, mercilessly pinned,
And nearly missed the Pit in stumbling flight.

The wondrous clash, the ebb and flow of battle,
The Maid had witnessed it with fluttering breast;
But when, triumphant, grand in fighting fettle,
The Angel turned . . . she heard herself addressed . . . .
She felt hot blushes flood her and unsettle
Her mind with recent memories again . . .
How irresistible the girl was then!

He flushed, this high-placed suitor's emissary,
And said his piece in That One's imagery:
"Rejoice, rejoice, elect of maidens, Mary!
Blest among women, grace is poured on thee,
And blest tenfold the first-fruit of thy womb,
He shall redeem the world, spell Satan's doom . . .
But I can only say, if you ask *me*,

His father's hundredfold more blest than he!"
The Envoy, in the proper pose of kneeling,
Squeezed the Lord's vessel's hand with generous heat;
She trembled, dropped her eyes, and sighed with feeling;
Which mute entreaty but a kiss could meet.
She blushed still more, fell still, and gave a shiver;
He reassuringly caressed her breast;
The Maid was thought to whisper "don't" and quiver;
At which point, though, he lovingly suppressed
All rearguard sighs by measures he knew best . . . .

What now? How bend the jealous wrath of God?
You need not fret, my gentle lady readers:
For every Cupid's prick you know a wad;
You have the happy cunning to mislead us,
Gullible grooms, and fool a sharp-eyed squad
Of experts when the time has come to place
The web of art on lovely failing's trace . . . .
From frisky mothers, girls already 'minus',
Take lessons in the arts of 'clamp-it-tight'
And feigned alarms, and with convincing shyness
Act out the part upon the crucial night.
Next morning, lateish, looking game though blighted,
One rises slowly, limps, is hardly seen;
"Thank God," breathe groom and mother-in-law, delighted,
While the old boy-friend taps against the screen.

Triumphant Gabriel, on wings unsteady
Is cleaving Heaven now with tidings heady.
As keenly as expectant fathers would,
God greets his envoy, sounding very ready:
"Well, Did you do it?" "I did all I could,
I interrogered—*you* know, questioned her,
Revealed the thing . . . " "And was she willing?" "Rather!"
Without another word the Heavenly Father
Rose from His throne, and awesome eyebrows drawn,
Dismissed them all, like Homer's god of thunder
When he resolved to tame his countless spawn.
But Hellas and her creed have long gone under,
There is no Zeus now, after Reason's dawn . . .

By lively recollections still uplifted,
Our beauty in her quiet snug retreat
Was not at ease upon the rumpled sheet.
'Twixt afterglow and fresh desire she drifted,
In ardent whispers called to Gabriel,
Prepared his love an open citadel . . .
And presently with languid foot she shifted
The sheet aside, and with a happy gaze
Looked down along her proud and lush undress,
Adoring her own dazzling nakedness;
Next, in a daydream sensuous and tender,
Brought on her own voluptuous surrender,
On waves of keenest, deepest pleasure floating . . .
Ah, Arch-Corrupter, how you must be gloating!

Abruptly through the window of our love
Flits, snow-plumed, downy-ruffed, the prettiest dove,
Flies overhead in whirring circles, making
Gay incantations, twittering at ease,
Then, guided by the maiden's outspread knees,
Dives on the cherry blossom! With much shaking
He pecks it, poking, writhing, stiff and sweet,
And butts away with little nose and feet.
He? HE, for sure! And Mary understood
Whom she was hosting in His pigeonhood.
She closed her knees, drew in those rosy layers,
Began to gasp and tremble, utter prayers,
She burst out crying—but the Doveling won,
In tiny cooing ecstasies He spun,
And sank in a brief spell of slumbering,
Half shielding love's dew-blossom with one wing.

He flew off. Worn out, Mary marvelled: "My!
Blest if I'm not a social butterfly!
One, two, three, bang! that's what you tell a lad by . . .
I've had too many callers to be bored:
Count them—all in one day I have been had by
The Tempter, an Archangel, and The Lord."

God-Father later, quite without persuasion,
Proclaimed as His the Hebrew maiden's son;
But Gabriel (that enviable one!)
Still would commune with her on safe occasion.
Joseph, like many, not at all forlorn,
Continued stainless vis-à-vis his wife,
Yet treated Jesus like his natural-born;
Wherefor the Father (God) did bless his life.

Amen! How end my chronicler's endeavor?
My own wild oats forsworn by now forever,
I sang you, Gabriel of the godly wings;
To you I dedicate my humble strings'
Perfervent and propitiatory cooing:
Take pity on me, listen to my suing!
Till now I was a heretic in love,
Young goddesses' immoderate pursuer,
Scapegrace, right hand of Satan, faithless wooer . . .
My true contrition, bless it from above!
With virtuous intentions I am gravid,
I mean to change: Helen has come my way,
Like Mary sweet and dear! My sould is avid
Forever to surrender to her sway.
Impart, I pray, enchantment to my speeches,
Tell me what stratagem will turn her head,
Lay secret fuses to her heart's deep reaches,
Or I shall ask the Evil One instead!
Meanwhile the days speed by, and time will alter
My poll with streaks of silver on the sly,
And earnest marriage rites with ring and psalter
Give me a charming consort by and by.
O honest Joseph's comforter resplendent!
I do beseech you then on bended knees,
O cuckolds' intercessor and attendant,
Bestow unstinted blessings on me, please!
Grant me serenity when things look shady,
Supplies of patience, over and again,
Untroubled slumber, trust in my good lady,
Domestic peace and good will to all men.

TSAR NIKITA AND HIS FORTY DAUGHTERS:
INTRODUCTION

Tsar Nikita and His Forty Daughters was written in 1822 in the colorful, raw frontier town of Kishinev in Bessarabia. Unlike the later *Gabri-Iliad* or *Gabriliad*, this rollicking piece of ribaldry does not seem to have been previously translated into English. The poem was driven underground by the censorship and was ultimately recovered from the memory of Pushkin's brother Lev.

TSAR NIKITA AND HIS FORTY DAUGHTERS

Tsar Nikita once reigned widely,
Richly, merrily, and idly,
Did no good or evil thing:
So his realm was flourishing.
He kept clear of toil and bother,
Ate and drank and praised our Father.
With some ladies he had squired
Forty daughters had he sired,
Forty maids with charming faces,
Four times ten celestial graces,
Sweet of temper, full of love.
Ah, what ankles, Heaven above!
Chestnut curls, the heart rejoices,
Eyes—a marvel, wondrous voices,
Minds—enough to lose your mind:
All from head to toe designed
To beguile one's heart and spirit;
There was but a sole demerit.
Oh? What fault was there to find?
None to speak of, never mind.
Or at most the merest tittle.

Still, a flaw (though very little).
How explain it, how disguise
So as not to scandalize
That cantankerous old drip,
Sanctimonious Censorship?
Help me, Muse—your poet begs!
Well—between the lassies' legs . . .
Stop! Already too explicit,
Too immodest, quite illicit . . .
Indirection here is best:
Aphrodite's lovely breast,
Lips, and feet set hearts afire,
But the focus of desire,
Dreamed-of goal of sense and touch,
What is that? Oh nothing much.
Well then, it was this in fact
That the royal lassies lacked.

This unheard-of malformation
Caused dismay and consternation
In each loyal courtly heart,
And much sorrow on the part
Of their Sire and stricken mothers.
From the swaddling-women others
Soon found out what had occurred;
All the nation when it heard
Ah'ed and oh'ed at such an earful,
Gaped and gasped, amazed and fearful;
Some guffawed, but most were leerier:
(This could land you in Siberia!).

Sternly Tsar Nikita summoned
Courtiers, mummies, nannies, "Come and
Hear the stricture I impose:
Any one of you who sows
In my daughters' minds suggestions
Or provokes unseemly questions,
Or as much as dreams to dare
Hint at that which is not there,
Deal in doubtful words and notions,

Or perform improper motions—
Let there be no shred of doubt:
Wives will have their tongues cut out,
Men a member more essential,
Intumescent in potential."

Stern but just, such was the Tsar,
And his eloquence went far
To induce a wise complaisance;
All resolved with deep obeisance
That the counsel of good health
Was to hold one's mouth and wealth.
Noble ladies went in terror
Lest their men be found in error
While the men in secret thought:
Oh, I wish my wife were caught!
(Ah, disloyal hearts and base!)

Our Tsarevnas grew apace.
Sad their lot! Nikita's Grace
Called his Council, put his case:
Thus and so—not unavowedly
But in whispers, not too loudly,
Pas devant les domestiques . . .
Mute the nobles sat and wondered
How to deal with such a freak.
But a gray-haired Nestor pondered,
Rose, and bowing to and fro,
Dealt his pate a clanging blow,
And with venerable stutters
To the potentate he utters:
"May it not, Enlightened Sire,
Be accounted wanton slyness
Or offend your Gracious Highness:—
Sunken yet in carnal mire,
A procuress once I knew,
(Where's she now? What does she do?
Likely in the same vocation.)
She enjoyed the reputation
Of a most accomplished witch,

Curing any ache or itch,
Making feeble members sound.
Pray let my advice be heeded:
If that witch could just be found,
She'd install the thing that's needed."

"Instantly," exclaimed and frowned,
Thunder on his brow, Nikita,
"Send for her and let me meet her,
Let the sorceress be found!
If, however, she deceive Us,
Of Our shortage not relieve Us,
Lead Us up the garden path
With sly tricks—she'll know Our wrath!
Let me be not Tsar but duffer
If I do not make her suffer
Death by fire—of which is token
This my prayer! I have spoken."

Confidentially, discreetly,
Envoys were despatched who fleetly
Sped by special courier post,
Searched the realm from coast to coast,
Scampered, scurried, faster, faster,
Tracking witches for their Master.
One year passes, nothing's heard,
And another, not a word.
Till at last a lad of mettle
On a lucky trail did settle,
Rode into a forest dread
Just as though by Satan led;
There he found the little cottage
Where the witch lived in her dotage.
Boldly passing gate and bar
As an envoy of the Tsar,
He saluted the magician
And revealed the Tsar's commission:
What the quest was all about,
What his daughters were without.
She, with instant understanding,

Thrust him back onto the landing,
Hustled him straight on and out:
"Shake a leg, don't look about,
Do not linger or I'll plague you,
Strike your limbs with chills and ague;
Wait three days and then come back
For your answer and your pack;
But no later than the crack
Of that dawn!" Then she remembers
To lock up, fans golden embers . . .
Three-score hours she brewed her spell,
Conjured up the Prince of Hell,
And as soon as she could ask it,
He produced a brassbound casket
Stocked with countless feminine
Wherewithals of men's sweet sin.
Curly beauties, choice examples,
Every size, design, and shade,
What a marvelous parade!
Sorting out her wealth of samples,
Soon the sorc'ress had arrayed
Forty of superior grade
All in damask napkin dressed,
And had locked them in the chest.
This she handed to the willing
Envoy with a silver shilling,
And he rides . . . till in the west
Sinking sun commends a rest.
Just a bite to stay one's hunger,
Spirit keeps the body younger,
Vodka keeps the spirit mellow;
This was a resourceful fellow,
And he carried in his sack
Victuals for the long way back.
So he took this pleasant course,
Loosed the harness of his horse,
And sat munching in the shadow,
While his charger cropped the meadow.
Happily he sat and mused
How the Tsar would be enthused

With what nestled in his basket,
Might appoint him, what a fluke,
Knight or Baron, Viscount, Duke . . .
What was hidden in the casket
That the witch was sending him?
Just that oaken lid to mask it
For the journey's interim . . .
Tightly grooved, though . . . all looks dim.
Terror of the Tsar's decree
Yields to curiosity,
The temptation's too delicious:
Ear laid close against the fissures,
Long he listens—but in vain;
Sniffs, familiar scent . . . Egad!
What profusion there, what wonder!
Just a glimpse could not be bad;
If one pried the lock asunder . . .
And before he knew, he had.
Whoosh! the birdies, swarming out,
Light on branches all about,
Tails aflirt. In vain our lad
Loudly calls them back to casket,
Throws them biscuit from his basket,
Scatters morsels—all no good.
(Clearly such was not their diet);
Why return if you could riot
Sweetly chanting in the wood,
To be cooped in gloom and quiet?

Meanwhile in the distance stumbles,
All bent double by her load,
Some old woman down the road.
Our poor envoy up and bumbles
Quite distracted in her wake:
"Granny, help, my head's at stake!
Look, there sit my birdies scattered,
Chattering as if nothing mattered,
How can I entice them back?"
That old woman craned her neck,

Spat, and with her crook did beckon:
"Though you asked for it, I reckon,
Do not fret or worry so:
All you need to do is show—
And they'll all come back, I warrant."
Our young fellow thanked the crone,
And the moment he had shown—
Down they fluttered in a torrent,
Swarming off their firs and birches,
And resumed their former perches
In the envoy's box; and he,
To forestall some new disaster,
Clapped them under lock and key,
And rode homeward to his Master,
Thanking God he had retrieved them.
When the princesses received them,
Each one promptly found its cage;
And the Tsar in royal glee
Graciously was pleased to stage
A gigantic jubilee.
Seven days they spent in fêting
And a month recuperating.
The entire House of Lords
He allotted rich rewards,
Nor forgot the witch herself:
On the Art Museum's ladders
Reaching for the highest shelf,
They brought down to send the elf
Skeletons, a brace of adders,
And in spirits in a jar
Half a candle famed afar.
And of course the envoy bold
Had his prize. My tale is told.

Some will ask me, eyebrows climbing,
Why I wrought such fatuous rhyming,
What the reason for it was?
Let me answer them: Because.

THE FOUNTAIN OF BAKHCHISARAY: INTRODUCTION

The Fountain of Bakhchisaray is stylistically the purest, and thematically the most "oriental" of Pushkin's verse tales of the South. "The South" refers here not only to the poet's "southern exile," spent mostly in Bessarabia and Odessa, but also, and more to the point, to the exotic and Islamic spell which the newly Russian southern territories (the Caucasus, the Crimea, and the vast Cossack borderlands with Ottoman Turkey) had cast over poetry and travel literature and thence over the public imagination. The South for Russia thus corresponds in its associations with the Orient of the "eastern poems" of Byron and Moore.

The poem was preceded by two verse tales not included in the present collection: *The Prisoner of the Caucasus* (1821), a somberly romantic story of bondage, love, and self-sacrifice amid the crags of Circassia, and *The Robber Brothers*, a fragmentary evocation of the Schillerian romance of not-ignoble brigandage, which took shape simultaneously with *The Fountain*. Pushkin worked on the latter poem intermittently from 1821. The year before, while traveling through the Crimea on his way to Kishinev in Bessarabia, he had had occasion to visit the ruined palace of the Crimean Khans at the site of the ancient capital of Bahçesaray (Turkish spelling; the meaning is 'garden palace'). In a letter he later exclaimed in dismay over the pathetic remnant—a faint trickle from a cast-iron pipe—which was all that was left of the legend-shrouded fountain in the once-famous pleasure garden of the Khans.

The Fountain was completed in 1823 and published the following year. It is still close in some ways to the "Eastern" poems of the English romantics: exotic and retrospective in place and era, mostly *andante* in tempo, intermittent in the flow of information. Rhetorical queries relaunch the plot at intervals, and an epilogue of author's reminiscing in present time sustains the general note of wistful lyricism and the power of the highly musical, wonderfully mellifluous verse. This last quality, and the absence of any hero other than all-assuaging time, separate the poem from Byron's stereotypic figures and his slap-dash poetics.

While the treatment of the male in the love triangle, Khan Girey, and that of the virginal Polish captive, Maria, is at best rudimentary, the figure of Zarema marks a distinct step forward in individuation, compared either with "the Russian" and his Circassian maiden in *The Prisoner* or with Byron's recurrent oriental heroines. In the few paragraphs of her confrontation with Maria her character—passionate, sensitive, direct—comes to stand out vividly against the somnolent vagueness of the backdrop. Her desperate plea to Maria is a splendid dramatic monologue in its variety of credible feeling, tone, and diction, highlighted by the fine fragments of recollection of her own capture.

Most of Pushkin's own infrequent remarks about *The Fountain* are perfunctory and deprecating. In a letter to Prince Vyazemsky of October, 1824, he says: "Between you and me, *The Fountain* is trash; but its epigraph is fine." Later, in one of his "rebuttals to criticism," Pushkin had this to say:

> *The Fountain of Bakhchisaray* is weaker than *The Prisoner* and, like it, is redolent of Byron, who had gone to my head. The scene between Zarema and Maria has dramatic validity; it was not criticized, I believe. A. Raevsky burst out laughing at the following lines:
>
> > At times, in peril's very jaws,
> > He'd raise his sword, and as he downed it,
> > Halt, peer distractedly, and pause
> > As if forgetting where he was,
> > And blanch . . .
>
> Young writers are unable as a rule to portray the physical movement of passion. Their characters are forever convulsed, laughing ferociously, gnashing their teeth, and so one. All this is ludicrous, like a melodrama.

In one of the more acute and lucid exchanges produced by the critical debate of the early century on the nature and legitimacy of the new "romantic movement," Pushkin's above-mentioned friend, Prince Peter Vyazemsky (1792-1878), came to the defense of romanticism and of Pushkin's *Fountain* in particular. In his "By way of a Foreword to *The Fountain of Bakhchisaray*" (1824) he cast his polemic in the form of a long dialogue between "Publisher" and "Classicist," which runs in part as follows:

Publisher:

The poem is based on a legend well-known in the Crimea to this day. The story has it that Khan Kerim-Girey abducted the beautiful [Countess] Potocka and kept her in the harem at Bakhchisaray; it is even suggested that he married her. It is a dubious tradition, and Muravev-Apostol in his recently published *Journey in Tauris* questions the likelihood of this story; on rather strong grounds, it would seem. However this may be, the legend belongs in the realm of poetry.

Classicist:

I see! So the muses in our day have been turned into purveyors of all sorts of cock-and-bull stories. What becomes of the worth of poetry if you feed it nothing but fairy tales?

Publisher:

History must not be gullible; poetry, quite the reverse. It often values what the former dismisses with scorn, and our poet did very well in adapting the legend of Bakhchisaray to poetry and enriching it with plausible inventions; and he did even better by making use of both elements with artistic perfection. The narrative preserves the local color as vividly and freshly as could be imagined. There is an oriental cast to the mise-en-scène, to the very emotions, and to the style. In the view of judges whose verdict may be deemed definitive in our literary criticism, the poet in this new work has shown the marks of a steadily maturing gift.

Classicist:

Who are these judges? We do not recognize any but *The Messenger of Europe* and *The Well-Intentioned*, for our writing conforms with them. Let us await what they have to say!

Publisher:

Await by all means! Meanwhile I will say that Pushkin's story is vivid and interesting. There is a great deal of movement in the poem. Into a rather narrow frame he has fitted a content replete, not with a plethora of characters and a string of varied adventures, but with art—the kind of mastery which enabled the poet to portray with delicate shading the main actors of his tale. Narrative movement depends on the activation of talent, as it were; style lends it wings or hampers it progress. In Pushkin's work the reader's interest is sustained from start to finish. One cannot acquire this secret except by the lures of style.

Classicist:

I strongly suspect, though, that all this action, in the customary way of the romantics, is only lightly sketched in. What happens in such cases is that the reader has to play the author's handy-man and finish telling things for him. Slight hints, murky riddles, that is the stuff furnished by the romantic poet for the reader to do what he likes with. The romantic architect leaves the layout and structure of the edifice to anyone's caprice: a veritable castle in **Spain, having neither design nor foundation.**

Publisher:

You are not content to see a beautiful building before you; you demand that its framework be visible too. In works of art the mere outlines of action suffice; why should one want to look into the private workshop too? A work of art is a work of make-believe: the less the prosaic connection between parts protrudes, the greater benefit accrues to the whole. Personal pronouns in speech hold up its flow, bog the story down. Imagination and invention also have their pronouns, of which the writer's craft tries to rid itself by dexterous ellipsis. Why say it all, drive everything home, when you have to do with people of acute and active mind? And there is no reason to give any thought to those whose minds are dull and inert. I am reminded of a certain classicist reader who simply did not comprehend what had happened to the Circassian maiden in *A Prisoner of the Caucasus* in the lines:

> And in the surge of moonlit waters
> A ring of ripples dies away.

He took the poet to task for not having made things easier for his powers of penetration by saying outright and in so many words that the Circassian girl had flung herself into the water and drowned. Let's leave prose to take care of its own. As it is, there is quite enough of it in everyday life and in the poems published in *The Messenger of Europe*.

In the same year, 1824, M. N. Korniolin-Pinsky published a rather perceptive review of *The Fountain* in issue No. 13 of *Syn Otechestva* (Son of the Fatherland), the chief literary organ of the partisans of the new romanticism. Raising a point related to the primacy of character over plot and description over action often attributed to the Russian novel later in the century, he joined Pletnev, Pogodin, and others in averring that in the new poetry continuity and coherence of action could without detriment to the whole yield here and there to evocative spontaneity and striking poetic detail, even to mystifying ellipses. An effective lyrical murk surrounds the details of the original abduction of both Zarema and Maria, the movement of the Khan's emotions, and the life of Bahçesaray in peace and war. But the murk deepens to mystery precisely at the point of the tragic consummation of the poem, the suggestive gap which replaces the murder of Maria by her desperate rival. It was this point which brought forth the following shrewd comment by the reviewer: "If he had shown us the shrinking beauty under the dagger of the frantic Georgian girl, he would have ruined our entrancement and hence his poem. Indignation would have banished from our souls all other feelings evoked by the poem."

THE FOUNTAIN OF BAKHCHISARAY

*Many have visited this fountain, as I
have done; but some are no more,
others are wandering afar.*

Sadi

With brooding eyes sat Khan Girey
Blue smoke his amber mouthpiece shrouded;
About their fearsome ruler crowded
The Court in sedulous array.
Deep silence reigned about the prince;
All humbly scanned the least reflection
Of irritation or dejection
On his beclouded countenance.
But now a gesture of impatience
From the imperious lord of nations
Made all bow low and melt away.

Enthroned alone remains Girey;
More freely labors now his breathing,
More clearly now his scowls betray
The surf of passion's inward seething.
Thus clouds, the brow of heaven wreathing,
Are mirrored in a changeful bay.

On what high issues is he poring?
What would his haughty mind essay?
To Russia will he fare with warring,
On Poland force his sword and sway?
Is he aflame with bloody vengeance,
Are plots uncovered in his host,
Do mountain tribes alarm him most
Or devious Genoa's subtle engines?

No—he has tired of armored fame,
That formidable arm is tame;
The lure of stratagems has faded.

Should rank defilement have invaded
His harem on betrayal's spoor,
A child of charms enchained have traded
Her ardent heart to a giaour?

No—Girey's wives, subdued of bearing,
Designs still less than wishes daring,
In melancholy stillness blush;
Their guard is vigilant and dreaded,
They harbor no deceit, embedded
Deep in their drear unsolaced hush.
In stealth their beauty blooms and wanes,
A sombre dungeon for its bower:
Thus blossoms of Arabia flower
Beneath the sheltering hothouse panes.
For them, disconsolately flow
Days, months, and years in changeless rhythm,
And, all unnoticed as they go,
Take youth and love and ardor with them.
Of even hue is every day,
And slow the current of the hours.
Sloth holds the Harem's life in sway,
And seldom sweet enjoyment flowers.
The youthful wives, by forced resort
To pastimes of whatever sort,
Will choose among their gorgeous raiments,
Engage in games and entertainments,
Or, deep in shade of sycamores,
By well-springs babbling near their quarters,
May sport in gauzy threes and fours,
Beribboned by the shining waters.
A baleful eunuch wanders here;
To counter him is vain endeavor:
His unrelenting eye and ear
Are fixed on all their movements, ever.
Their changeless order bears his seal.
The sum and essence of his functions
Lies in his master's word and weal,
Nor the august Koran's injunctions
Does he observe with greater zeal.

His soul spurns love; a graven idol
Of unconcern, he does not bridle
At hatred, scorn, reproach; he brooks
The taunts which wanton mischief utters,
Disdain, appeal, submissive looks,
Unspeaking sighs, and languid mutters.
No stranger he to women's hearts,
He knows how wily are their arts
At large or in the dungeon's throe:
Eyes melting, tears' appealing source,
Are impotent to stay his course;
He ceased to trust them long ago.

When, fragrant hair in loose undress,
The youthful captives, on an outing
To feel the heart of day the less,
Have gone to bathe, clear fountains spouting
About their lovely nakedness,
He, all enjoyment's guard unswerving,
Is there, impassively observing
That welter of unveiled delight.
He stalks the shaded harem night,
Inaudible his feline gliding;
Across the carpets' soundless deeps
To the obsequious door he creeps,
In secret aisle on aisle bestriding;
What sensuous slumber might reveal
He summons to his shrewd ordeal,
Each whisper of the darkness scouting;
Quick breathing, sighing, languid pouting—
He dockets with relentless zeal;
And woe to her whose slumbrous mutters
Perchance another's name impart,
Or who to trusted ear unshutters
Unlawful stirrings of her heart!

What sorrows marks the Ruler's bearing?
The hookah wafts its fumes no more;
The Eunuch, not a tremor daring,

Awaits his signal at the door.
The pensive potentate has risen,
The portals gape. In silence grim
He enters the secluded prison
Of wives but lately dear to him.

    His visitation biding blithely
Round playful fountains, sprawling lithely
On silken rugs, our beauties lark;
One frisky troop beguile their leisure
By watching with a childish pleasure
The darting fishes glint and spark
Against the marble's lucent dark;
Some, doubly willful and capricious,
Drop golden earrings to the fishes.
Slave maidens, weaving all among,
Serve cooling sherbet, tart and fruity,
And to an air of tuneful beauty
Make all the Harem sweet with song:

TARTAR SONG

1

    "Man's way on earth the Heavens checker
By turns with wretchedness and tears:
Blest is the Fakir, eyeing Mecca
At evenfall of weary tears.

2

    Blest they who hallow Danube's valley
Afresh with mortal sacrifice:
To them, with lips on fire, will rally
The lovely maids of Paradise.

3

But blest, Zarema, more than these,
Who, spurning worldly clash and riot,
In the seraglio's peaceful ease
May lull you, sweetest one, in quiet."

They sing . . . Zarema, though, is far,
The Harem's queen, love's brightest star!—
Alas, all pale and overwrought,
She does not hear her praise. Distraught,
A palm by tempest bent and spread,
She sadly hangs her lovely head.
No thing can hearten her or spur:
Girey has ceased from loving her.

Betrayed! . . . But how can one believe you
Excelled in charms? By whom conceive you
Outshone? Around your lily brow is laid
A double coil of raven braid;
Your wonder-working eyes seem able
To blind the day, make night more sable;
Who sounds with fuller voice than you
The transports of enflamed desire?
Whose gifts of passion could outdo
Your fierce caresses' festering fire?
Enchantment tasted in your arms—
Who would essay another's charms?
Yet Khan Girey has been eluding
Your spell, from cruelty or scorn,
Those cooling hours from dusk to morn
He has been solitary, brooding—
Since first the Polish princess, doomed
To harem life, was here entombed.

Fair Mary had but little time
Been planted in this alien orchard—
A lovely flower, till lately nurtured
To blossom in her native clime.

She was her graybeard father's pride
Joy of his years' receding tide.
The maiden's every youthful whim
Was the indulgent father's order.
A sole wish animated him
That Providence should but accord her
Life's bright spring; that each day be passed
So that no shadow of displeasure
Should mar the comfort of his treasure,
That even as a bride at last
She should remember, tenderhearted,
Her maidenhood, those joyous days
That like a fleeting dream departed.
All spoke for her: her quiet ways,
Her movements, lithe and swift to view,
And eyes, a languishment of blue.
Kind Nature's gifts of heart and brains
With art's accomplishments she mated,
And with her harp's bewitching strains
Their homely feasting animated;
For her fair hand there came contending
The rich in gold and in estate,
And many a youth, in secret rending
His heart for her, bemoaned his fate.
But to her spirit Love was late
To make his way with soft incursions;
Her unsequestered leisure hours
In the paternal grounds and towers
Were spent in innocent diversions.

How long? Alas! The **Tartar swarm**
On Poland's marches poured in rivers:
Not with such rushing fury quivers
The fire across a field of corn.
By warlike devastation savaged,
New-orphaned lay the blooming land,
The dear pacific pastimes banned,
Oak groves and hamlets charred and ravaged,
The noble castle's keeps unmanned.
Maria's morning room is muted . . .

The crypt wherein, in marble dressed,
Ancestral relics lie at rest,
Embossed with princely crown and crest,
Sees a fresh sepulchre recruited . . .
The orphaned princess snatched by arms,
A grasping heir succeeds upon her,
By now a galling yoke's dishonor
His rule has brought to ravished farms.

The Khan's serail is now confining,
O grievous thought! the young princess.
Mute bondage has Maria pining
In tears of utter hopelessness.
Girey indulges her distress:
Her laments, sobs, despairing pleas
Disturb the Potentate's brief slumber,
And he has waived for her a number
Of the Seraglio's stern **decrees**.
The Harem beauties' gloomy warder
Does not patrol her night or day,
Nor does his company and order
Attend her to her slumber bay.
The contumely of his eyes
To her pure visage did not rise;
She used a pool, remote and lonely,
Attended by a slave girl only,
To bathe; the Khan himself was prone
To spare his captive's frail composure,
Permitting her to live alone,
In the Seraglio's last enclosure:
You'd think, in that secluded cell
One not of earth had come to dwell.
Within, a light is ever shining
Before Our Lady's image fair,
Assuagement for the spirit's pining:
There pious Faith confounds despair
And makes with Hope a saving pair;
And all inclines the soul to ponder
A gentler shore, a refuge yonder.

In this spare lodgement, set apart
From envious wives, she grieves her heart.
And while the rest have never craved
But unreflecting dissipation,
This nook, miraculously saved,
Hides virtue's sacred resting station.
Thus heart, by wickedness bespoken,
Amidst incontinence of vice
May clutch a single sacred token,
Discern a glint of paradise . . .
. . . .
. . . .

   The night has fallen; shades of sorrel
Now tint the smiling Tauric vale;
Far in the bosky hush of laurel
I hear the tuneful nightingale;
The starry choirs revolve, ashimmer,
The moon rides up; from cloudless height
It washes knoll and forest night
And lowlands with its langorous glimmer.
Their faces veiled in snowy swathes,
From house to lowly house there ply
The twilight of Bakhchisaray
On feet as light as nimble wraiths
The simple **Tartar women, roaming**
To barter gossip in the gloaming.
The Court is stilled; the Harem wing
Lies in assuagement lapped, untroubled;
Its slumber no unpeaceful thing
Can threaten: vigilance redoubled,
The Eunuch turns his nightly rounds.
Asleep, as now, his spirit, hobbled
But loosely, stays alert to sounds.
Scant respite to his chafing senses
Allows betrayal's restless fear.
Now someone's scrape or lisp he fancies,
Now exclamations does he hear;
Night sounds imagined or deceiving
Arouse him to a restive crouch,

His head and hearing tensely weaving . . .
But all is still about his couch.
The fountain's dulcet purl and bobbing
Alone enlives the marble close,
And nightingales, in darkness sobbing,
Which ever wait upon the rose;
Long does the Eunuch listen then—
Till sleep exacts its toll again.

How rich the night of Orient sky
How lush the shaded splendor of it!
How genially its hours flow by
For the disciples of the Prophet!
Sweet languors from their arbors well,
In their enchanted lodgement dwell,
Their harem, safe in stout defenses,
Where by the magic of the moon
All throbs in a mysterious swoon,
Voluptuous rapture of the senses!

The wives are sleeping. All but one.
She rises, breathless; tiptoes on;
She finds the door and, fingers questing,
She opens it; her footfall light
Advances in the murk of night . . .
Across her path the Eunuch's resting
In swathes of sleep that come and pass.
A heart of iron is his merit:
His tranquil sleep deceives, alas! . . .
She shimmers past him like a spirit.

A door ahead; her fingers blundered
As, tremulous, they groped to catch
The drawbolt of the trusty latch . . .
She entered, gazed about her, wondered . . .
An awed misgiving blanched her cheek:
A candelabra's lonely glimmer,
Its mournful light now bright, now dimmer
On a gilt frame, a visage meek,

Our holiest Maid's, and, sacred token
Of love, the Cross. O Georgian! These
Awaken strings which have not spoken
So long—in accents soft and broken
They sound forgotten melodies . . .
Before her the Princess was lying,
Her slumbrous breathing seemed to blow
Her cheeks a warmer, livelier glow
And cause a wistful smile to grow
Upon the trails of recent crying.
Thus walks the moon her silver lane
Through blossoms ravaged by the rain.
A son of Eden, downward sweeping,
It seemed, had furled his pinions here,
And in his sleep shed tear on tear,
The captive's wretched fate beweeping . . .

Zarema—oh! what touches you?
Her heart is gripped by pangs of rue,
Her knees bend under as if heeding
Another's will. "I beg of you,"
She prays, "have mercy, hear my pleading . . . ."
Her movements, sobs, abrupt behest
Have chased Maria's tranquil rest.
She fears who knows what mischief masked
In this appeal of a young stranger,
And trembling, sensible of danger,
She helps her to her feet, and asks:
"Who are you? . . . Lone nocturnal ranger,
Why are you here?" "I come to you;
Save me; such is the lot I drew
That you are now my sole redress.
Long did I savor happiness,
Live unassailed by care or doubt . . .
The shadow even of my bliss
Is gone; I perish. Hear me out.

This is not home; my childhood haven
Is far away . . . but what remains

Of bygone scenes, my mind retains
Live to this day and deeply graven.
Impenetrable forest lowers,
I see great mountains, ether-girt,
Hot falls which from the mountains spurt;
And laws and customs far from ours.
By what ordainment, by whose hand
I came to leave my native land
I know not; I recall the heaving
Of seas, a man high on a spar
Above the sails . . . Alarm and grieving
Have stayed aloof from me so far;
In peace which nothing seemed to mar
I bloomed in Harem shade, expecting
The call of love on me—my first—
With humble heart and unreflecting.
My fantasies, in secret nursed,
Came true. For peaceable indulgence
Girey renounced the clash of war;
When he forswore its gory fulgence,
The Harem saw him as before.
In dark suspense, we were paraded
Before the Khan. His countenance
Turned to me, shone: he was persuaded,
He summoned me . . . and ever since
Enchanted bliss without remission
We sipped; not once from that glad day
Did slander, scheming competition,
Tormenting jealousy, suspicion,
Or boredom mark us for their prey.
But you appeared to him, Maria! . . .
From that time on, alas, his soul
Turned black with traitorous desire!
Girey, rank perfidy his goal,
Is callous to my castigation,
The heart's lament he would ignore,
Finds neither converse nor sensation
To give Zarema as before.
You do not share his lapse from duty,

I know, and guiltless is your mind . . .
So listen to me: I have beauty;
Here, only you may boast the kind
That I might stand in peril of;
But I was wholly made for love,
And you can't love him in my fashion;
With barren beauty void of passion
Why stir a vulnerable heart?
Leave him to me; Girey is mine;
On me his burning kisses smart;
Most awesome vows from him I treasure,
Not just of late his thought, his pleasure
Seek me and with my own combine;
His faithlessness will be my death . . .
I weep—look!—prone before you, reaching
Humbly to touch your feet, beseeching
You (whom I dare assign no breath
Of blame) to heal my sorrow, teaching
Girey to be what once he was . . .
Gainsay me not, by word or sign;
Though dazed by you, Girey is mine;
By pleading, spurning give him pause,
Pride, grief—whatever—make him heed;
Swear to me (though for the K'oran
Amid the captives of the Khan
I all but lost my childhood creed,
My mother prayed the Christian way
Like you . . .) by this your faith I say:
Back to Zarema turn Girey . . .
There's hope . . . but mark me: if I lose it—
I have a dagger, and I use it.
The Caucasus has been my sire."

  With this, she vanished; and Maria
Avoided watching her depart.
The voice of mutinous desire
Is foreign to her maiden heart.
She cannot fathom its narration.
It frightens her and makes her ill.
What tears, entreaty, imprecation,

Might rescue her from degradation?
What looms ahead? Must, by his will,
What bitter youth awaits her still
Reek with a concubine's disgrace?
O heaven—what if Girey had left her
To droop in this forsaken place;
Or if his purpose had bereft her
Of her sad life's remaining lease—
With what serenity Maria
Would leave behind life's joyless grind!
What moments had been dearer, higher,
Had long been lived and left behind!
What in this waste but begs release?
Her time is come, her place is shown,
And with a smile so like her own,
They call her home to heavenly peace.
. . . .

The days have fled; Maria's gone,
To earth committed what was human,
An angel now, the friendless one
Her longed-for haven helps illumine.
What was it thrust her to her tomb?
Sad durance, whence all hope was banished,
Disease, or else some other doom?
Who knows—but tender Mary's vanished! . . .
The vacant Court in doldrums fades,
By Khan Girey once more forsaken;
His **Tartar squadrons he has taken**
To lash abroad with evil raids;
To slaughter, seemingly the same,
He rides again, blackbrowed and cruel,
But in his heart, a desolate flame
Of other feelings draws its fuel.
At times, in peril's very jaws
He'd lift his sword, and as he downed it,
Halt, peer distractedly and pause
As if forgetting where he was,
And blanch as if by fear confounded,

Then whisper something—and it seems,
Tears scored his cheeks in scalding streams.

   The Harem, utterly neglected,
Knows not the favor of his stay;
Within, their womanhood rejected,
Beneath the Eunuch's frigid sway
The fretful wives grow old. Their orders
Long since exclude the Georgian girl:
By the Seraglio's tongueless warders
Cast to the waters' silent swirl.
The very night the Princess died,
Her own deliverance was hastened.
Sin as she did, from love and pride,
She was most pitilessly chastened!

   Laid waste with sword and firebrands
Caucasia, and the peaceful lands
Of Rus' with plague of war infected,
Back home the **Tartar chieftain came;**
A marble fountain he erected
To honor poor Maria's name,
Deep in a corner of the Court.
Mohammed's crescent moon surmounting,
A cross was set atop the fountain
(Symbols conjoined from lack of thought,
They still affront in the recounting).
There's writing, too; the probing whirls
Of time have not erased it yet.
Behind its curious curves and curls
Within the stone the waters fret,
Then gush and rain in tearlike pearls,
Undried, unsilenced evermore.
Thus mothers mourn in grief unmeasured
Sons done to death by savage war.
This tale of woe from ancient lore
The maidens hereabouts have treasured;
Each age the mournful mark reveres,
And knows it as *The Fount of Tears.*

Departed from the north at last,
High merriment for long put by,
I visited Bakhchisaray,
Its palace, slumbering in the past.
By soundless lanes and deviations
I roved, where erstwhile, scourge of nations,
The fiery-blooded **Tartar dined**
And from more ghastly depredations
In more luxurious ease reclined.
Luxuriance to this day enthralls
Those vacant pleasances and halls;
The roses glow, the waters jingle,
The tendrils of the vine commingle,
And gold still glistens on the walls.
Frail lattice still shuts off each chamber
Where, in the spring of years confined,
Distraitly fingering beads of amber,
The harem wives in silence pined.
I saw the Khans' sepuchral mounds,
The potentates' last resting grounds.
Those pillars rising from the sod,
Topped with their marble turban-winding,
Made sensible the secret grinding,
I fancied, of the mills of God.
Where now the Khans? The Harem where?
All now was silent, all was dreary,
All had been altered . . . but not there
Was what bestirred the spirit's query:
The breath of rose, the fountain's gush
Induced, unwilled by me, forgetting;
Unwilled by me, there surged a rush
Of feelings questioning and fretting,
And through the palace, shadow-light,
A maiden glided in my sight! . . .

Whose shade, companions, did I see?
Tell me: whose tender image haunted
My pensive mind so earnestly,
By naught deflected, nothing daunted?

Did pure-souled Mary cross my path,
Was it Zarema's fiery passion,
Who, deathless in her jealous wrath,
Bestrode the Court in spectral fashion?

I know a gaze as dear and fair,
And beauty still in nature anchored;
To her my heart-deep thoughts repair,
For her in exile I have hankered . . .
Madman! Enough of this! Forbear,
Do not perversely ask to languish,
To frantic dreams, love's hopeless anguish,
You have paid tribute, and to spare—
Come to your senses; convict pining,
How long are you to kiss your chain,
And with your lyre's immodest whining
Broadcast your madness, and your pain?

To peace and to the Muse devoting
My heart, oh! soon I'll relish here
The smiling banks of the Salgir,
On neither love nor glory doting!
I'll half ascend the coastal height
And, full of memories to aching,
Let Tauric waves in crest and breaking
Regale again my eager sight.
O magic shore! O visions' balm!
All there inspirits: peak and pine,
The graceful valleys' sheltering calm,
The rose and amber of the vine,
Cool brooks and toplar shade near by . . .
All this will lure the rider's eye
As his familiar mount may sidle
Along the shore with slackened bridle
Upon a windless morning's spree;
And, turning emerald, the brine
Will scintillate for him and shine
Where Ayu Dağ falls off to sea . . .

THE GYPSIES: INTRODUCTION

The Gypsies (begun in 1823/24 in Odessa, finished in October, 1824, at Mikhailovskoe) is a terse **anti-Rousseauian** drama built on **Rousseauian** premises. It posits a tragedy wrought in a humble "golden age" society by the sense of pride and false honor bred in natural man by civilization. These are the "fateful passions" of the rueful closing lines of the epilogue. Once implanted, they possess man and may destroy him and others despite his own urge towards a life of frugal innocence, so that the normally central tragic issue of personal flaw or guilt becomes almost irrelevant. Aleko, the haunted hero who bears a variant of Pushkin's own name, is twice undone by the elemental passion of possessive jealousy: once (it is barely hinted in the nightmare scene) during his life in urban civilization, a second time in the free, simple environment which he has himself sought in a vain attempt to escape human law and "enlightened corruption"—a term which stands for civilized sophistication, seen as a curse in the vein of Rousseau. Of the triad of principal actors, only the artistically subdued central figure, the old gypsy, has conquered, at great cost, the helpless serfdom of the human condition and thus, achieving full harmony with the frugal nature and a life reduced to the bare essentials, attained the peace and wisdom of resignation. This achievement, however, has no explicit parallel among the other followers of the nomad life, whether "naturals" or romantic fugitives from the city—for *ot sudeb zashchity net*: there is no refuge from the fates.

The Gypsies is the most mature and thoughtful of Pushkin's southern narrative poems. In it he has completely discarded the romantic vagueness of background and the arid habit of narcissistic self-projection, which he had come to condemn in the Byronic poem and its thinly disguised author-hero—both powerful influences upon him in the earlier years of his "southern exile."

THE GYPSIES

Between Moldavian settlements
In clamorous throng the gypsies wander.
Tonight they spread their tattered tents
Encamped beside the river yonder.
Gay is their camp, like freedom gay,
Their sleep beneath the stars untroubled;
Amid the wheels of van and dray,
Their sides with hanging carpets doubled,
The campfire burns, and over it bent
They cook their meal; at pasture scattered,
The horses graze; behind the tent
A tame bear lies at ease, unfettered.
A lively bustle stirs the scene:
The peaceful cares of **tribesmen keen**
To move at daybreak, women singing
And children's shouts around the wains,
Above the traveling anvil's ringing.
But now the night with slumbrous balm
Descends on the nomadic camping,
And nothing stirs the prairie calm
But barks and horses' neighs and stamping.
Extinct at last the winking lights,
All lies in stillness, moonbeams shimmer
Alone from heaven's distant heights
And set the silent camp aglimmer.
But in one tent an aged man
Still lingers by the charcoal pan,
His limbs at dying embers warming,
And his old eyes alertly scan
The steppe, where mists of night are forming.
His youthful daughter, scarcely grown,
Has gone to roam the prairie yonder.
In willful freedom bred to wander,
She will be back; but day has flown,
And soon the moon will have receded
From heaven's far-beclouded fold—
Zemfira's still abroad; unheeded
Her father's poor repast grows cold.

But there, she's coming; and together
With her, strange to the old man's gaze—
A lad comes striding through the heather.
"My father," thus the maiden says
"I bring a guest, found in the distance
Beyond the barrow as I went;
I bade him slumber in our tent.
He wants to share our own existence,
And I shall be his gypsy love;
For where he dwelt, the law pursues him.
His name—Aleko. He will rove,
He vows, where I rove; and I choose him."

OLD MAN

My welcome to you; if you meant
To rest till morning in our tent,
Or if indeed you came preparing
A longer sojourn—I am glad
To share my shelter and my bread.
Be ours—and our own lot preferring,
Espouse our humble, wayward faring,
And share my wagon too; and so
At dawn we shall set forth together;
Choose any of the trades we know;
Forge iron, or to market go
With songs and dancing-bear atether.

ALEKO

I choose to stay.

ZEMFIRA

He will be mine;
And who is there to drive him from me?
But it grows late . . . the new moon's rim
Has sunk from sight; the plains are dim
With mist, and sleep will overcome me . . .

* * *

Day breaks. The elder ambles nearer
About the sleep-enveloped tent.
"The sun is up. Arise, Zemfira,
Wake up, my guest; it's time we went!
Come, children, end your blissful slumber . . . "
Out pours the tribe in noisy swarms,
The tents are struck, and wagons lumber
As the accustomed cart train forms.
All moves at once, by wonted norms
Across the barren lowlands swaying,
The donkeys carry children playing
In baskets slung behind the reins,
Husbands and brothers, wives and maidens,
All ages line the wagon trains,
Hails, clamor, tunes of gypsy cadence,
The dance-bear's growling and his chain's
Impatient jangle, colors sparkling
From tattered motley rags of dress
On gnarled or tender nakedness,
The dogs' unending howl and barking,
The bagpipe's skirling, axles' creak—
All squalid, savage, all unsettled,
But how vivacious, highly mettled,
How alien to our pastimes bleak,
How foreign to those vapid pleasures,
Stale as a slave song's tuneless measures!

* * *

The youth in gloom of spirit viewed
The level steppelands, now deserted,
His reason fearfully averted
From the deep sources of his mood.
Black-eyed Zemfira's love to treasure,
The wide world his to roam at leisure,
The lofty sun above him gay
In festive noontime glamour shining—
What sets the youthful heart to pining,
What private torment, what dismay?

Little bird, God's wingèd neighbor,
Knows not toil or heart's unrest,
Nor in unremitting labor
Weaves a long-enduring nest;
Seeks a twig-perch when it darkens
And till sunrise folds its wings;
Come the dawn, God's voice it hearkens,
Shakes its feathers down and sings.
Spring, the year's adornment, fading,
In its turn the summer's blaze,
Tardy autumn will be shading,
Shrouding all in rain and haze,
Fretful sloth to humans bringing—
Past blue seas denied to men,
Southward bound the bird is winging
Till the spring returns again.

He, like that careless feathered singer,
A transient exile, would not linger
In safety by a sturdy nest,
Clove to no custom, sought no rest.
For him no beaten road was needed,
No inn bespoke, no route to chart,
Aroused by each new morn, he ceded
His day to God, life's cares, unheeded,
Stirred not the torpor of his heart.
At times, like far-off constellations,
He glimpsed renown's alluring ray,
And rare delights and dissipations
All unexpected came his way.
Though crashing thunderbolts not seldom
Above his lonely head would strike,
The same oblivious slumber held him
In storm and quietude alike.
His life ignored blind Fate and yielded
To her malignant guile no toll;
But God! what sway the passions wielded
Within his unresisting soul!
How in his ravaged breast their torment

They used to wreak and rage their fill!
How briefly, how much longer dormant,
Will they flare up once more? They will!

* * *

ZEMFIRA

Tell me, my friend; you are not grieving
For what you will not know again?

ALEKO

Know what again?

ZEMFIRA

   I mean your leaving
The cities, your own countrymen.

ALEKO

What should I grieve for? If you knew it,
Could comprehend—why would I rue it,
The bondage of the stifling towns!
There man in throngs, hemmed in by fences,
Tastes not the morning cool, nor senses
The vernal perfume of the downs;
There love is furtive, thought in bridles,
There liberty is bought and sold,
They bow in worship before idols
And beg for shackles and for gold.
What did I leave? Betrayers' babble,
Rank prejudice's smug decree,
The hounding of the mindless rabble
Or else replendent infamy.

ZEMFIRA

But there they have such spacious mansions,
With rugs of many-colored plaid,
And festive games and lively dancing,
And girls there go so richly clad!

ALEKO

What of the city's noisy mirth?
Where love is not, there is no pleasure.
The girls . . . Of how much greater worth
Are you than they, for all your dearth
Of costly garments, pearls, and treasure!
Don't ever change, my lovely fair!
And I . . . have but a single mission,
Your pastimes and your love to share,
An exile by my own volition.

OLD MAN

You like us and the life we lead,
Though nurtured by a wealthy nation.
Not always, though, is liberation
Dear to a man of tender breed.
Here an old tale is still related:
A dweller of the South[1] once came
Amongst us, by the Emperor fated
To live in exile here, the same
As you (the legend stated,
But I forget his curious name).
Though old in body, far from strong,
His guileless soul was younger, firmer—
He had the wondrous gift of song,
His voice like to the water' murmur.
And long, beloved of everyone,
Here on the banks of Danube dwelling,
He lived, and gave offense to none
But charmed them with his storytelling.
As shy and feeble as a child,

He knew not how to make his living,
And fed on creatures of the wild,
On fish and fowl of strangers' giving.
When storm-winds raged and winter came,
The rapid flow in frost entrapping,
They used to guard with furry wrapping
The saintly stranger's aged frame.
Yet years and habitude could never
Endear our humble, toilsome way,
But, pale and gaunt, he strayed forever
Amongst us and was wont to say
That an immortal's vengeful passion
Pursued him for some old transgression.
Deliverance his only thought,
Throughout his span, with piteous crying
The exile, restless and distraught,
Bestrode the banks of Danube, sighing
For his far city; lastly, dying,
He charged them earnestly to send
To the warm land of his allegiance
His sorrowing bones—this alien region's
Reluctant guests unto the end!

ALEKO

Is such the fate, then, of your sons,
Majestic Rome of song and story!
Thou bard of the immortal ones,
Love's singer, tell me, what is glory?
Sepulchral echoes, honor's hail,
Renown from age to age redawning?
Or, told beneath a smoky awning,
An errant nomad's artless tale?

* * *

Two years have passed. The gypsies wander
Upon their wonted peaceful quest,
As ever finding here and yonder
Both hospitality and rest.

Civilization's bonds disdaining,
Aleko wanders free as they;
Exempt from cares and uncomplaining,
He shares their ever-ranging day.
He is the same, so are his dear ones,
Their life is his; to all appearance
He scarce remembers former years.
He loves the dusk of their nocturnal
Bivouacs, sweet indolence eternal,
Their tuneful speech upon his ears.
Fled from the lair where once he bedded,
The shaggy sharer of his tent
In hamlets on the steppe-trail threaded,
Near some Moldavian settlement,
Performed his ponderous dance and snorted
Before a cautious gathering
And gnawed the noxious iron sling.
While, on his traveler's staff supported,
The elder with a lazy swing
Would set the cymbaled hand-drum ringing,
Aleko sang, Zemfira bringing
The crowd's free-given offering.
Night falls; all three prepare their diet
Of unreaped millet gleaned and crushed;
The old man sleeps—and all is quiet . . .
The tent within is dark and hushed.

* * *

The ancient's failing pulses quicken,
New life the vernal sunshine brings;
And by the cot his daughter sings
Of love. Aleko listens, stricken.

ZEMFIRA

Graying man, cruel man,
Spare me not fire or knife,
Stab you can, burn you can,
Firm I am, spurn your strife.

And your love I deny,
And your wrath I defy,
For another I love,
For his love I will die.

ALEKO

Be still. Your singing wearies me,
I do not like this uncouth air.

ZEMFIRA

You don't? But it is not for thee
That I am singing them. Why care?

Stab you may, burn you may,
Not a word will I say,
Graying man, cruel man,
You shall not learn his name.

How much fresher than spring,
Hot as summer's-day gold,
Is my lad young and bold,
Is his love that I sing.

What caresses we shared
In the still of the night!
How we laughed at the sight
Of the gray in your hair!

ALEKO

Enough, Zemfira! Hush, be quiet . . .

ZEMFIRA

So thou hast read my song's intent?

ALEKO

Zemfira!

ZEMFIRA

Scold, then! Why deny it?
It is for thee my song is meant.

Goes off, singing "Graying man . . . "

OLD MAN

Yes, I remember—that old ditty
Was first in my young manhood sung,
And often since in mart and city
It has delighted old and young.
When we were roaming Kağul shire,
Mariula some cold night, mayhap,
Would sing this ditty by the fire,
Rocking our daughter on her lap.
The years gone by with every hour
Grow dark and darker now, I find
But that refrain some secret power
Has graven deep into my mind.

* * *

Night; all is still. The moon has brightened
The southern heaven's azure span;
Zemfira wakens the old man:
"Oh, father, listen! I am frightened.
Such troubled sleep Aleko sleeps!
He groans as if in pain, and weeps."

OLD MAN

Keep silent, daughter. Do not touch him.
I often heard the Russians tell:
At midnight a domestic elf

May haunt the sleeper's rest and clutch him
To choke his breath; at dawn the spell
Is loosed. Sit by me, calm yourself.

ZEMFIRA

Oh, Father! Now he sobs: Zemfira!

OLD MAN

His very dreams reach out for thee:
Than all the world he holds thee dearer.

ZEMFIRA

His love is wearisome to me.
For freedom pines my soul and mutters—
Already . . . Hush! I hear him moaning . . .
It is another name he utters.

OLD MAN

Whose name?

ZEMFIRA

Oh, listen! Hoarsely groaning,
Gnashing his teeth as one insane!
I must awaken him.

OLD MAN

In vain;
Break not a nightbound spirit's spell
Before its own time.

ZEMFIRA

It is broken.
He's rising, calling . . . he has woken.

I'll go to him—sleep on; farewell.

ALEKO

Where have you been?

ZEMFIRA

                I have been sitting
With Father; there was plaguing thee
An evil sprite; thy soul, unwitting,
Knew agonies. It frightened me,
For in thy slumber thou wert gritting
Thy teeth and calling me.

ALEKO

                I dreamed
Of you. Between us, so it seemed . . .
I fancied horrors past endurance!

ZEMFIRA

Trust not dream fancies—they depart.

ALEKO

Ah, I trust nothing—not the art
Of dreams, or that of sweet assurance,
I do not even trust your heart.

            * * *

OLD MAN

  Wherefore, unruly youth, confess,
Wherefore forever sighing, pining?
Here men are free, the heavens shining,
And women famed for comeliness.
Weep not—grief will undo you. Rather . . .

ALEKO

Zemfira does not love me, Father.

OLD MAN

She is a child, friend; be consoled.
Perversely, foolishly you languish.
Your love is drudgery and anguish,
A woman's is all play. Behold!
Across the vaulted darkness soaring,
The heedless moon serenely strays,
On all creation gently pouring
Her undiscriminating rays.
She calls upon a cloudbank yonder,
Bedews it with a silver haze—
Lo! to another she will wander,
Again for but a fleeting gaze.
How fix on one among the stellar
Redoubts **and bid** it: Cease to range!
How fix a maiden's heart and tell her:
This you shall love, and never change?
Console yourself, my friend.

ALEKO

                              How tender
Her love! How willingly she sank
To my embraces as we drank
The wilderness' tranquil splendor!
Forever playful, childish-gay,
How often has she sweetly chattered
Or with her magic kisses scattered
Dark fancies, banished gloom away,
And to the moment's joy restored me!
And now? Zemfira gone astray!
Zemfira grown unkind toward me! . . .

OLD MAN

Attend, my son, and you shall know
What once befell me long ago:
When yet the Danube did not echo
To Moskal² arms encroaching here
(An ancient grief, you see, Aleko,
I must recall), we lived in fear
Of the Great Turk; and from the aerie
Of lofty-towered Ak-Kerman
A Turkish pasha ruled the prairie
Of the Budzhak³ still. I was young,
My fervent spirits sparkled brightly,
And of my curly tresses none
Was yet with silver threaded whitely.
Among our youthful beauties one
There shone . . . and long my eyes upon her
In worship gazed, as on the sun,
And in the end, at last, I won her . . .

Alas, my youthful years were gone
Like fallen stars as soon as kindled!
But sweet fulfillment's season dwindled
More swiftly still; for not above
One year I held Mariula's love.

Not far from the Kaǧulan waters
We met a tribe; they staked their ropes
And pitched beside our canvas quarters
Their tents upon the mountain slopes.
Two nights that band spent near us, breaking
Their trek, and on the third decamped;
With them, Mariula left, forsaking
Her baby daughter, while I dreamt
In peaceful sleep. At dawn's first shining
I woke—my love was gone! I flew
To search, I called—no trace. Repining,
Zemfira cried, and I wept too!
That dark hour taught me to abhor
All this earth's maidens; I forbore

Henceforth to let my eyes admire,
Nor my lone idleness desire
The solace of a tender guest.

ALEKO

You gave not chase, then, to arrest
The faithless ingrate and to chasten
Her vile abductors, did not hasten
To plunge a dagger in their breast?

OLD MAN

To what end? Who would vainly try
To hold young love, free as a bird?
On each in turn is bliss conferred
What was, returns not.

ALEKO

No—not I
Would thus have cravenly resigned
My rights in a usurper's favor;
Or at the meanest I would savor
A sweet revenge. Were I to find
My foe on the deep sea, I swear,
Unarmed, asleep—I would not spare
The knave my foot: straightway, unblanching,
Into the raging waves would launch him;
The sudden terror of his waking
With savage laughter I would cheer,
And long his thrashings would be breaking
Like gleeful music on my ear.

* * *

YOUNG GYPSY

One more . . . one more kiss . . .

ZEMFIRA

> Time is fleeting,
My man mean-spirited and cross.

GYPSY

Just one . . . but longer! One last greeting.

ZEMFIRA

Farewell, or he might follow us.

GYPSY

When shall we have another meeting?

ZEMFIRA

> Tonight, then, when the moon takes cover,
Upon that tomb, beyond the mound.

GYPSY

She plays me false—will not be found!

ZEMFIRA

Run! Here he is! . . . I'll come, my lover.

* * *

> Aleko sleeps, but in his mind
A vague and troubling vision lingers,
Till with a cry he wakes—to find
All darkness. His mistrustful fingers
Reach out . . . and shrink as they uncover
Cold blankets—far off is his lover . . .
Half-rearing with a shuddering start,
He listens: silence; sick at heart,

His limbs now chill, now fever-damp,
He rises, leaves the tent, goes walking
Between the wagons, grimly stalking
The slumbering fields about the camp.
Deep gloom; the moon is mist-beclouded,
The faltering starlight barely hints
The faintest trail of dewy prints
Toward the mounds in distance shrouded.
He follows with impatient haste
The path these ominous footprints traced.

White in the hazy dusk before him
There gleamed afar a roadside tomb . . .
And there his dragging footsteps bore him,
Weighed down by prescience of doom,
With quivering lips and shaking knees;
Until—is it a dream he sees?—
Nearby is heard a whispering sound,
And at his feet twin shadows hover
Upon the desecrated mound.

FIRST VOICE

It's time . . .

SECOND VOICE

No, wait . . .

FIRST VOICE

It's time, dear lover.

SECOND VOICE

Don't go—let us await the day.

FIRST VOICE

It's late.

SECOND VOICE

Be bolder, love, be joyous.
One moment more!

FIRST VOICE

You will destroy us.

SECOND VOICE

One moment!

FIRST VOICE

While I am away,
My husband may wake up! . . .

ALEKO

He may.
No, stay, you two, where are you flitting?
The graveside here is fine, is fitting.

ZEMFIRA

Run, dearest, hurry . . .

ALEKO

Where away?
Oh, no my bonny lad, you stay!
Lie there!

Thrusts his knife into him.

ZEMFIRA

Aleko!

GYPSY

I am dying!

ZEMFIRA

Aleko, you will be his death!
Look: you are all with blood bespattered!
What have you done?

ALEKO

As if it mattered.
Now go and drink you lover's breath.

ZEMFIRA

Ah, no—I am not frightened of
Your rage! I scorn it, I abhor it,
Your bloody deed, I curse you for it . . .

ALEKO

Then die you too!

Strikes her.

ZEMFIRA

I die in love . . .

* * *

Resplendent Venus, star of morrow,
Across the dawning orient shone.
Upon the tomb beyond the barrow,
Blood-dabbled, knife in hand, alone
Aleko sat. And thus they found him,
Hunched by those dead, his stare insane.
Abashed, the gypsies shrank around him;

Some sidled to inter the twain
Not far away. In mournful train
The women followed one another
To kiss their eyelids. On the slain
In numb bereavement her old father,
Bleak desolation in his heart,
Sat gazing mutely and apart.
They lifted and bore off the supple,
Now lifeless, forms and laid the couple
Into the chilly earthen womb.
Aleko from the farther tomb
Looked one . . . but when the two were covered
With that last offering of earth,
Still mute, he teetered forward, hovered,
And sprawled headlong upon the turf.

Then spoke the ancient by his side:
"Depart from us, oh man of pride!
We are but wild, a lawless nation,
We keep no rack or hempen knot,
Need neither blood nor lamentation—
But live with slayers we will not.
The heathen freedom you have known,
You claim it for yourself alone;
Your voice henceforth would awe and grieve us,
For we are meek and kind of heart,
And you are fierce and wicked—leave us,
And peace be with you as we part."

He spoke—and with a bustling start
The light encampment rose as bidden
To leave the night's dread vale behind.
And soon the prairie's depth had hidden
The nomad train. A single cart,
Its frame with wretched cover vested,
Stood in the fateful field arrested.
Thus late in autumn one may find,
On plains where morning mists are clinging,
With cries above their gathering-stead

A tardy crane-flight southward winging;
But one, pierced through by mortal lead,
Forlorn in empty fields is lagging,
Its wounded pinion sadly dragging.
Dusk fell; behind the wagon's awning
That night no flickering fire arose,
And no one till a new day's dawning
Lay down there for a night's repose.

EPILOGUE

Thus song-craft with its potent magic
From memory's beclouded haze
Will conjure visions, now of tragic,
Now of serenely shining days.

Where long, so long, the conflagrations
Of warlike ardor did not cool,
Where once the Russian showed his nation's
Imperious borders to Stambul,
Where our old eagle double-headed
For parted glories still is dreaded,
There in the steppelands I would see
On some abandoned rampart's traces
The gypsies' peaceful camping places,
Wild freedom's humble progeny.
And often through those untamed shires
Behind their lazy troops I fared,
Their simple nourishment I shared,
And fell asleep before their fires.
As on those leisured treks I came,
Their cheerful ringing tunes I cherished,
And long with fond recital nourished
Sweet Mariula's tender name.

Yet you, too, Nature's sons undaunted,
Are strange to happiness, it seems!
Your ragged shelters, too, are haunted
By omens and oppressive dreams,

Deep in your wilderness, disaster
For wandering tents in ambush waits;
Grim passion everywhere is master,
And no one can elude the Fates.

THE BRIDEGROOM: INTRODUCTION

The stanza of this ballad (1825), with its haunting alternation of dreamy singsong, hearty rollick, and ominous gallop, is, of course, borrowed *in toto* from G. A. Bürger's (1747-94) famous "Lenore," perhaps the most impressive work of infant Romanticism. Lenore's ghostly ride bewitched both Goethe and Schiller and scored an international triumph second only to the noble vapors spread by Goethe's own *Werther.* A characteristic stanza of "Lenore" goes as follows:

> Schön Liebchen schürzte, sprang und schwang
> Sich auf das Ross behende;
> Wohl um den trauten Reiter schlang
> Sie ihre Lilienhände;
> Und hurre hurre, hopp hopp hopp!
> Ging's fort in sausendem Galopp,
> Dass Ross und Reiter schnoben,
> Und Kies und Funken stoben.

It is interesting to note also that Natasha's "nightmare" in "The Bridegroom" in atmosphere and some particulars closely prefigures Tatyana's dream in *Eugene Onegin* V, 11-21, which was written in the same period.

THE BRIDEGROOM

Three days Natasha'd been astray,
Who was a merchant's daughter,
When running home in wild dismay
At last the third night brought her.
Her mother and her father plied
The maid with questions, tried and tried;
She cannot hear for quaking,
All out of breath and shaking.

But fret and wonder as they did
And stubbornly insisted,

They could not fathom what she **hid,**
And in the end desisted.
And soon Natasha grieved no more,
But flushed and merry as before
Went with her sisters walking
Beyond the gate and talking.

Once at the gate of shingled ash
The maidens sat together,
Natasha too, when in a flash
Past speeded, hell-for-leather,
A dashing troika with a youth;
And rug-clad roans he drove, forsooth,
Drove standing up, bespattered
All in his path and scattered.

He, drawing closer, glanced upon
The maid; her glance replying,
He like the whirlwind galloped on,
The maid was nigh to dying.
And arrow-straight she homeward fled,
"It's he, I knew him well!" she said,
"Stop him, it's he, no other,
Oh, save me, friend and brother!"

Her kinfolk listened, grave and sad,
And shook their heads with ruing:
"Speak out, my lass," her father bade,
"And tell us how you knew him.
If something untoward occurred,
Speak openly, say just a word."
Natasha's back to crying,
No further word replying.

Next day a marriage-gossip came,
Came unexpected rather,
She spoke Natasha fair by name,
Fell talking to her father:
"You have the wares, we want to trade;

My buyer is a fine young blade,
Is lithely made and comely,
Not evil-famed or grumbly.

"Has wealth and wits, to never a man
In low obeisance bending,
But rather, like a nobleman
He lives with easy spending.
He's like to give his chosen girl
A fur of fox-skin and a pearl,
Gold hoops for golden tresses,
And stiff brocaded dresses.

"Last night he saw her on his ride
Out by the town-gate linger;
Let's shake, take ikons and the bride
And to the altar bring her!"
There over tea and cake she sits
And hints and yarns and snares their wits,
While the poor bride's uneasy,
All fidgeting and queasy.

"So be it, then," her father said,
"Go forth, God speed you, dearie,
Take wreath, Natasha, and be wed,
Alone upstairs it's dreary.
Comes time for maids no more to flit,
For swallows, too, their chirps to quit,
It's time to nest, to nourish
Young bairns at home and cherish."

Natasha tried to have her say,
Her back to wall and rafter,
But all ashudder sobbed away,
Now racked with tears, now laughter.
The gossip in dismay runs up,
Makes her sip water from a cup,
And all the rest she dashes
And on her forehead splashes.

Natasha's kinfolk moaned and wept.
But she, back in her senses,
Announced: "I honor and accept
What your high will dispenses.
It's time that to the feast you bade
The groom, and many loaves were made,
Mead choice of brew and hearty,
The Judge bid to the party."

"Command, Natasha, angel child,
To please you, I am ready
To give my life!" A feast is piled,
Prodigious, rich, and heady.
Now worthy guests arrive apace,
They lead the bride to take her place;
As bridesmaids sing with weeping,
A sledge and team come leaping.

Here is the bridegroom—all sit down,
Cup touches cup with ringing,
The toasting bowl goes round and round
To drunken shouts and singing.

THE BRIDEGROOM

"I say, my merry friends, abide,
I say, why is my pretty bride
Not serving, eating, drinking,
All lost in mournful thinking?"

Said bride to groom: "I'll tell my plight
As best I may be able:
I find no rest by day or night,
I weep abed, at table.
A horrid nightmare wears me out."
Her father wonders: "What about?
Whatever kind it may be,
Tell us, my own dear baby!"

The maiden said: "I dream that I
Walk where the wood grows thickly,
It's late, and from a cloudy sky
The moonlight glimmers sickly.
I've lost my way; in pine and fir
No living creature is astir,
The trees alone are brushing
Their crowns with wispy rushing.

"But clear as day I now make out
Ahead a hut emerging;
I reach it, knock: no answer, shout:
No sound; I hail the Virgin,
I lift the latch, go in, advance,
Inside a candle burns; I glance—
All gleams with heaping measure
Of gold and silver treasure."

THE BRIDEGROOM

"What is so bad about your dream?
It means you'll be in clover."

THE BRIDE

"I ask your leave, sir, it would seem
The dream is not yet over.
On gold and silver, rugs untrod,
Brocade and silks from Novgorod,
I stood in silence gazing
With wonder and amazing.

"Now hoofbeats clatter, voices roar,
Here someone comes a-riding;
I quickly up and slam the door,
Behind the chimney hiding.
Then voices swell in mingled din,
Twelve lusty lads come trooping in;
With them in modest duty
A fair and pure young beauty.

"Without a bow they throng the place,
The ikons never heeding,
Sit down to dine without a grace,
And, cap on head, start feeding.
The eldest brother at the head,
The youngest at his right hand fed,
At left in modest duty
There sat the pure young beauty.

"Hubbub and clink, guffaw and scream,
Exuberant carousal . . . "

THE BRIDEGROOM

"What is so bad about your dream?
It bodes a gay espousal."

THE BRIDE

"Your pardon, sir, it is not done.
The drunken dit goes roaring on,
But as they cheer and riot,
The maid sits sad and quiet.

"Sat mute and neither ate nor sipped,
In bitter tears and fretting,
The eldest brother, whistling, gripped
His knife and fell to whetting;
The fiend glanced at the maiden fair,
And sprang and seized her by the hair:
I saw him kill and fling her
To chop off hand and finger."

"Sheer raving, fancy run amuck,
I would not let it grieve me!
Yet," said the groom, "it bodes good luck,
My tender maid, believe me!"
She gazed at him both hard and long:
"To whom, pray, did this ring belong?"
She asked, and, half-arising,

All stared with dread surmising.
The trinket, slipping, clinked and bounced,
The bridegroom blanched and trembled.
The guests stood awed. The Judge pronounced:
"Stop, bind him, all assembled!"
The fiend was tried, in fetters strung,
And shortly from the gallows hung.
Natasha rose to glory!
And therewith ends my story.

COUNT NULIN: INTRODUCTION

During Pushkin's prolonged isolation at the remote little family estate of
Mikhailovskoe in the mid-twenties he completed *The Gypsies* and
continued his labor of love on the steadily expanding *Eugene Onegin*. But
new literary interests had awakened. He intensified his exploration of
Shakespeare, which had begun to engross him in his southern exile, studied
the era of dynastic upheavals preceding the Romanovs in Karamzin's
History of the Russian State, and dramatized it in his pioneering romantic
tragedy in blank verse, *Boris Godunov*. At the same time, constant contact
with the life of the rustic squirearchy and peasantry increasingly drew his
mind to humbler and earthier themes, and from the poetic forms that still
came most naturally to him to the neglected claims of prose. *Count Nulin*,
completed in two days in 1825 and published after his return from exile,
reflects some of these new influences and tastes. It is in small part a remote
parody of the well-worn classical tale of the rape of Lucretia by Tarquin,
which Pushkin had lately encountered again in Shakespeare's poem; and if
this makes his story a miniature mock-epic, it is "classical" at two removes.
But the transposition into a totally different milieu and idiom is almost
complete, the parodical intent so faint as to be nearly irrelevant, and the
treatment one of evocative contemporary realism in detail and setting. To
the reader, whether he is familiar with the hoary Roman legend or not,
Count Nulin need be no more, and no less, than a briskly moving, elegantly
turned anecdote in verse on the comic discomfiture of a Frenchified titled
dandy stranded for a night in the Russian countryside; spiced at the very
end with an astringent grain of worldly innuendo.

COUNT NULIN

It's time, it's time! The horn resounds,
The whips, done up in hunting habit,
Are mounted by first light, the hounds
Strain at the leash for fox and rabbit.
The squire on his veranda base

With arms akimbo scans the action,
His nice "important duty" face
Alight with honest satisfaction.
He sports a coat in Cossack taste,
A Turkish knife tucked in his waist,
A rum flask, in his bosom placed,
A horn, hung from a bronzen straplet.
His wife peers out in shawl and chaplet,
Her eyes, yet barely open, glare
At that equestrian affair,
The whips' and beaters' noisy tussle . . .
Now they lead up his horse out there;
Up stirrup, withers, all abustle
He hails her: Don't wait up for me!
And canters off in joyful hustle.

In late September, you'll agree,
(I speak in lowly prose, you see),
The countryside is drear: foul weather,
Snow, autumn winds, the roads a mess,
And howling wolves. But these, I gather,
Elate your huntsman! Comfortless,
Through godforsaken fields he prances,
Wet through and cursing, yet, confess,
Delighted to take random chances
Of night's rest and malign success.

But what, the while the husband's wooing
Diana, is his lady doing?
There's all too much to do, worse luck:
Salt down mushrooms, feed goose and duck,
Both lunch and dinner to be seen to,
An eye to keep on loft and vault,
Always some place one has not been to
Where something might be found at fault.

Our heroine, heedless of disaster . . .
(Why, I forgot to give her name.
Natasha—thus her lord and master
Called her—but we can't do the same:

Natalia Pavlovna) . . . I'd rather
Natalia Pavlovna were more
Inclined to stir herself and bother
About this kind of wifely chore,
But she'd been reared, I need not mention,
Not mindful of ancestral law,
But in a noble spinsters' pension
Run by a Madame Falbalat.

She's sitting by the window, sore
At odds with Letter Ninety-four
Of that four-volume tranquilizer,
The Love of Armand and Eliza:
From Family Letters of the Pair,
A novel classical and hoary,
A lengthy, monstrous lengthy story,
High-mindedly exhortatory,
And quite without romantic flair.

Natalia Pavlovna to start with
Had thought it middling hard to part with,
But shortly found herself agog
At an embroilment then proceeding
Outside the place where she was reading
Between a he-goat and a dog.
A gang of urchins were guffawing,
And underneath her sill a flock
Of turkey-hens with mournful cawing
Stalked in the wake of a wet cock.
Three ducks were splashing in a puddle,
A woman picked her muddy path
To hang some wash across the lath;
The weather worsened; of a sudden
It seemed that snow was threatening . . .
Then you could hear a sleigh-bell ring.

He who has led a drear existence
Deep in the country, friends, will know
How sleigh-bells tinkling in the distance

Can set the doubting heart aglow.
A friend on a belated visit,
Playmate of one's wild youth? . . . or is it . . .
Great God, could it be she? No . . . still . . .
Close, closer yet . . . your heartbeat chases
The jingling sound . . . but past it races,
Grows fainter . . . dies beyond the hill.

Natalia Pavlovna has hurried
Onto the balcony, all flurried
By the glad sound: there! By the mill
Behind the brook a coach comes flying,
Crosses the bridge—you see? Oh, please,
This way! No, turning left . . . She sees
It go and nearly bursts out crying.

Oh joy! A sudden slant and, jarred,
The coach capsizes. "Fil'ka, Vas'ka,
Go quickly, yonder's a kolyaska,
Run it at once into the yard,
And ask the owner in for dinner!
I hope he's whole! Find out, you ninny,
Don't stand there, run!" Away he raced.

Natalia Pavlovna posthaste
Whips up a storm of ringlets, closes
The curtain, quickly redisposes
A chair, puts on a shawl and waits.
"How long, good Lord?" At last the gates
Admit a travel-worn, much battered,
In weary journeys mud-bespattered
And barely dragging *équipage*.
Behind it, a young esquire stumbles,
His French valet, undaunted, mumbles,
Sustaining him: *allons, courage!*
This tandem passes double-jointed
Through porch and hall; the lord they show
Into a room, in haste appointed,
The door flung wide as it will go;
While Picard bustles and arranges,

And his young master slowly changes,
Shall I just tell you who he was?
Count Nulin, back from foreign shores,
Where he had flung to winds of fashion
His income and his future ration,
Now to Petropolis bestirred
To strut there like some gorgeous bird,
Complete with sundry dress suits, waistcoats,
Hats, cloaks, young ladies' fans and mascots,
Spyglasses, corsets, little baskets
Of studs, bright ties, chic pantaloons,
Some of Guizot's[1] appalling rot,
A sheaf of villainous cartoons,
A new romance by Walter Scott,
The Paris court's risqué *bons mots*,
With Béranger's[2] last tuneful varia,
Paer's[3] and Rossini's latest aria,
And this and that, and these and those.

  All's ready. Lunchtime comes and goes;
The hostess finds her patience tested.
At last the door admits her prize.
Natalia makes as if to rise,
Deplores, politely interested,
His fall, and could he walk, in fact?
The Count declares himself intact.
They're served. The Count is seated, ponders,
Then brings his instrument to bear
And enters colloquy with her;
He rails at Holy Russia, wonders
How one can live amidst her snows
And yearns for Paris—ah, God knows!
"The theatre?" "Oh, barer, colder,
C'est bien mauvais, ça fait pitié.
Talma[4] stone deaf, about to molder,
And Mamselle Mars[5]—zut! getting older . . .
None but Potier[6] , *le grand Potier*,
Still sheds, alone among his nation,
His pristine brilliance on the scene."

"What writer now holds domination?"
"Still d'Arlincourt[7] and Lamartine."
"Here, too, they have been imitated."
"You don't say! Really? Then I bet
Taste's growing more sophisticated!
God grant we'll be enlightened yet!"
"How high are waists now?" "More than lowish,
Almost to . . . this point, more or less,
Here is a pattern I possess . . .
If I may just inspect your dress . . .
Yes, flounces, ribbons . . . all quite modish."
"We get the *Telegraph* sent out."
"No wonder then! . . . Now you might favor
Some charming vaudeville, no doubt."
He sings. "But Count, do you not savor
Your lunch." "I'm done." "Well, then we might . . . "

They've risen. She performs the duties
Of hostess with uncommon cheer.
The Count, forgetting all the beauties
Of Paris, marvels: what a dear!
Time flies unchecked. The Count is fighting
Some slight unease. The lady's eyes
Now seem expressively inviting,
And now opaquely unrequiting . . .
Here's midnight, to their great surprise;
Long have the footman's snores been blowing,
Long has the neighbor's cock been crowing;
The watchman beats his iron tub;
The candle ends are barely burning.

Natalia Pavlovna gets up:
"*Adieu*, bed waits, time for adjourning.
Sweet dreams." The Count is loath to stand,
And, kissing tenderly her hand,
Perceives . . . what do you think? A quiver . . .
(A flirt will stop at nothing, though!)
For our young scamp, may God forgive her,
Has slyly pressed his hand, you know.

Undressed, Natalia's being ushered
To bed by her Parasha's hands.
Friends, you must know that this Parasha
Shares in her lady's moods and plans:
She sews, she washes, crimps her tresses,
Begs for discarded hats and dresses,
With master now will freely clown,
Now just as freely dress him down,
And lie to her young mistress bravely.
And now she is discoursing gravely
About the Count and his concerns—
Lord knows how in one day she learns
The mass of trifles now outpouring.
At last her mistress stemmed the flow,
And saying: "That's enough, you're boring!"
Asked for her cap and robe, and so
Was soon alone and gently snoring.

The Count, too, is by his valet
Peeled down to shirt and negligee.
He lies down, asks for a Havana,
Picard brings in accustomed manner
Carafe and cup of silver plate,
Cigar box, candlestick of copper,
Tweezers, alarm clock with a stopper,
And a romance in uncut state.

The Count finds his attention flagging,
Though his eyes read; his soul is not
Content in bed with Walter Scott,
A secret restlessness is nagging
At his composure, and he thinks:
"Could I have fallen for that minx?
Might it be possible . . . how splendid!
That would be grand, though unintended . . .
The lady likes me, I don't doubt."
And Nulin puts his candle out.

Restless, as in a raging fever,
By Satan, busy as a beaver,
Beset with sinful waking dreams,
He glows. Imagination seems
To conjure up in all its phases
Last night's events. Her speaking gazes,
The rather rounded, ample shape,
The wholesome country-pink compexion,
That truly feminine inflection,
The flush of health no rouge can ape.
He sees that dainty foot protruding,
Recalls—of course! had she not shown . . . ?
Her hand, one could not help concluding,
Had casually squeezed his own;
Who but a fool . . . yes, he should never
Have missed that moment's mood! However,
There was a chance still. He supposed
Her door would not as yet be closed . . .
With instant resolution, fumbling
Into his gown of silken hues,
Here comes for his Lucretia (stumbling
Across a falling chair), previews
Of love's sweet harvest his attraction,
The latest Tarquin, braced for action.

Thus you may see a crafty cat,
The dainty darling of the servant,
Steal down the stove bench, eyes observant,
To stalk a mouse. His ears laid flat,
His lids contracted, tail-end twitching,
He inches, freezes, talons itching
On each sly paw . . . until, scritch-scratch,
He pounces on the luckless wretch.

The Count, in amorous elation,
Gropes forth by blind manipulation,
With flaming passion all aseethe,
At creaking boards in trepidation,
And scarcely taking time to breathe.
By long pitch-dark perambulation

He finds that door, and with light touch
Bears on the handle: not so much
As one faint squeak; discreetly nosing
Into the gap, he sees light seep
From a dim lamp, but half disclosing
The room; his hostess blithely dozing,
Aslumber, or pretending sleep.

He enters, lingers, interposing
A step back . . . plump! is at her feet;
And she . . . but here I would petition
The gentlewomen of St. Pete[8]
To picture how this apparition
Had our Natalia petrified,
And if she should . . . Well, you decide!

She, speechless at the visitation,
Stares at him wide-eyed, and the Count,
With floods of ardent protestation
Lets his emboldened fingers mount
Upon the coverlet: which action
Caused her a moment's stupefaction;
But she revived and, mortified
By outrage and indignant pride
(And panic too, perhaps, one wonders?),
She swung on Tarquin with a thundrous
Ear-box. Oh, yes, a slap—in fact,
A haymaker, to put it mildly!

Thus contumaciously attacked,
The Count changed color, glaring wildly;
Who knows but that his rattled wits
Might have provoked him further, given
That blistering rebuff—but driven
From dreamless sleep by barking Spitz,
Parasha crossed the hall; and damning
The roof that sheltered him that night
And that young vixen's artful shamming,
He turned to ignominious flight.

For the ensuing who, what, whether—
You may imagine as you choose
How they ran out that night together!
I will not offer any clues.

    Arising taciturn next morning,
Count Nulin dresses slowly, yawning,
And manicures his rosy nails,
Though not too thoroughly or gently,
Ties his cravat but negligently,
Nor yet with moistened brushes sails
Down well-trimmed waves on glossy trails.
I wonder what he may be thinking;
But here he's called for coffee-drinking.
What now? Not having mastered yet
His sleepishness and sullen pet,
He goes.

        Miss Mischief, tightly pursing
Her rosy mouth, beneath bent brow
Hides wicked gleams, but starts conversing,
As best her twitching lips allow,
Of this and that. Abashed and harassed,
But slowly growing less embarrassed,
He answers in a lighter vein,
And after thirty minutes scarcely,
His little sallies flow less sparsely,
And he is half in love again.
Hush—in the hall there's some commotion,
Who's this? "Good Lord, I had no notion . . . "
"Natasha!" "Meet my husband! Here,
May I present: Count Nulin, dear."
"Delighted, sir . . . what awful weather!
Well: at the smith's as I passed through,
I saw your coach—as good as new!
Down by the orchard in the heather,
Natasha, we tracked down a hare,
The brown kind . . . Hey, some vodka! Try us,
Count, it's from far away somewhere;
You'll stay for lunch—don't you deny us!"

"No, really, . . . I've already missed . . . "
"Oh, nonsense, Count, I must insist,
My wife and I . . . no, do be seated,
We dote on guests!"
                    But rudely cheated
Of every hope by these appeals,
The gloomy count digs in his heels.
Picard, already well refueled
Against the trip, turns up endueled
With baggage, while two men approach
To screw the chest down in the coach.
Now it drives up to the veranda,
Picard has stowed all odds and ends;[9]
The Count departs. Here, in all candor,
The tale might well conclude. Quite true;
But let me add a word or two.

The carriage still on the horizon,
Our lady lost no time advising
Her husband of the whole affair,
And soon, indeed, was advertising
My Count's great exploit everywhere.
But who was it that really rocked
With laughter at Natalia's tale?
Guess, if you like, but you will fail!
"Her husband?" Lord, no! He was shocked.
He sputtered, called the Count a whelp,
A jackanapes, he'd make him yelp,
Would sic his pack at the young jackass
To skin him for that shameful fracas.
No—Lidin laughed a great deal more,
The squire aged twenty-three next door.

Now without fear of contradiction
We claim, in our own day and house,
A lady faithful to her spouse,
My friends, is no outlandish fiction.

POLTAVA: INTRODUCTION

To the first edition of his dramatic poem *Poltava*, completed in its final redaction on October 3, 1828, Pushkin added the following foreword:

> "The battle of Poltava is one of the most important and most fortunate events of Peter the Great's reign. It freed him of a most dangerous foe; it strengthened Russian dominion in the south; it secured the new institutions in the north and proved to the state the success and absolute necessity of the transformation which was being accomplished by the Tsar.
>
> The Swedish king's error has become proverbial. He is reproached for rashness, his drive into the Ukraine is termed senseless. There is no prevailing over critics, especially after failure. Yet for all that, Charles had by this move avoided Napoleon's error: he did not march on Moscow. And could he have expected that Little Russia (the Ukraine), always restless, would not be swayed by the example of her Hetman and not revolt against the recent overlordship of Peter; that Loewenhaupt would be put to rout three days in a row; that, finally, 25,000 Swedes commanded by their king would take to their heels before the runaways of Narva? Even Peter wavered a long time, evading an all-out battle "as a right perilous business." In this campaign, Charles XII trusted his luck less than ever before: it yielded to the genius of Peter.

The Caesarian brevity and artful detachment of Pushkin's preface hides a multitude of sins and silences, both Peter's and his own. This introduction attempts to examine the poem in the double context of, first, the poet's active role in Russian national myth-making, and, second, the spectacle of events unclouded by notions of a Russian manifest destiny.

Poltava is Pushkin's greatest dramatic poem. Condensed from a plethora of drafts into three terse, majestic cantos of equal size, the poem stands between *Boris Godunov* and *The Bronze Horseman*, and also at the end of the series of *poemy* of the 1820s which had taken on a markedly somber and thoughtful cast with *The Gypsies*. *Poltava* retains from the antecedent *poemy* a predominantly narrative mode. It shares with *Boris Godunov* the choice of a major crisis in Russian history as its underlying text, and the ampler use of dramatic dialogue than marked even the later "southern" *poemy*; it has in common with *The Bronze Horseman* the tripartite form and a central numinous role assigned to Peter I. But this work is more dynamic, pithy, and *actuel* than *Boris Godunov* and more stridently assertive in its myth-making than *The Bronze Horseman*. The "autocratic titan" appears in both the "Petrine" poems. He presides over *Poltava* as inventor and shaper, over *The Bronze Horseman* as emblem and brooding guardian, of a homegrown mystique of Russian manifest destiny. That fertile fiction has served, tentatively since the historical Peter I and brashly since Pushkin's artifacts of him, to ennoble domestic despotism, administrative centralism, claims of hegemony over older Slavic statehoods, and at times, imperialistic dreams.

But however arbitrarily stylized its characters and politically bigoted its would-be "historical" fable, *Poltava* brilliantly evokes the conflict— military and, less avowedly, cultural and ideological—which first settled the modern balance of power in eastern Europe between Russia, the Ukraine, Poland, and Sweden; and its starkly drawn love intrigue enriches and dramatizes the public theme. Pushkin's psychodramatic recreation, or transformation, of the power struggle and its three leading personages, Peter, Charles XII, and Mazepa, contrasted in his era with the conceptions of "the same" events and careers held by occidentally oriented participants, historians, and thinkers, notably Voltaire. But as is always the case with complex cultural evolutions later considered "epochal," Pushkin's *poiesis*, his imaginative *creation* of these events won out; it has irreversibly become part of his community's self-understanding. Similar "historicizing" effects have been achieved by fictions such as Tolstoy's *War and Peace* for Napoleon's débâcle, Hugo's *Les Misérables* and Dicken's *A Tale of Two Cities* for the Great Revolution (French and British edition, respectively), and on a smaller scale, *Eminent Victorians* and *The Great Gatsby*.

Thus understood, *Poltava* is not only a harsh and passion-ridden masterpiece by a mature poet, but also an important cultural document for students of international literature of Mazepa's era, "history," and legend; for students of Pushkin's political make-up and development; and for observers of the inspired poetic myth-making which if successful becomes history.

Pushkin's dramatic poem on the turbulent events of 1704-1709, unlike the romantic-fantastic treatments of various semi-mythical "Mazeppas" by Westerners like Voltaire, Byron, and Słowacki before and after him, takes its title not from Mazepa but from the battle of Poltava, which in effect ended the struggle among Sweden, Poland, Muscovy, the Ukraine, and Turkey in the Northern War. This choice of title, while seldom examined by readers or critics, is significant. It would seem plausible enough had the poem been an account of the climactic period of the war and Peter I's political and strategic role in it. Such is far from being the case, though. For all the titular emphasis on Peter's military triumph at Poltava, and for all the fine poetic glow and martial glitter with which the battle scene late in the work is surrounded, Pushkin's poem as a whole is overwhelmingly preoccupied not with Tsar Peter, nor with the meteoric destiny of the Swedish king, not even with the victory which, for better or worse, converted Muscovy into Russia. Instead, its focus is on the independent (hence "treasonable" by Moscow's lights) political designs and, entwined with these, the late-blooming amorous involvement of the saturnine Ukrainian challenger—who as it turned out has almost no effect on the decisive battle.

Why, then, "Poltava" and not "Mazepa"? Neither of the two monarchs who are the real antagonists at Poltava is granted a speaking part in the great poem, save Peter's two words to launch his troops into battle and Charles' single sentence to rouse Mazepa during their joint escape towards Turkey. There are two possible reasons, it would seem, for this strange incongruence between contents and title. One is that Pushkin sought, with only partial success, to confront us in *Poltava* with a deterrent example of one at odds with history and the will of Providence—as Aleko, the anti-hero in *The Gypsies*, is fatally at odds with the natural law and the moral temper of his chosen society. But in that case, why cling to the detestable, God-forsaken schemer throughout the long drama, rather than have him recede at an earlier point in the poem before the "higher" mission and superior statesmanship of Peter—as Aleko is outshone by the humble stoicism of the gentle wanderers who took him in? The other possiblility is that Mazepa, despite contrary appearances or even intentions on the part of his creator, became or remained the protagonist by default, the residual (anti-)hero as it were; for neither Peter (with his cavalier treatment of Ukrainian traditions and interests and his repellent cruelty, now towards Kochubey, now towards Mazepa) nor the now ill-starred and sickly Charles could well engage the moral or romantic partisanship of the reader. Mazepa apparently could—even for Pushkin the Great-Russian patriot. The seemingly impassioned denunciation of Mazepa early in his poem (lines 227 ff.) comes inadequately motivated; its fulminant rhetorical splendor protests and detests too much. Its moral impact is further weakened by the catalogue of Ukrainian aspirations and grievances, reproved but not disproved by the poet, which he puts into the mouths of spirited Cossacks at the court of Baturyn (lines 158 ff.). Are we perhaps to detect in some of the internal contradictions of the Poltava poem an early example of Pushkin's spasmodic, dutifully but imperfectly suppressed sympathy for the defiers and victims of Russian imperial power, as it flickers up in *The Captain's Daughter* (Pugachev), *The Bronze Horseman* (Eugene), and in Pushkin's ambivalent judgments of Mickiewicz?

However, this may be, Pushkin's powerful though morally equivocal drama has brought it about that the figure of Mazepa, ill-lit at best by historians inimical or indifferent to Ukrainian-Cossack statehood, is now reflected in European poetry and historiography with a double distortion. The West irrelevantly took to its romantic bosom a Mazepa that never was or never mattered; Pushkin tried (though his poetic genius caused him to fail) to turn him from a troubled statesman facing insuperable odds into a black villain and, absurdly, traitor to a fatherland which was not his. The Western accounts, whether historical sketch (Voltaire), narrative poem (Byron), or closet play (Slowacki), pin Mazepa's name to a rococo page or a young quasi-Taurian or Scythian Ulysses of their imagination—a naked philanderer who is swept from Poland into the Ukraine strapped sunny side up to a wild stallion's back by an irate cuckold. Of Mazepa's career as commander, enlightened ruler, and statesman these works say nothing. Pushkin, in his turn, depicts under a misleading title the last phase of the life and career of an embittered elderly chieftain of the left-bank Ukraine. His Mazepa is crafty, vindictive, perfidious, yet unaccountably noble and glamorous; a laureled campaigner in Peter's wars yet—passing strange!— implacably hostile to Moscow. He presides over ill-defined hordes of hotheaded Slavic horsemen, noble savages some of whom, perversely but rather romantically, refuse to accept Muscovite claims to sovereignty and military leadership over Cossackdom. Pushkin, like the historians he mainly relies on, fails to paint into the background of *Poltava* the vital fact that these ill-founded claims had throughout the campaigns before Poltava and for thirty years or more before the Northern War been continually expressed by Muscovite economic exploitation, callous waste of Cossack cannon fodder, and other forms of Great Russian *Herrenvolk* behavior— with the implicit goal of enserfment and (as a later age would call it) denationalization of the Ukraine.

The Romance between Mazepa and Motrya Kochubey

A brief but fervent attachment came to link Mazepa, then aged 65 or more, and young Motrya (also styled **Matrёna** and Maria) Kochubey, the eighteen-year-old daughter of Mazepa's friend and Judge General, Vasily Kochubey. Mazepa and Kochubey lived in close neighborly and comradely (as well as official) relations at Baturyn, Mazepa's capital and residence near Putivl on the Seym river. Things came to a crisis in March when Mazepa, truly in love with Motrya and sure of her fervent attachment, asked the Kochubeys for Motrya's hand. He was indignantly repulsed on the grounds that both decorum and Orthodox religion (he was Motrya's godfather) utterly precluded such a union. Mazepa, as the most generous patron and benefactor of the church in Ukrainian history, had good reason, though, to hope for a dispensation.

Motrya presently fled from her parents' house, where she was constantly humiliated and maltreated, to Mazepa. He received her kindly, but for the sake of her reputation and peace of mind sent her back immediately under the escort of the Russian resident at Baturyn. In secret messages to her, some of which have fortunately been found and published, he sent her costly presents of jewelry, lovingly commiserated and reasoned with her and kept assuring her of his love and need for her. In the spirit of Romeo, not Hamlet, he advised her to take refuge in a nunnery if life became intolerable at home. He would claim her from the convent as soon as he could make arrangements for it (i.e., presumably, obtain an episcopal or metropolitan dispensation for her release and their marriage). Motrya, whose part in the correspondence has not been preserved and can only be deduced from his answers, either did not or could not take this advice. The episode ends there as far as historical documentation is concerned, except for a record that Motrya was subsequently married.

The first crucial distortion of Mazepa's role in this touching romance as Pushkin, perhaps in good faith, represents it, is of course Mazepa's alleged complicity in Motrya's elopement (Canto One) and his acceptance of "Maria" as his mistress. This first distortion draws in its train the aggravated cruelty of Mazepa's throwing his old friend and, in effect, father-in-law to the wolves, and then seeking a psychological pardon or immunity from his unsuspecting daughter for the imminent judicial murder of her father. Actually, of course, it was Kochubey who betrayed the Ukrainian cause in Mazepa's person; there was no treason in Mazepa "betraying," i.e., repudiating, a Russian cause which was firmly committed to the destruction and absorption of the nascent, or renascent, all-Ukrainian state.

The second momentous distortion (not directly affecting the Motrya story) in the background of Pushkin's narrative is his virtual silence about the systematic Muscovite degradation of the Ukraine. This crucial omission is of a kind with and complements his silence about the remarkable progress of the Ukrainian economy, her church life, and her western-oriented institutes of learning under Mazepa's wise and active patronage. But for the tragedy of Poltava, this gifted and humane ruler might have been termed "the Great" by East European history, while Peter, for all his westernizing, might in many minds have joined the company and epithet of Ivan IV.

Another, more technical yet significant distortion is Pushkin's shifting of the time of the Mazepa-Motrya romance by four or five years to the eve of Mazepa's open defection. This enables Pushkin to weave a strong strand of fresh personal vendetta into the motivations of both Kochubey and Mazepa and to depict Mazepa as particularly heartless in coolly arranging behind her back to orphan Motrya; when in actual fact Kochubey's denunciation came at a time when Motrya not only was no longer under Mazepa's protection (if she had ever been for more than a few hours) but probably was married to someone else.

Since Mazepa's alleged inhumanity towards Motrya Kochubey stands Pushkin in good stead in darkening the Hetman's image in *Poltava*, it is fortunate that twelve undated notes from Mazepa to Motrya have survived in the Moscow archives; we owe this to the fact that Kochubey used them to help document his denunciation when he betrayed the Hetman to Peter. What follows below is in part a paraphrase, in part a full translation of these secret messages[1] sent by the Hetman to Motrya when she had been persuaded to return to her parents' custody:

Letter 1

A short note of three sentences, expressing grief at her absence and sending tender greetings: " . . . tenderly I kiss the whole of you."

Letter 2

My dear heart: I am distraught to learn from your maid that you are angry at me for not having kept your Grace in my house, and having sent Her back to Her parents. But give a moment's thought of your own to what would have ensued. Firstly, your parents would have broadcast to the whole world the report that I had forcibly abducted their daughter by night, and would have claimed that I was keeping you by my side as a concubine.

Further, in keeping Your Grace at my house, neither you nor I would have known what conduct to adopt. We should have been compelled to live like a newly-wed couple, whereupon the Church's thunderbolt and execration would have forced us to part. What would I have done then? Would I not have suffered if Your Grace had complained of me?

Letter 3

This letter begs for an early meeting and professes in most urgent terms both his love and his doubt of her: . . . . "If you love me, do not forget me; if you do not love me, don't remember me! But recall your words. Did you not promise to love me and hold out your white hands to me?

And I will repeat it to you a hundred times more: I beg you, let me know where I might meet with you, and were it but for a single minute, for the happiness of both of us—as you yourself promised me at one time. If that is impossible, take off your necklace, I beg of you, and send it to me."

Letter 4

This expresses love for Motrya "to the point of madness" ("I have never loved anyone in the world like this . . . "), and in effect exhorts her to be patient despite the impossibility of his taking her openly to his side. He also inveighs against her parents' ill-will and obduracy.

Letter 6

. . . "No news! Have they stopped harassing you? I am going away for a week and am sending you a gift by my servant Charles."

Letter 7

"Well then, if they disown you, your accursed parents, take refuge in a convent, and I shall know what must be done about you . . . . Let me know what you need by this girl [evidently one of their go-betweens]."

Letter 9

This notes in bitter accents that "Your Grace has completely changed towards me. You know it: let your will be done! Act as you see fit. You will regret it later. Just remember your words, the sworn pledge you gave me as you left the palace, when you received a diamond ring from me, my finest and most cherished jewel. You said then: 'However things may turn out, the love between us will not perish.' "

Letter 10

Mazepa curses the enemies who have separated them. He sadly longs for news "of the matter well-known to yourself."

Letter 11

Mazepa recalls private talks of love in the Hetman's apartments (apparently on only one occasion!) and her vowing love and fidelity no matter whether they would be together or apart. Mazepa speaks again of his longing for Motrya and urges a meeting. He threatens his enemies: "I shan't tolerate their machinations much longer, but will pay them back and send them to the places they deserve. Which? You will see for yourself."

Letter 12

This takes an outwardly calmer yet more impassioned tone: I am sending you this little book and this ring adorned with diamonds. See fit to wear it and remain faithful until God allows me to report a better outcome to you . . . . I kiss your coral-red lips, your white hands, and all your gleaming body, my adored beloved."

The style of these letters shows traces of the Ukrainian *duma*, one of the genres Mazepa used as a poet; lexical stereotypes like "your white hands" and "coral lips" are characteristic of this form. The polonizing baroque style of his public prose is absent, though. The letters ring true; and they convey some of the imponderables of the relationship. Further details harmonizing with them are found in Kochubey's denunciation, where he complains that Mazepa has demanded and received a lock of Motrya's hair, and that Motrya had sent the Hetman a night-gown [presumably one of hers, as a love token]. While Motrya's letters are missing, the above fragments of the correspondence all but destroy the image of Mazepa as an old lecher and callous seducer.

The incongruity sensed here, as in other places, is not so much between Pushkin's muse and the Clio of non-Russian sources. Pushkin does testify in Canto One to the ardor and depth of both Mazepa's and Maria's love. It arises within the work itself between conflicting impressions of Mazepa which Pushkin conveys. He comments on the enduring power of mature love, cites the desperate strength of Maria's infatuation, and dwells on the fact that she, not Mazepa, took the initiative, in the passage of retrospection in which her parents' eyes are opened to Maria's conduct (p. 327). Yet earlier Pushkin has hinted at an abduction (the eight hoof-prints: four from Maria's horse, and four from Mazepa's? Maria's groom's? Mazepa's groom's? Voynarovsky's?); and later, in Canto Two, he allows Mazepa only perfunctory and selfish qualms over his deadly justice for Maria's father and has him deplore the hindrance she is to him in his world of action and danger. Then there is the passage emphasizing the pressure exerted on Mazepa by the insurrectionist Ukrainian factions, who saw treason, of course, not in severing the bonds with Muscovy but in maintaining them despite all injuries and humiliations suffered in those endless Russian wars. The fairness of this passage contrasts strangely with Pushkin's famous diatribe of execration against Mazepa in the middle of Canto One (pp. 330-31).

These are gritty and puzzling disharmonies. Throughout *Poltava*, defying the vigor of its narrative flow and the harsh magnificence of the verse, there rings in the reader's ear a small but strident note of clashing sympathies. This is not wholly the effect of that Shakespearian art which, as many have observed, makes whoever spoke his piece last, be he ostensibly hero or villain, capture the audience's sympathy. For in *Poltava* it is evidently the poet himself who speaks with discordant voices, not the nature of man; and the music, splendid though it is, turns subtly dissonant from the cracks which run through what is after all, despite the poem's title, its outstanding figure.

The sensational love affair between the majestic old Hetman and the most eligible young beauty in the realm obviously made exciting gossip in and about Baturyn over the few weeks it lasted. Obviously, too, it must have created a temporary rift between the two closely associated families. Credible testimony, however, informs us that Mazepa presently resumed social relations not only with Kochubey personally, his comrade-in-arms and continued holder of the highest office in the Hetman's giving, but also with his wife, both at the Kochubey house and elsewhere. In Kochubey's own denunciations of Mazepa in 1708 one of the pettier charges asserted that Mazepa had remarked at the recent christening of a Jewish apostate that "Moscow planned to enslave the Ukraine." What is interesting here is Kochubey's mention that he and his daughter had been with Mazepa at the time. Other charges also mention or imply contacts between Mazepa and either of the Kochubeys.

To a poet wishing to dramatize the last years of Mazepa's life, the temptation is irresistible to find in this colorful and poignant intrigue the chief motivation for Kochubey's attempt to betray Mazepa and the Ukrainian cause. It also supplies the serious "love interest" otherwise lacking in Mazepa's attested career—at least since the legendary gallop home from Poland at age eighteen. But if such a dramatist also wishes, as Pushkin claimed *he* did, to respect chronology and authenticity, he is constrained to saddle Kochubey with a five-year-long grudge, carefully dissimulated. And for what injury? For the impulse of Mazepa, a prince in his sixties and a distinguished soldier, but even more famous for the breadth and refinement of his European learning and the grace and polish of his manner, to dare to accept briefly, and to return, the ardent girlish affection of a young baroness. True, Kochubey's daughter could have been Mazepa's granddaughter, and was in fact his goddaughter—an even closer kinship in the eyes of the Orthodox church. If this long-faded romance was not what chiefly motivated Kochubey in his denunciation of 1708, then he was simply one of the few Cossack leaders who had made their personal peace with the forcible russification of their country, and who was anxious by way of the Tsar's favor to buy Russian insurance for his wealth and position. In effect, he was implicitly renouncing Cossack liberties and Ukrainian national identity in order eventually to become a Russian landed proprietor and serf-owner.

Pushkin's Poltava, Byron's Mazeppa, *and* Ryleev's Voynarovsky

What is the relationship between *Poltava* and the two narrative poems featuring Mazepa which preceded it, Byron's *Mazeppa* (1818) and Ryleev's *Voynarovsky* (1825)? Does *Poltava* show traces of an attempt, prompted in part by Ryleev's treatment, to *corriger l'histoire*, lend more color to an already hundred-year-old Great-Russian mythology about Peter I and the Ukraine, and incidentally to pay a poetic compliment to the Tsarist government of the day? Byron's work was probably too uninformed and too remote from relevant history to warrant any "answer." But it does seem that Pushkin felt impelled by *Voynarovsky*, which with little claim to historical accuracy sings of the Cossack struggle for freedom, to "set matters straight" through *Poltava*—using the sources available to him, which were almost exclusively Russian or Tsarist Ukrainian in origin and viewpoint.[2]

It seems clear that to Pushkin, Mazepa was bound to be the dangerous apostate from the all-Russian creed he himself espoused, the benighted "minor Slav" fanatic, one of the company he fulminated against in "To the

Slanderers of Russia" and elsewhere. Mazepa's native habitat was the Ukraine; much of his education and adolescent cultural affiliation was Polish-Latin, though not Roman Catholic, and his democratic, even populist sympathies, intermittent as they were, ran counter to the landowners' interests and tastes both in the Ukraine and in Great Russia: *pospolity narod*, the common people, is a term very frequently encountered in Mazepa's *universals* (decrees) and letters. *Odi profanum vulgus et (arceo) timeo* characterizes Pushkin's sentiments regarding this social stratum; and when the *vulgus* is Ukrainian or Polish, the *odium* is redoubled.

Byron's *Mazeppa*, published in 1818, is almost entirely irrelevant to any historical or literary enquiry into the Mazepa theme as treated by Pushkin. It is negligible historically in that Byron confines himself entirely to romanticizing the dubious legend he found in Voltaire's writings concerning young Mazepa's alleged non-stop return from Poland to the Ukraine, lashed bareback-to-bareback to a spirited and justly indignant horse, supplied for the purpose by a wrathful, magnificently antlered husband. Mazepa in Byron's poem cuts no very heroic, though certainly a very pathetic figure; hence there was little in this poem for Pushkin either to debunk (as his bias might have impelled him to do) or to imitate—for his fascination with Byron was long over. Byron's *Mazeppa* is linked to Pushkin's *Poltava* at best by Pushkin's epigraph to *Poltava*—consisting of three unquestionably apt lines of Byron's about the luck of battle passing to the Tsar's side—and by a certain number of shared formal features. But these are of the kind adapted by Pushkin from Byron and others many years before and now functioning as his own.

Byron's *Mazeppa* is a narrative poem of 870 lines cast in irregularly rhymed iambic tetrameters, with the narration gathered loosely into twenty chapter-like units averaging some forty verses. *Poltava* shows the same metrics, but constitutes a heroic, or anti-heroic, poem almost twice the length of Byron's and divided symmetrically into three equal panels of a triptych, which function as three acts of a drama. Pushkin's drama operates with seven speaking roles, counting the Tsar; Byron's with three, counting the horse. Byron's work expends virtually all its poetic breath on its central flashback—young Mazepa's legendary embroilment in Poland and his inexhaustible sufferings athwart the runaway steed in often inclement weather. This *pièce de résistance* is framed exiguously by its setting—the flight to Turkey, fifty years later, of Mazepa and King Charles after Poltava. One evening Mazepa tells the story to the king, who, wounded and feverish, is unable to sleep. In the end, to the reader's drowsy relief, the narrative does send Charles to sleep as well.

A far stronger incentive for poetic response—protest or refutation—

on Pushkin's part is offered by Ryleev's *Voynarovsky*—a Russian poem by a Decembrist poet of Pushkin's acquaintance, published only a few years earlier. *Voynarovsky* (1825), named for and focusing on the deeds and sufferings of Mazepa's nephew and trusted deputy, is a romantic poem of ca. 1,000 lines. It is divided into two parts and resembles *Poltava* in its metrics and in the canto-like size of its units. It resembles Byron's *Mazeppa* only in that the main fable is delivered in a retrospective narrative by the protagonist, and reduces the rest of the poetic matter to a narrow frame of author's narration. While Ryleev's Hetman Mazepa is not the eponymic hero and plays a memorable, but essentially parenthetical part in the central flashback, neither is he a villain; far from it. He is a mysterious, powerful figure, forced in 1709 to reveal himself as a patriot in a cause which may be doomed, but which is noble and inspiring. The romantic terms and elements in the following passage from *Voynarovsky* are strikingly similar to those used by Pushkin when he depicts Mazepa on the verge of his difficult decision, with the important difference that by Pushkin Mazepa's enforced silence and secrecy are put to work as repellent aspects of his treachery:

Ryleev:

All of Ukraine in joyous riot
Thronged into ranks and flew to war;
Alone Mazepa's features bore
Shades of dejection and disquiet.
From underneath the beetling brows
A savage flame began to flicker,
. . . .
. . . .
Mazepa stayed in deep seclusion,
Kept silent—and assembled troops.

Pushkin:

The Cossack land was mutely seething.
A spark had smoldered long; and breathing
To fan the bloody feuds of yore,
The spokesman of a people's war
Sought from the Hetman for sedition
A freer rein with angry snarls,
And their incontinent ambition
Impatiently awaited Charles.
The mutinous "it's time!" was muttered
Around Mazepa near and far;
Yet the old Hetman never uttered
A thought disloyal to the Tsar . . .

When Mazepa presently reveals his mind to his nephew, Voynarovsky, Ryleev makes it quite clear that Mazepa's cause is a noble one: The Ukraine and her ancient liberties. Having first sworn his nephew to the pledge that he would sacrifice anything and everything to the homeland—Voynarovsky stipulating "all save my honor"—Mazepa continues:

"Ukraina's son I see in you:
An upright citizen I knew
In Voynarovsky long ago.
I loathe the men of frigid thought
Who put the native country last;
They war against the sacred past:
They hold the nation's woes for naught,
High sentiments they are denied,
They lack the spirit's hot strong breath,
And from first childhood unto death
It is their lot to cringe and hide.
You're not of that kind, that I knew.
But my Ukraine—it's in no way
To slight your feelings when I say
I hold her dearer than do you.
As it befits the youthful hero,
For love of the ancestral soil
You stand prepared to sacrifice
Your wife, your children, and yourself . . .
But I . . . but I, for vengeance thirsting,
To break her chains I am about
To sacrifice my honor even.
It's time to bare a secret now.
I hold great Peter in respect,
But—bowing down to Destiny,
I am his foe henceforward, learn!
This is a daring step, I know,
And chance will have the issue of it.
Unsafe the prospect—what awaits me
Is either fame or calumny!
I am decided, though: let Fate
Augur the Motherland misfortune,
The hour is near, and near the struggle
Of freedom battling Tyranny!"

It is perhaps worth noting that Ryleev makes Mazepa express these sentiments not on some public occasion, where politics might have influenced the message and demagoguery its style, but in the course of a tête-a-tête with an intimate—suggesting that his emotion is genuine and his habits of stealth and dissimulation are dictated by necessity.

There are in this somewhat ingenuous poem numerous further passages reminiscent in their lofty feeling and abstract nobility of language of nothing so much as of Schiller's *Tell*, where a similar national crisis is resolved happily. The above colloquy between the doomed patriots, Mazepa and Voynarovsky, culminates in a final reflection whose magnanimity and rueful wisdom contrast impressively with Pushkin's oddly shrill and ill-motivated vituperation of Mazepa in corresponding passages:

> Oh, how inconstant are our blessings,
> How we are underlings to Fate!
> In vain does courage seethe within:
> The sacred struggle nears the end.
> A single moment wrought it all,
> A single moment snatched away
> Forever from my native land
> All hope of happiness and peace . . .
> Mazepa to submit in spirit?
> I will not be a slave to Fate;
> Should I not battle Destiny
> When I gave battle to a Tsar?
> Yes, Voynarovsky, I shall harness,
> As long as life and breath will serve,
> All my resource, try any means
> At hand to aid our native land;
> And I am tranquil in my soul:
> Peter and I—we both are right;
> I live for glory, as does he,
> And for the welfare of my land."

This is the light thrown on Mazepa in a number of such passages by Ryleev in 1825—just before the Decembrist revolt that would ruin him. His fellow poet and political ally, Bestuzhev, on the other hand, takes a more conventional Russian view of the Hetman in a two-page biographical sketch of Voynarovsky's career directly preceding Ryleev's poem. With an eye to the censorship, no doubt, he calls Mazepa "the famous traitor." This alibi is much fortified by a second, longer introduction by A. Kornilovich, headed "Biography of Mazepa," which represents Mazepa's career as a long chain of betrayals, culminating in the corruption and abduction of Motrya Kochubey and the "high treason" of 1708-9.

POLTAVA

> *The power and glory of the war,*
> *Faithless as their vain votaries, men,*
> *Had passed to the triumphant Czar.*

Byron

DEDICATION

This is for you—but will the rhythm
Of this dark music touch your ear?
And will your modest nature fathom
    My heart's unruly striving here?
Or will the poet's bold submission
Of verse, as once of love, again
Pass by without your recognition,
As unacknowledged now as then?

    Know it again, at least, the rhyme
That once, I think, was dear to you—
And know that since that parting chime,
Whatever changing fate I knew,
The memory of words last spoken
By you, and your sad wilderness,
Have been my only sacred token,
Sole refuge, ultimate redress.

CANTO ONE

Renowned and rich is Kochubey,[1]
His grasslands more than eye can ramble;
There teeming herds of horses stray
At pasture, and unguarded amble.
His ring of manor parks surrounds
The cossack farms[2] about Poltava;
There every costliness abounds,
Wrought silver, furs, and shot-silk gowns,

On show or under lock and cover.
But Kochubey is rich and blithe
Not by his herds of long-maned ponies,
Nor gold, Crimean Tatars' tithe,
Nor fruitful landed patrimonies;
These the old magnate counts for less
Than his young daughter's loveliness.[3]

And well he may: she shines in beauty
Above Poltava's fairest maids,
Fresh as the primrose, tender duty
Which April pays to sylvan glades.
Lithe is she as the poplar's blades
On Kiev's hills, her gait as gliding,
One moment, as the silken shift
Of swans on lonely tarns adrift,
Then like the roe-deer's eager striding.
Her bosom gleams like ocean spume,
While dusky ringlets make a gloom
Of clouds above her noble forehead;
Her eyes are starry bright, the bloom
On cheeks and lips is petal-florid.
Nor was it loveliness alone
(A transient blush) which folk admired,
By which most winsomely she shone:
She had a sweetness all her own,
Wherein reserve and sense conspired.
This is why Russia and Ukraine
Send eager suitors to the palace;
But fearful, as from ball and chain,
She shrinks from wedding crown and chalice.
All suitors are refused—but then
The very Hetman sends his men.[4]

True, he is old. Both years and sabers
Have marked him well, yet grievous labors
Left passion buoyant as before;
Love sways Mazepa's soul once more.

The youthful heart so briskly ranges,
Is swift to cool and quick to burn,
Love will depart, love will return,
And day by day its temper changes.
Not with this forward, easy air,
With upsurge so abrupt, so ardent,
Is seasoned heart about to flare,
By time's relentless probing hardened.
It is refractory, and slow
In passion-heat to fuse and glow,—
But kindled late, will be on fire
Till life's term shall itself expire.

As chamois cleave to mountain faces
Beneath the eagle's rushing wing,
Thus, tremulous, Maria paces
And bides, alone, what fate must bring.

At last her mother seeks her, clutching
Her head in disbelief; and touching
Maria's fevered hand, she cries:
"Oh shameless! This is past forgiving . . .
Old lecher! . . . no, while we are living,
He shall not have his sinful prize!
The wretch, who to his ward should rather
Be counsel, friend, baptismal father,
Let his disordered fancy rise
To be her wedded lord, none other."

Maria shrank; a grave-like taint
Appeared to stain her rosy vigor,
And as if touched by mortal rigor
She fell unconscious in a faint.

Restored again, she all but shuttered
Her senses from the world, and uttered
Not one word. Both her parents sought
To chase her spirit's morbid languor,
The writhings of a mind distraught,

And rid her soul of fear and anger . . .
In vain. All that day and the next
Marie, in tears or proudly vexed,
Of neither food nor drink partaking,
Would droop, her brightness overcast,
And quite estranged from sleep. At last
They found her bedchamber forsaken.

None knew just when and in what way
She could have vanished. But next day
A fisherman recalled the clatter
Of hoofbeats, sounds of cossack chatter,
A woman's voice; and trails were grooved
Across the dewy fields, eight-hooved.—
Not just fresh chestnut locks, the down
On youthful cheeks unlined and florid—
An older man's austerer frown,
A silver-shaded, deep-cleft forehead,
In beauty's mind has cast, not once,
Seeds of a passionate response.

And stricken Kochubey soon faces
The dread, unfathomable news:
She's slighted Nature's, honor's dues,
Was in the miscreant's embraces!
Disgraceful, loathly! Stunned, the two
Forbid their minds to think it true.
Then only did they come to gather
The truth, appalling, naked, whole,
Then only did they come to fathom
The young transgressor's secret soul.
Then only was it manifested
Why she had willfully contested
The claims of the familial bond,
Would sigh and mutter in seclusion
And with remote disdain respond
To every wooing squire's effusion;
Why no one but the Hetman held
Her ear at any festive table,
When shouts rose to a merry babel

And beakers foamed and overwelled;
Why she intoned whenever able
The cossack songs composed by him[5]
When yet his destiny was dim,
His name unknown to fame or fable;
Why, flouting girlish rule and grace,
She watched the charging squadrons race,
Loved growling drums and rough opinion
About the horsetail-crested mace,[6]
Ukrainian emblem of dominion . . .

Lord Kochubey has wealth and fame,
Could effortlessly cleanse his name:
His followers and friends are legion,
A word from him could rouse the region;
Armed with a vengeful father's grief,
He could attain the haughty thief
In his own Court, work retribution
With his strong forearm as he ought . . .
But a more recondite solution
Preoccupies the magnate's thought.

Then stood we at the clouded stage
In youthful Russia's destined courses
When she, exerting all her forces,
With Peter's genius came of age.
Harsh was the taskmaster of glory
Fate had assigned her: no small meed
Of lessons unforeseen and gory
Were dealt her by the royal Swede.
Yet the ordeal of searching trials,
Fortune's harsh blows and long denials,
Steeled Rus. The heavy hammer thus
Shapes iron while it shatters glass.
Bold Charles for idle fame was charging
Along a yawning chasm's margin.
On ancient Rus he turned his sword
And swept away the Russian rallies
As whirlwinds scour the arid valleys

And rake the dusty meadow-sward.
He came, the very path pursuing
By which more lately sought us out
A man of fate, and in so doing
Made famous but his staggering rout.[7]

The Cossack land was mutely seething.
A spark had smoldered long, and breathing
To fan the bloody feuds of yore,
The spokesmen of a people's war
Sought from the Hetman for sedition
A freer rein with angry snarls;
And their incontinent ambition
Impatiently awaited Charles.
The mutinous "it's time" was muttered
Around Mazepa near and far,
Yet the old Hetman never uttered
A thought disloyal to the Tsar.
As ever saturnine in manner
He calmly flew his Hetman's banner;
To all appearance unaware
Of strife, he feasted free of care.
"Where stands the Hetman?" hotheads queried.
"He is enfeebled, sapped by time,
Age and adversities have wearied
The fervent vigor of his prime.
Why should he clutch, with fingers shaking,
The hetman's mace? What is it for
But to make signal for the breaking
Of Moscow's hateful hold by war?
If but the grand old Doroshénko,[8]
Of Samoylóvich's young resource,[9]
Or our Paléy,[10] or Gordeyénko[11]
Commanded now the country's force,
Then snow-sheets would not hump in clusters
On far-flung graves of Cossack folk,
By now the grieving homeland's musters
Might have thrown off the alien yoke."[12]

Aglow with mutinous desire,
Thus rash young manhood played with fire
And, courting heady risks, lost sight
Of the Dominion's servile plight,
Forgot Bogdan's auspicious quarrels,
Those sacred truces, martial laurels,
The glories of ancestral might.
The way of ripeness, though, is chary,
It looks askance at risks involved,
Which scheme is sound and which unwary
Is not incautiously resolved.
Who probes the watery abysses
Beneath unyielding ice confined?
Who may descend with questing mind
Into the murky precipices
Of deviousness? Its deep pursuits
Long-stifled passions' tardy fruits,
Lie undiscoverably buried,
Till plans slow-grown from earliest roots,
Abruptly ripening, are carried.
The wickeder Mazepa's schemes,
With smoother fraud his actions larded,
The more his aspect is unguarded,
The simpler his demeanor seems.
How he is effortlessly clever
At wooing and unriddling hearts,
Converting minds to his endeavor
While privy to their secret arts!
How disingenuously trusting
At feasts, with what a genial glow,
His vigor to old age adjusting,
He mourns the days of long ago,
With friends of freedom talks petition,
With foes of government, sedition,
With the oppressed sheds tears of rage,
With the dull-minded plays the sage!
Not many, surely, then suspected
The flinty soul that was his share,
That, bent on vengeance, he elected

The foulest means as soon as fair,
That by his rancor's lifelong scoring
The ghostliest grudge was never laid,
To what forbidden heights of soaring
His seasoned arrogance had strayed;
That he recalled no benefaction,
That he revered no sacred action,
That from his heart all love was banned,
That he would squander blood like water,
That he held freedom fit for slaughter,
That he avowed no fatherland.

Long has the chieftain ruminated
A loathsome plot, in stealth designed;
But hostile gaze has infiltrated,
Has perilously pierced his mind.
"No, brazen scoundrel, thieving varlet,"
Broods Kochubey and grinds his teeth,
"I'll spare your godless roof the scarlet:
My daughter's chamber lies beneath.
You shall not roast in blazing ashes,
Nor gasp your last beneath the slashes
Of cossack sabres. No, you scum—
In Moscow, lashed to rack and drum,
Amidst most searching body-trials,
A-choke on blood and vain denials,
You are to execrate the day
When in her christening array
You held our baby, and the revel
Where I poured full your cup of love,
And, most, the night when, bird of evil,
Your talons struck our straying dove!..."

And yet, time was when friendly dealing
United ataman and laird,
When common issue, noble feeling,
Like salt and bread and oil they shared.
As one, they charged at cannon blazing
Across the fields of victory,
Had met on many a past occasion

In long and private colloquy;
Guile had allowed but this companion
A glimpse into the brooding canyon
Of spite on self-assertion bent,
Had seemed to hint impending changements,
Negotiations, disarrangements,
In words of dubious intent.

Then, true, Mazepa had inspired
In Kochubey devotion. Now,
To fever-pangs of outrage fired,
He lives for but a single vow;
A single all-engrossing mission
Absorbs him, day and night the same:
Through execution, or perdition,
To wash away his daughter's shame.

Yet the shrewd engines of his rancor
Were in his breast securely pent.
"To melancholy's gnawing canker,
Aye, to the grave his temper leant.
He bore Mazepa little ire,
His child was guiltier by far;
Yet he would not condemn Maria,
But cite her to God's judgment-bar.
She had disgraced her proud connection,
Forsworn celestial law and man's . . . "
Meanwhile, with eagle eyes he scans
His household circle, for selection
Of intimates by doubt unhaunted,
Suborned by no one, nothing daunted.
His wife is privy to his mind:[13]
In utmost stealth he has designed
The deadliest of denunciation,
And the exasperated wife,
With woman's loyal fury rife,
Still goads her raging lord's impatience.
At night, beside his couch, a grim
Penumbral shape, she whispers him

Of retribution, breathes reproaches,
Sheds tears, then heartens him and coaches,
Demands his oath; to her fierce creed
Grim Kochubey now vows the deed.

He lays his plans; and like a brother,
Bold Iskra[14] joins him with a will.
"We shall prevail," they tell each other,
"Mazepa's fall is fated. Still—
With all we know the Tsar to feel,
What fearless, righteous detractor
Shall tender, flushed with civic zeal,
Against this favored malefactor
Impeachment for the common weal?"

Among the cossacks of Poltava
Whom the unhappy girl had spurned
One had from adolescence burned
With thwarted passion's pent-up lava.
Amidst Ukrainian cherry-groves
Now early, now at dusk he roves,
In hope of his adored's appearing,
In agues of expectancy,
The native river's slanting lea
And lets a moment's meeting cheer him.
He loved her bare of hope, and so
Had never pressed his suit upon her:
He could not have survived her no.
When suitors jostled for the honor
Of wooing her, he stayed aloof
From their array, his sorrow muted.
But when among the cossacks proof
Of Mary's infamy was bruited,
And obloquy began to prey
Upon her name with gleeful rending,
Her spell throughout his never-ending
Distress retained its former sway.
Yet when they happened in his hearing
To name Mazepa, he would pale,
And anguish, secretive and searing,

Would film his visage like a veil.
. . . .
By waning moon and glint of star
Who rides his steed so late, so far?
Whose progress neither veers nor varies
Across the eye-defying prairies?

The cossack rider's northward bound,
No respite has he sought or found
'Mid open steppe, through woodlands coursing,
Or at a rushing river's forcing.

His iron trappings glint like glass,
His sidebags jingle as they pass;
Not breaking step at ford or crossing,
The charger speeds, his long mane tossing.

Gold rubles are the courier's right,
Steel is the plucky lad's delight,
His steed of eager blood comes nearest,
His dolman cap, though, he holds dearest.

For it he'll render, come the need,
Red gold, blue steel, and blooded steed,
He'll brave all fighting odds to shield it,
Fight unto death before he'll yield it.

Why is the cap so dear to him?
A screed is sowed into its brim,
For Peter's eyes; its gist—grave reason
To have Mazepa seized for treason.

Meanwhile, perturbed by nothing yet,
Quite unaware of any threat,
Mazepa weaves his sly devising.
A priest, whose word counts like his own,[15]
Foments a popular uprising
And lures him with a parlous throne.
Like thieves at furtive assignations
They hold nocturnal consultations,

Promote betrayal with a heart,
Encode a ciphered manifesto,[16]
Place the Imperial head at mart,
And barter feudal oaths with gusto.
There comes of late—whence, no one knows—
To Court a certain alien vagrant,
Attended as he comes and goes
By Orlik,[17] long the Hetman's agent.
His emissaries carry on
From place to place their subtle poison,
Here help Bulavin's[18] cossacks, noising
Revolt among the clans of Don,
There turn the treatied Hordes to flout laws,
There, past the Dniepr's cataracts,
Enrage fierce companies of outlaws
With tales of Peter's self-willed acts.
Mazepa   peers in each direction,
To every quarter sends report,
By threat of force plants disaffection
For Moscow at the Tatar court.
The King in Warsaw finds dispatches,
The Pasha in Ochakov's walls,
The Tsar and Charles in camp. He hatches
Astute intrigue with never a pause;
Each snare with barbs more finely snagging,
He steadies the impending blow,
His evil purpose never flagging
And quenchless his felonious glow.

But how he gloated, how he shivered
When at his feet abruptly quivered
The bolt that missed him! When to *him*,
The very arch-foe of the realm,
The Russian government remitted[19]
The plaint of treason written out
In his Poltava! sent without
Reserve, as to one preacquitted!
When by the cares of war distraught,
Shocked by this slander (as he thought),

The Tsar himself ignored the warrant
And sent the Judas word he meant
To wreak a fittingly abhorrent,
An exemplary punishment!

Mazepa, sounding hurt and bitter,
Appeals in humble words to Peter:
"Let God, let people judge the truth;
Had he, poor chieftain, from his youth
Toiled for the Tsar, two decades rounding,
And, honored with his grace abounding,
Had prospered wondrously, just so
(How mindless is the spite of mortals!)
That now, at the sepulchral portals,
He might learn treachery, might throw
Filth on a stainless reputation?
Had he not spurned with indignation
King Stanislaw's[20] embrace, had ground
His heel on kingly robes half-fitted,
Had notes and drafts-of-state submitted
To Peter, as in duty bound?
Had he not turned to bait and barter
With Great Turk and Crimean Tartar[21]
A stone-deaf ear? Aflame with zeal,
He was, as ever, glad to seal
With life's last drop his lifelong labors
In any cause the Tsar declared;
And here enraged detractors dared
To soil his name to Tsar and neighbors!
And who, pray? Iskra, Kochubey!
So long his comrades, tried and tested! . . . "
All insolence, he then requested,
With much display of reptile tears,
Death warrants for those noble peers[22] . . .

Maria—pitiful Maria,
Circassian maidens' loveliest!
The callous fiend, the monstrous liar
You have been cradling at your breast!

What enigmatic charm or merit
Has made your proud and tender spirit
So malleable to the control
Of that uncouth and wolfish soul?
His wiry locks, with silver sprinkled,
His brow, profoundly cleft and wrinkled,
The deep-set eyes, like glittering sherds,
The spice of cunning in his words,
Have grown the dearest in creation,
Have dulled your mother's sensed reproof;
They, and the couch spread by temptation,
Have turned you from your father's roof.
The crafty conjuror has wrested
All choice from you with elfin eyes,
His guilt-assuaging speeches vested
Contumacy in freedom's guise;
You shine on him your fondly doting,
By love irradiated face,
You worship him with happy gloating—
And glory in your own disgrace.
You take strange pride in shame's effacement,
As though new-virgined in his arm;
For maiden modesty and charm
Have changed their signs in your abasement.

What's honor, shame to Mary now?
The gossip of the manyheaded?
When safely in her lap is bedded
The Hetman's formidable brow,
When he forgets his cares, though laden
With fateful hazards and fatigues,
Or shares the furtive, bold intrigues
Of statecraft with the guileless maiden?
Thoughts of the past stir no regret;
A single image wanders yet
Across her soul like cloud-shade—token
Of rue—her parents, grieving, broken;
She sees them, through a mist of tears,
Round out their bitter, childless years,
And hears reproaches never spoken . . .

Oh, had she come to know at once
What couriers had for days been riding
To tell Ukraine! But for the nonce
They kept from her the murderous tiding.

CANTO TWO

Mazepa glowers, preoccupied
By dark implacable reflection.
Upon her greybeard's deep abstraction
Maria gazes tender-eyed.
She settles at his feet, embraces
His knees with an endearing speech;
In vain: those black and secret places
Her love is powerless to reach.
Before her earnest gaze his eye
Strays into clouded inattention;
Blank silence is his sole reply
To love's appeal, to love's shy mention.
At last, amazed and deeply stung,
The girl leapt to her feet and flung
These words at him, by passion driven:

"Mazepa, hear me! For your sake
I left all else; I have but striven
For one prize, placed my whole life's stake,
My heart, once and forever given,
On you—your love. And I did lose
All else, my world . . . No matter—whose
Concern but mine? I don't regret it.
That solemn midnight stillness when
You made me yours (could you forget it?) . . .
You swore an oath to love me then.
Why have you broken it already?"

MAZEPA

"Beloved, hush—you are unjust.
Dismiss unreasoning mistrust;

Black fancies make the heart unsteady:
Your soul, so swift to feel, I fear
Is darkened now by vain suspicion.
Maria, know: I hold you dear
Above all fame, beyond ambition."

MARIA

"No! You have secrets now! Before,
Just weeks ago, we never parted;
Now you shrug off my fondness, or
You strain, and still remain halfhearted.
You court the magnates of the plain—
Routs, councils, stealth . . . I don't exist!
Through long lone nights you entertain
The Jesuit, give that beggar tryst . . .
My warm caresses meet with cold
Constraint, are illtimed or fatiguing . . .
You drank a toast, so I am told,
To Dulskaya one night. Intriguing . . !
Who is this Dulskaya?"

MAZEPA

           "No . . . you??
Jealous? One of my years and temper
Would crave the condescending simper
Of some smug beauty? Would it do
For me—gruff, greyhaired, not unlettered—
To ape the mindless, smitten sigher,
Parade ridiculously fettered,
Or burn with simulated fire?"

MARIA

"What good is this evasive plea?
No . . . make your answer straight and clear."

MAZEPA

Your peace of soul is dear to me.
So be it, then. Maria, hear:

Great plans have long been in the making,
And now the flood is at the tide:
To us a glorious dawn is breaking:
Soon fateful battle must decide.
Bereft of pride, of free election,
We bent our heads in futile spite
Beneath the Pole's unsought protection,
The harness of the Muscovite.
Self-rule in free, in sovereign manner
Is due us—overdue by far:
I hoist Ukraina's bloody banner
Of liberty against the Tsar.
All waits: the Commonwealth* and Sweden
Will join their forces to our own;
'Mid clash of arms and heroes bleeding
I soon may raise myself a throne.
I count firm friends in noble houses;
The Princess Dulskaya espouses
The cause; that priest, that beggar bring
Affairs to imminent fruition
As go-betweens in the transmission
Of word and writ from either king.
There—now you have my grave admission.
Are you content? Is your suspicion
Allayed?

MARIA

        My dearest, no: quite banned . . .
You are to rule our native land . . !
How bravely will your silver glisten
Ringed by a crown!

---

*This refers to the Polish state, which was a "crowned republic." Both "commonwealth" and
"rzeczpospolita," the abiding name of the Polish state, are direct translations of the Roman
res publica, 'public weal', eventually 'republic'.

MAZEPA

But understand:
All's moot yet, storm-clouds gather . . . Listen:
None knows what lies in store for me.

MARIA

Oh, by your side I know no terrors—
You are so mighty! I can see
A throne ahead.

MAZEPA

What if—the gallows?

MARIA

The gallows then for you and me . . .
Would I prize life itself above you?
No! You are marked for majesty.

MAZEPA

You love me, then?

MARIA

I, do I love you?!

MAZEPA

Tell me: who is more dear to you,
Husband or father?

MARIA

If I knew
I could not say . . . A fearful question,
And idle, too . . . when what I sought

Was to forget my kin . . . I brought
Disgrace on them. Yet the suggestion
My father might have cast me off
Strikes terror to my heart . . . Enough!
It was for you.

MAZEPA

Then you do favor
Your father less? Say so.

MARIA

O Savior!

MAZEPA

Which is it? Answer!

MARIA

You decide.

MAZEPA

No, speak: were life to be denied
To either of us, or accorded;
And you were made the arbiter—
To which of us would you prefer
The gift of life to be awarded?

MARIA

Oh, stop tormenting me! You try
My heart, you play the Fiend.

MAZEPA

Reply!

MARIA

Your face is white, your accents chilling . . .
O don't be angry! I am willing
To yield up anything you say.
But speeches like this make me tremble.
Let it be over.

MAZEPA

       Just remember,
Maria, what you said today.

The night of the Ukraine is still,
The skies alive with starry glitter.
The drowsy ether lacks the will
To shake its languor; barely twitter
The silver poplars' wispy strands.
The crescent moon serenely stands
High over Biala Cerkiew, gilding
The hetmans' luscious garden lands
And time-revered seignorial building.
And all about is sunk in sleep;
The Hall, though, stirs with sounds of action,
And at the window of a keep,
Engrossed in desolate reflection,
Leans Kochubey against the bars
And frowns, unseeing, at the stars.

      The scaffold waits. But not with horror
He contemplates the fateful morrow.
The wound of life in him is deep:
What can death augur? Wished-for sleep.
He longs to join those blood-stained musters.
Long, long he broods. Yet—God of Justice!
To writhe at that false prince's bar,
A trussed and muzzled ox unloaded,
Turned over by a trustful Tsar

To Tsar's betrayer to be goaded;
Lose life, and lose it like a knave,
Drag friends and clan into the grave
To curse him with their dying breath;
Guiltless beneath the axe, to see
The traitor's wink of shameless glee . . .
And enter the embrace of death
With none to leave, for sole estate,
A sacred legacy of hate! . . .

Then he recalled Poltava town . . .
The dear old round of friends and kin,
His past life's splendor and renown,
The songs Maria used to sing;
The house where he was born and nourished,
Where he had toiled and sweetly dreamed,
Which held all he had ever cherished
And wantonly—as now it seemed—
Had cast aside . . .
But here the turnkey
Unlocks his door with grinding clinks:
He's here! the luckless captive thinks,
My guide upon the fearful journey
Beneath the token of the Cross—
Strong scourer of sin's stain, the fervent
Caustic of soul's distemper—servant
Of Him they crucified for us,
Whose sacred Host he bears, supplying
My dearth . . . whereby I gather strength
For hardier, more undaunted dying
And gain eternal life at length!

His heart with sorrow overflowing,
The stricken prisoner prepares
To call the Boundless and All-knowing
To witness with his contrite prayers.
But quite another meets his sight—
Far from some holy anchorite . . .
Before him wolfish Orlik stands;
And spreading bitterly his hands,

The weary sufferer groans and glowers:
"What brings you, harbinger of hate?
Why must Mazepa desecrate
The quiet of my final hours?"

ORLIK

Your hearing is resumed. Speak on.

KOCHUBEY

You have my answers. Now be gone,
Leave me in peace.

ORLIK

      One more admission
Demands the Hetman.

KOCHUBEY

      But to what?
What is there left that I have not
Confessed as asked? My deposition
Is judged deceitful. They detect
Vile schemes. The Hetman is correct.
What more is owing?

ORLIK

      We have reason
To think that of your boundless wealth
You planted many a hoard in stealth
On the estate[23] before your treason.
The headman's axe is bound to fall,
And your possessions, one and all,
Are forfeit—this the law imposes—
To feed the war. My Lord discloses
What is still owing: to reveal
The treasure which you still conceal.

KOCHUBEY

You are correct, again: three hoards
Have been to me this life's rewards.
The first has been my honest name;
The torture brought that down in shame.
The other, priceless, was the honor
Of my dear child. I doted on her,
I trembled for it night and day;
That hoard Mazepa stole away.
The third, still safely in my hands, is
Sacred revenge, my final hoard.
That—I shall pass unto the Lord.

ORLIK

Old man, dismiss such empty fancies.
This is no time for games. Prepare,
Near as you are now to departing
This world, your mind for sterner fare.
So—will you freely tell, or smarting
From torture? Where's the gold?

KOCHUBEY

                Coarse knave,
Will nothing choke that yokel query?
It's time—past time—to fill my grave;
You and Mazepa then may weary
Your claws on the estate I leave,
With bloodstained paws perform your audit
Of spoils, root in my cellars, cleave
The halls and orchards where I stored it . . .
Why, send my child into the lead!
She'll mark off all the hollow spaces,
Conduct you to those hiding-places;
But for the love of God I plead
To spare me further crude offenses . . .

ORLIK

Reveal the hidden treasures! Talk!
Where are they? Out with it! You baulk?
Then you prefer . . . the consequences?
Think—one last time . . . Your final chance!
No answer? Torturer, advance![24]

The headsman came . . .
                O night of torment!
Where hides Mazepa from the darts
Of conscience now, the asps long dormant
In this most recusant of hearts?
In the apartments of young Mary
(Who slumbers, blessèdly unwary
Of doom), beside his godchild's bed,
Sits motionless, with sunken head,
The Hetman, ponderously brooding,
Grim thoughts upon his mind intruding,
Each blacker, blacker than the last.
"On Kochubey the die is cast;
He is past saving. For the nearer
The Hetman's object, the more proud
And unassailably endowed
With power he must seem—and the clearer
His enemies' decline . . . No doubt!
Both the informer and his lout
Shall die." But to the sleeper wanders
His eye, and "Lord on high!". . he ponders,
"What will become of her? The blow
Must fall, and she be orphaned by it . . .
Her soul is mercifully quiet
Thus far; the mortal secret, though,
Must now come out. The hissing cleaver
That falls tomorrow will be heard
Throughout Ukraine; a noisy fever
And clash of minds must shake her world . . !
I see it now: one who is fated
To master destiny's great tide,

Let him stand up to it unaided
And take no consort to his side.
Can to one chariot be knotted
The war-horse and the timid deer?
In my rash folly I forgot it,
And now must pay for it, I fear . . .
Of all pure boons in nature's giving,
Of all that could make life worth living,
The poor child freely made a gift
To my gaunt age . . . and I for dower
Gave her—what short, what deadly shrift!"
He looks at her: how like a flower
She blossoms there, a dewy rose;
How slumber lulls her reverently,
How sweet her parted lips; how gently
Her peaceful breathing ebbs and flows.
Tomorrow, though . . . His breath comes faster,
He shudders, and his eyes grow dark . . .
And stealthily advancing past her,
He enters the deserted park.

The night of the Ukraine is still,
The skies alive with starry glitter.
The drowsy ether lacks the will
To shake its languor; barely twitter
The poplar twigs with silver gleams.
Distraught, oppressed by haunting dreams,
Mazepa roams; the starry skies—
A million marking, noting eyes—
Pursue him with their mocking stares;
The poplars in their swaying pairs
Are lisping, bowing to their sisters
Like justices exchanging whispers.
The summer's dim nocturnal spell
Hangs airless, like a dungeon cell.

Just then he hears a feeble tone
As from the castle . . . like a moan.
Is it a drowsy mind's delusion?
A tortured groan? a hunting owl?

Some forest creature's far-off howl?
In his bemusement and confusion,
The fierce old man cannot restrain
An answering cry—of cheer or rally,
Such as on many a warlike sally
He traded in the heat of fray
With bold Zabela, noble brother
In arms, and Gamaley, another;
And, yes, with him; with Kochubey . . .

The morning sends its glow ahead
Across the east in flares of red.
Soon hillocks, vales, and pastures quiver
With sparks from forest crown and river . . .
The cheery noise of day began,
Awakening the tribe of man.

Maria feels—still breathing gently
In veils of sleep—a step intently
Approach her couch; someone is there
Touching her feet and pressing lightly . . .
Awake but barely yet aware,
She smiles and shuts her eyelids tightly
Against the brilliant morning glare.
Maria, with a drowsy nestling,
Gropes for the hand, her voice caressing:
"My love . . ?" The answering whisper, though,
Betokens quite another visit . . .
She starts, sits up to look—who is it?
Her mother!

MOTHER

Quiet, child, no sound;
Don't ruin us! Last night I found
A secret way to reach you, staking
All on one hope: with tears to sue
For stay of sentence. Only you
May stop their murderous undertaking.
Save Father.

DAUGHTER

Save—what father? Who?
Stay of what sentence?

MOTHER

Are you saying
You still don't . . . Come, no! You are staying
At court, not in some desert place;
You must know; know the Hetman's wrath
At enemies who cross his path;
His power to blight those who oppose him;
The favor which the Sovereign shows him . . .
But I can see it now: you chose
That man above your kinsmen's sorrow;
I find you lolling in a doze
As they decree the deed of horror,
As the attainder bill is read,
The cleaver honed for Father's head!
Yes—we are strangers to each other . . .
Yet, Mary! As I am your mother,
Fly, kneel before him, kiss his sleeve,
Be our dear angel of reprieve!
Your suppliant hand alone can reach him,
Snatch Father from the scaffold's rim;
He must relent when you beseech him:
You gave your honor up for him,
Your kin, your God . . .

DAUGHTER

My head is reeling . . .
Mazepa . . . Mother here, appealing
For mercy! Father to be slain!
No—either I have gone insane
Or these are nightmares.

MOTHER

No! Not raving,
Not dreaming—would it were so, child!
You—yet to hear?? That Father, wild
With grief at your dishonor, craving
Savage retaliation, warned
The Tsar against the Hetman, braving
The wrath of treachery suborned;
That by vile torture they extorted
Confession of intrigues aborted,
Of slander shameless, reasonless;
That, snared by wanton righteousness,
He was remanded as a victim
To the despoiler, who had tricked him;
That in a hollow square (unless
The Lord sends down some portent dreaded)
He must this morning be beheaded;
That meanwhile he is in duress
Here in the prison keep.

DAUGHTER

No. Never!
This very day . . . poor Father? Dead?

And bloodless, like a stark cadaver,
The girl falls back upon the bed.

Caps bright with color; lance-tips winking;
The drum-beat rumbles; Serdyuks[25] prance;
The regiments fall in, advance.
The throng heaves wildly; hearts are shrinking;
Into it, crowded roadways, coiling
Like serpents, merge their moving strands.
High in the square the scaffold stands;
On it the headsman loiters, spoiling
In glad impatience for his prey:
Now in rehearsal he will lay

His white hands on the cleaver's grip,
Now trade the rabble lip for lip.
The steady, sullen roaring blends
High shrieks and laughter, oaths and chatter.
But then an exclamation sends
All into silence; only clatter
Of hoof-beats fills the awestruck square.
The Hetman's mightiness, escorted
By notables and serdyuks, parted
The masses on his raven mare;
And from the Kiev road that minute
There rolled a cart, and seated in it—
All anxious gazes drawn its way—
In it, unmoved by fear or grief,
His soul sustained by firm belief,
There rode the guiltless Kochubey,
And with him Iskra, calm, resigned,
A lamb to sacrifice consigned.

The wagon came to rest. Deep boom
Of chanted orisons arose;
The censers raised a pall of fume;
The people spoke a silent prayer
For the unhappy souls' repose,
The martyrs—for their foes. And there,
They mount . . . Kochubey, on the trestle,
Has knelt and crossed himself, and bowed
Onto the block. The seething crowd
Now freezes, hushed . . . A flashing whistle,
The head leaps off and with a thud
Falls down. The people gasp . . . the second
Comes thumping after as if beckoned.
The grassy knoll is bronzed with blood;
The gloating headsman, nothing loath,
By shocks of hair has gripped them both,
And either hand at arms outspread
Shakes on the crowd a staring head.

This closes the event. Uncaring,
The throngs dissolve and go their way,

Already nonchalantly airing
The timeless topics of each day.
The place of carnage empties quickly.
Then, up that road, still peopled thickly,
Two women struggle through the press,
Way-weary, dust-streaked, stained of dress;
Straight to the square they seem to hurry,
Eyes haunted, desperate with worry.
"You're late," a passing stranger said
And gestured backward with his head
Where in the distance men were knocking
The fateful scaffolding apart,
While cossack lads below were rocking
An oaken coffin up a cart.

    Mazepa, wintry-faced, ahead
Of all his mounted suite had ridden
Away from the beheading, bidden
By an unfathomable dread.
None will approach him, peer or squire,
And not a word he utters there;
All white with lather speeds his mare.
Arrived at home: "Where is Maria?"
Mazepa asks; but what he hears
Sounds wary, vague . . . His soul entire
A prey to unacknowledged fears,
He walks into the rooms assigned her:
Her quiet chamber, though, is bare.
He strides into the park to find her,
Distraught, he wanders everywhere—
The broad lake, shady paths and borders,
All empty, not a trace or clue . . .
She's gone! He summons servants, orders
His nimble serdyuks to pursue;
They leap to it. Their ponies, saddled,
Dance snorting, sidling out, are straddled,
Down the four winds, full-tilt, they race
Amid shrill huzzas of the chase.

The precious moments pass and wane;
None brings Maria back again.
Why she had fled and by what path
Nobody knew or dared have stated.
Mazepa glared in silent wrath;
The household shrank, intimidated.
He locked himself in Mary's room;
Torn between fierce chagrin and gloom,
There he still sat as night was sinking,
Hunched by her bedside, never blinking,
By some unearthly ache undone.
Next morning on their separate courses
The chase came homing one by one.
Of these men—slumped on shambling horses,
Their stirrups, girths and saddlecourses
By creamy lather weirdly frosted,
Blood-beaded, black with sweat, exhausted—
Not one came forward to relate
Words of Maria or her fate.
Forgetful time was swift to smother
Her imprint like a buried leaf
And left her lonely stricken mother
To exiled penury and grief.

CANTO THREE

His soul's perplexity and grief
Do not restrain Ukraina's chief
From furthering his brash ambitions:
His temper merely hardening,
He joins with Sweden's haughty king
In a renewed exchange of missions.
Meanwhile, more surely to disarm
The fangs of untoward suspicions,
He takes to bed—with much alarm
Of febrile tremors and a swarm
Of tutting personal physicians.
"The fruits of passions, toil, and war:
Aches and afflictions never bettered,

The heralds of the end, have fettered
Him to his sickbed. At death's door,
Life's fleeting pageant now forsaking,
He soon would humbly be partaking
Of sacred food..." A priest is led
To act the questionable function;
And lo! mysterious Final Unction
Anoints the guileful silver head.

Time passed—and Muscovy looked out
For her unbidden guests in vain;
Prepared on graves of earlier rout
To solemnize the freshly slain ...
When Charles abruptly turned about
And fell with arms upon Ukraine.

The day has come. Behold the haggard
Old martyr rise again—o wonder!
The piteous wreck who lately staggered
His groaning way to six-feet-under!
Now he is Peter's potent foe;
Now see him, hale and keen-eyed, dashing
Along the squadrons, sabre flashing,
Urge on his fiery steed, and so
Off to where Desna's waters flow.
Just so, decrepit and weighed down,
A crafty cardinal of yore,
Once vested with the triple crown,
Grew straight and whole and young once more.

The word has spread as if on wings,
Through all Ukraine it hoarsely rings:
"He has gone over, has betrayed,
At Sweden's footstool he has laid
The Cossack mace ... " The war-flame rages.
Here breaks the dawn, in blood and fire,
Of internecine war.
                    Who gauges
The Tsar's outraged, imperial ire?[26]

The church-ban thunders in the temples,
Mazepa's effigy is maimed:
In loud debates by free assemblies
A rival Hetman is proclaimed.
Back from the wastes of Yenisey
The exiled kin of Kochubey
And Iskra are brought home, reprieved:
Tsar Peter joins with them in weeping
And renders wry atonement, heaping
New land and rank on the bereaved.
Mazepa's foe, fierce old commander
Of raids, rides up to Peter's standard,
Paléy, from penal exile spared:
Rebellion quakes as if uprooted.
The bold Chechél is executed,[28]
Alike the Zaporozhian laird.
And you, to whom his whole existence
Is armored fame, and helmet—crown:
Your day is near, for in the distance
You see Poltava's bastions frown.

There also sped his adversary,
His forces gathering tempest-like;
The two encampments in the prairie
Kept wily vigil for the strike.
Thus will a warrior of high mettle,
Much mauled in bold engagements past,
With blood-lust drunk before the battle
Confront the chosen foe at last.
And stung, the Northern Lion sees—
No longer bands of refugees
At Narva straggle from the fray,
But gleaming ranks in fighting fettle,
Obedient, firm, adroit in battle,
And bayonets in tight array.

Still he resolved: at dawn we fight.—
The Swedish bivouacs slept, unstirring.
But in a certain tent that night
Two men were eagerly conferring.

"No, no: believe me, Orlik mine,
Too callow visions did we nourish;
Both frail and rash was the design,
We have small hope to see it flourish.
Of its own weight my purpose falls.
Alas ... I made a grievous blunder:
I staked too greatly on this Charles.
He's fiery, brave, a nine-day wonder
Who, brilliant for a month or so,
Is apt to carry all before him;
Who rides to pot-luck with a foe[29]
And greets a bombshell with guffawing;[30]
He will steal up to enemy posts
No worse than cossacks, boldly raiding,
And popping pistols at his hosts,
And bullet-holes for bullets trading;[31]
But he too clearly lacks the weight
To stay that sovereign titan's course;
He would throw back the wheel of fate
As he wheels back a troop of horse;
He is impatient, stiff-necked, blind,
Reckless, and arrogant of mind;
He trusts God knows what star, assesses
The adversary's present strength
But by a past campaign's successes,
And breaks his stubborn neck at length.
I feel ashamed: a gipsy soldier
Contrived to sweep me off my feet;
I have been dazed, though much the older,
By gallantry and self-conceit,
Like some young ninny ... "

ORLIK

Let the war
Decide. Things have not gone so far
As to rule out negotiation.
The wrong is not past reparation;
Defeated in the field, the Tsar
Will not reject conciliation.

MAZEPA

No, it's too late. Past all return
The Tsar and I have been divided.
My course was long ago decided
And irreversibly. I burn
With long-pent hate ... In Peter's quarters,
When at Azóv the Tartar fought us,
We drank one night, before the siege.
The wine leapt sparkling in the beakers,
So did the spirit of the speakers ...
I spoke too boldly for a liege.
The youngsters, mortified, sat gasping;
The Tsar spilt wine and, flushed with rage,
Cursed at me, insolently grasping
My whiskers silvery with age!
By helpless fury stricken dumb,
I swore an oath, and vowed his doom.
This oath I bore as woman's womb
Bears out the child. Its term has come.
Yes, mind my words: he will be fated
To recollect me while he breathes;
For Peter's scourge I was created,
The thorn in his triumphal wreaths.
He'd give old cities, life's most touching,
Most precious moments, just to hold
My pride to ransom, to be clutching
My whiskers, as that night of old.
Meanwhile—we have not yet been humbled!
The dawn will show which must go down.

With this composed himself and slumbered
The traitor to the Russian crown.

In flares of dawn the east is burning.
Along the ridges, down the dales
The cannon growl. With purple churning
The smoke of salvos skyward sails
And drapes the slanting sun in veils.

The squads have closed their ranks and bristle;
Into the brush the marksmen steal;
Bombshells go hurtling, bullets whistle,
All muskets taper to cold steel.
The Swede, long triumph's favored son,
Falls on our trenches at a run;
Swift waves of horse roll off and clash;
The infantry steps out and follows,
Its steady onslaught fills the hollows
And backs the cavalry's mad dash.
The fateful acres thrum and rattle
And blossom out in flares and dust;
But, clear to all, the scales of battle
Already shift to favor us.
The Swedish squadrons, raked by volleys,
Now wallow disarrayed and gored;
Count Rosen yields the narrow gullies,
The fiery Schlippenbach his sword.
And rank on rank we are compressing
The Swede, aground his banner drags;
The god of battle's patent blessing
Is blazoned on our eager flags.

Then Peter's booming voice resounded
Like the Almighty's instrument:
"To work, with God!" And from the tent,
By his close favorites surrounded,
Emerges Peter: living fire
His blazing eyes; his step resilient;
His visage fearsome; he is brilliant,
Embodiment of godly ire.
A war-steed presently is brought;
High-bred, but docile to his weight,
As if it sensed the touch of fate,
The charger shudders; eyes athwart,
It struts amid the dust of battle,
Proud of the hero in its saddle.

A blazing sun—at zenith soon;
The fighting rests, like scythes at noon.

Some cossacks curvet round the flanks.
The squares regroup and dress their ranks.
The music's martial clangor ceases.
From bordering hills the hungry roar
Of spurting cannon sounds no more.
And there! the echoing plain releases
Hurrahs like thunder from afar:
The regiments have seen the Tsar.

He gallops past the troops, and keener
His might and zest than very war.
His eyes devour the hushed arena,
And thronged about him in the fore
You see that brood of Peter's eyrie:
Those who in travail long and weary,
In toil of empire and armed strife,
Were sons and comrades of his life.
There's Sheremétev, noble earl,
There's Bruce, and Baur, and Repnin,
And he, low-born but fortune's pearl,
Half chancellor, half sovereign.*

Before the blue and silver glitter
Of his batallions poised for war,
Borne motionless upon a litter
By faithful servants, pallid, sore
From recent wounds, emerged King Charles,
And after him his premier jarls.
He paused there, silent, deep in thought.
His eye was dim, as if he fought
Some lately felt unease that vexed him;
It seemed, the issue he had sought
To take to battle now perplexed him . . .
Abruptly, with a languid sign,
He launched his troops against our line.

*This restrained reference is to Peter's powerful and corrupt boon companion and marshal, A. D. Menshikov (1673-1729). He excelled in penal expeditions and campaigns of extermination and had just massacred the entire civilian population of Baturyn, Mazepa's capital.

And in mid-plain, 'mid swirls of powder
Those armies clashed; and ever louder
The battle raged—Poltava Day!
The fiery hail of musket balls
Deflected by those living walls,
As falling ranks to fresh give way,
They lock bare steel. Like flying thunder
Black clouds of horsemen fan asunder,
With clang of curb and sword attack,
Collide with crashing, swing and hack;
And, flinging corpses heap on heap,
Hot balls of iron hurtle, leap
Into the stumbling ranks and thud,
And plough the ground and hiss in blood.
Swede, Russian—stabbing, splitting, slashing,
Commingled uproars, drumbeats clashing,
Groans, hoofbeats, neighing, cannon's boom,
And universal death and doom.

Amidst the martial din and riot
The war lords, in that inner quiet
Where skill and inspiration merge,
Watch the formations wheel and surge
And augur victory and ruin,
Their placid colloquies pursuing.
But near the Tsar of Muscovy
What white-maned warrior there? Supported
By cossack lads, his ardor thwarted,
Aflame with noble jealousy?
With an old hero's keen devotion
He scans the war-game's every motion;
No more for him to leap astride,
From exile orphaned now and sere:
No longer will the cossacks hear
Paley's loud summons far and wide!
But why are his old eyes afire?
Why like the shades of night does ire
Becloud his rugged features now?
What furrows on his noble brow?

Has he espied through smoke and dust
His foe Mazepa and had cause
To hate his age with fresh disgust,
Stripped bare of arms as now he was?

    Mazepa gazed in deep abstraction
At the vicissitudes of action
Amidst insurgent countrymen,
His serdyuks, councillors, and kin.
Close by, a shot. Mazepa, turning,
Saw Voynarovsky with—most strange—
A musket still in smoke; and, squirming
In a red pool, shot a close range,
A cossack brave; nearby, an idle
Sweat-blackened horse, swift to careen,
Rid of the wonted weight and bridle,
Into the lurid battle scene.
All that grim day the youth had hunted
The Hetman down, a murderous glare
Hot in his eyes, his sabre bare.
Now the old man rode up and wanted
To question him: he scarce could raise
His eye, but his congealing gaze
Still threatened Russia's adversary,
As color drained from him in death:
And the caressing name of Mary
Was heard to fade upon his breath.
But triumph's near, hurrahs are shouted:
We've broken through; the Swede is routed!
O wondrous hour! O glorious sight!
One onrush more brings headlong flight.[32]
The cavalry pelts off, pursuing,
Swords dull with slaughter, and the chewing
Of death lies black upon the field
Like locusts on a summer's yield.

    Exultant Peter—proud, vivacious,
His eyes aglow with martial fame.
And his triumphal fête is gracious:

Amidst the cheering troop's acclaim
He bids the lords beneath his scepters,
Both Swede and Russian, to his tent;
And gaily mingling prey and captors
Lifts high his cup in compliment
To the good health of his "preceptors."

But where's our foremost, fiercest coach?
Surely the first to be invited,
Whose last and cruelest approach
The victor of Poltava blighted?
And where's Mazepa, fiend unblest?
Where did the Judas flee his dreaded
Deserts? Where is the royal guest?
Why is the traitor not beheaded?[33]

Across the steppeland lone and bare
Hetman and King, two homeless rangers,
Are speeding. Fate has yoked the pair.
His hot chagrin, his pressing dangers
Combine to steel the royal heart.
Deep though his wound, it feels no part
Of him as, straining in the saddle,
He flees the Russians, head inclined,
And puts his servants' faithful huddle
In fear of being left behind.

The steppeland's limitless horizon
With keen-eyed scrutiny comprising,
His álly flanks the King in flight.
Ahead, a manor . . . At the sight
Mazepa sets his mare to charging
Like one who sees some evil elf,
As if to put a safer margin
Between that manor and himself.
This park, unwalled now at the fringes,
That orphaned house, forlorn estate,
The portals swinging on their hinges—
Have they some story to relate?

Ah—did you, profligate, debaucher,
Flinch as you saw the gate, the orchard,
The mansion, once a happy house,
Where often, genial and heated,
By happy host-folk kindly treated,
You used to banter and carouse?
You recognized the lovely parklands
The artless angel dwelt amid,
The garden whence she was in darkness
Borne off by you? . . . You did, you did!

Hid in the cloven bank of Dnieper,
As shadows on the steppes grow deep,
The foes of Peter's Rus, Mazepa
And Charles, have briefly paused for sleep.
The hero's soul indeed found easement,
Forgot Poltava dared and lost;
Mazepa muttered, though, and tossed,
His night of spirit past appeasement.
Abruptly in the brooding gloom
His name was called; he started, shifted,
Then, waking, saw a figure loom
Bent over him, a fist uplifted.
He cringed, as from the axe of doom:
Lank hair disheveled all and scattered,
Sunk eyes aglitter, garments tattered,
There stood before him, pale and lean,
A shape of mist and lunar sheen . . .
"No . . . am I dreaming? Is it . . . Mary?"

MARIA

No, quiet, hush! keep quiet, dear;
Father and Mother have just barely
Dropped off to sleep, they still may hear.

MAZEPA

Maria! Oh . . . unhappy Mary!
Come to your senses! Some strange spell . . .

MARIA

O listen! What weird tales they carry!
You know the kind of thing they tell?
She gave it out ("hush, child," she told me)
That my poor father was . . .was dead.
And, very secretly, she showed me,
God save us all! A greying head . . .
Where can we run from evil tongues?
And do you know, that head the woman
Was showing wasn't even human,
But like a wolf's . . . like that: with fangs!
It was to fool me, like . . . a joke.
It's wicked to tell lies to folk.
And why? So that I would take fright
And not run off with you to-night!
It is not right.

       In rueful horror
Her flinty lover heard her sorrow.
Still prey to wild imaginings,
She mused: "And yet—such foolish things—
I do recall a square . . . some pageant;
And crowds, and corpses lying there.
Yes—Mother took me to that fair.
But where were you? Why are we parted,
Why do I haunt the night, the dead?
Time to go home, the day has started;
Come quickly . . . Oh: I see my head
Is full of empty noise and bother . . .
Old man, I took you for another,
I know that now. No—I must go!
Your gaze is wry, your warmth pretended;
Why, you are loathesome . . . He is splendid!
His eyes have such a loving glow,
His words are tender, to be trusted;
His whiskers are as white as snow,
But yours . . . yours are . . . all blood-encrusted! . . . "

She gave a strident peal of laughter
And, nimbler than a hind in flight,
Jumped up, and as he started after,
Had vanished in the depth of night.

The shadows thinned. The east grew red.
The cossack campfire flickered, spread.
The cossacks poured the wheaten gruel,
While servants, down the river's course,
Watered the mounts and gathered fuel.
King Charles awakened. "Ho! to horse!
Mazepa, rise! The mists are thawing."
The Hetman, though, has been awake
Long since. Despair is gnawing, gnawing
His heart, his breathing choked with ache,
He mounts, and rides unspeaking, bitter,
Beside the King; his eyes beneath
Their rank tufts make a fearsome glitter
As he forsakes his native heath.

A hundred years have passed since then—
What now remains of those proud men,
So strong of licence and of lust?
Their generation turned to dust,
And dust has claimed the bloody spoils
Of passions, victories, and toils.
Of all the names which shone and went,
The annals of our iron era
Have raised but you, Poltava's hero,
Upon a timeless monument.
Down where a flock of windmills girds
Bendéry's slopes in peaceful rows,
Where soldiers' graves are ringed by herds
Of thick-horned water buffaloes,
The remnant of a dwelling, sherds
Of masonry and crumbling plaster,
And, overgrown by mossy weed,
Three stairs half-buried in the pasture
Bear witness to the royal Swede.
For standing there, the highly strung

Daredevil with his handful flung
The charging Turk aback and cast
His sword beneath the horsetail mast.
But vainly would you seek to trace
The Hetman's final resting-place:
Mazepa's name has long been dead!
At high cathedral service merely
His solemn ban is thundered yearly
And wakens echoes hoarse and dread.
Yet folk remember reverently
Where in the boneyard of the just
The pious brethren bedded gently
Two suffering martyrs' holy dust.
Dikanka* shows an ancient lane
Of murmuring oaks, by mourners planted;
To this day they have gravely chanted
To grandsons of the wrongly slain.
The guilty maid, though, these narrations
Omit. Her sin, her tribulations,
Her wanderings in mortal pain,
Of these tradition offers barely
A distant echo. Only rarely
Might some blind singer of the plains
The youthful cossack maids regale,
And strumming on the village common
One of the Hetman's chanties, summon
The errant maiden and her tale.

*Kochubey's hamlet and estate.

PUSHKIN'S NOTES TO *POLTAVA*

1. Vasily Leontevich Kochubey, judge-general, one of the ancestors of the present-day counts.

2. Khutor: a villa.

3. Kochubey had several daughters; one of them was married to Obidovsky, nephew to Mazepa. The one mentioned here was named Matrena.

4. Mazepa did indeed sue for his goddaughter's hand, but was refused.

5. Tradition attributes to Mazepa a number of songs which popular memory has preserved to this day. Kochubey in his denunciation likewise mentions a patriotic ballad allegedly composed by Mazepa. It is remarkable not merely in a historical sense.

6. Horsetail standard and mace are the emblems of the Hetman's office.

7. Cf. Byron's "Mazeppa."

8. Doroshenko, one of the heroes of ancient Little Russia, an implacable foe of Russian overlordship.

9. Grigory Samoilovich, son of the Hetman exiled to Siberia at the start of Peter I's reign.

10. Simeon Paley, Colonel of Khvastov, a famous raider. Upon Mazepa's complaints over his unauthorized incursions he was exiled to Eliseisk. When the former was revealed to be a traitor, Paley as his inveterate enemy was duly recalled from exile and was present at the Battle of Poltava.

11. Kostia Gordeenko, tribal ataman of the Zaporozhe Cossacks. Subsequently he went over to Charles XII. He was captured and executed in 1708.

12. 20,000 Cossacks had been sent to Livonia.

13. Mazepa in a letter takes Kochubey to task for being dominated by his "proud and highminded" wife.

14. Iskra, Colonel of Poltava, Kochubey's comrade, who was his intimate and shared his fate.

15. The Jesuit Zalensky, Princess Dul'skaya, and a certain Bulgarian archbishop exiled from his country were the chief agents of Mazepa's treason plot. The last-named, in the guise of a beggar, traveled between Poland and the Ukraine.

16. "Universals"—the term for a Hetman's general proclamations.

17. Philipp Orlik, Secretary-General, Mazepa's intimate, after the latter's death (in 1710) received from Charles XII the empty title of Hetman of Little Russia. He subsequently embraced the Moslem religion and died at Bendery about 1736.

18. Bulavin, a Don Cossack, who led an insurrection about this period.

19. The Privy Secretary Shafirov and Count Golovkin, friends and patrons of Mazepa; at their door should by rights be laid the horror of the informers' sentencing and execution.

20. In 1705; cf. the notes to Bantysh-Kamensky's *History of Little Russia*.

21. At the time of the abortive Crimean campaign Kazy-Girey had proposed Mazepa's making common cause with him in attacking the Russian army.

22. In his letters he complained that the informers had been tortured too mildly, insistently demanded their execution, and compared himself with innocent Susanna, slandered by the profligate elders, and Count Golovkin with the prophet Daniel.

23. Kochubey's village, Dikanka.

24. Already sentenced to death, Kochubey was tortured at the Hetman's military headquarters. The unfortunate man's answers show that he was interrogated about treasures he had hidden.

25. Troops maintained by the Hetmans personally.

26. The strong measures taken by Peter with his customary despatch and energy kept the Ukraine from defection.

"On the 7th of November, 1708, by Imperial decree, the Cossacks according to their custom in free ballot elected as Hetman the Colonel of Starodub, Ivan Skoropadsky. On the 8th there arrived in Glukhov the Archbishops of Kiev, Chernigov, and Pereiaslav.

And on the 9th these prelates publicly pronouned the Church ban over Mazepa; the same day the effigy (a puppet) of the same traitor Mazepa was carried forth and, the insigne of the order that had been fastened on it with its ribbon having been taken off, delivered to the hands of the executioner; who attached a rope to it and dragged it down the street and through the square right to the gallows, and hanged it there. And at Glukhov on the 10th were executed Chechel and the rest of the traitors . . ." (Peter the Great's Diary).

27. A Little-Russian word. In Russian: executioner. (Translator's note: the word is Polish; "Little-Russian" is the Russocentric name for Ukrainian.)

28. Chechel put up a desperate defense of Baturin against Prince Menshikov's troops.

29. To King August at Dresden; see Voltaire, *Histoire de Charles XII.*

30. Oh, Your Majesty! a shell! "What has a shell to do with the letter that is being dictated to you? Write!" This happened much later.

31. At night, Charles on personal reconnaissance of our camp attacked some Cossacks sitting by a fire. He charged them point-blank and shot one of them with his own hands. The Cossacks fired three shots after him, severely wounding him in the foot.

32. Thanks to the excellent dispositions and actions of Prince Menshikov the outcome of the main battle was a foregone conclusion. The action lasted less than two hours. "For," as *Peter the Great's Diary* has it, "the invincible Swedish gentlemen soon took to their heels, and the entire enemy army was totally shattered." Peter in times to come would forgive Danilych [Menshikov's patronymic—used in disparaging or condescending address only; tr.] a great deal on account of the services rendered that day by General Prince Menshikov.

33. L'Empereur Moscovite, pénétré d'une joie qu'il ne se mettait pas en peine de dissimuler (there was good reason for rejoicing) recevait sur le champ de bataille les prisonniers qu'on lui amenait en foule et demandait à tout moment; ou est donc mon frère Charles? . . . Alors prenant un verre de vin: A la santé, dit-il, de mes maîtres dans l'art de la guerre!—Renschild lui demanda: qui étaient ceux qu'il honorait d'un si beau titre.—Vous, messieurs, les généraux Suédois, reprit le Czar.—Votre Majesté est donc bien ingrate, reprit le Comte, d'avoir tant maltraité ses maîtres.

34. The headless bodies of Iskra and Kochubey were delivered to their relatives and buried in the Kiev monastery; the following inscription was carved on their gravestone:

"O passer-by who dost not know of us,
Who have been laid to rest eternal here,
Bid surcease unto suffering and death;
And tell this stone to sing to thee of us,
And how for truth and faith to Sovereign
We drained the cup of agony and death,
True to the last, Mazepa's victims we;
And having been cut down by axe to head,
Repose here now with Mary, Mother and Queen.

In the year 1708, on the 15th day of July, the noble Vasily Kochubey, Judge-General, [and] Ioann Iskra, Colonel of Poltava, were beheaded at military headquarters at Borshchagovets and Kovshevo near Bela Tserkov. Their bodies were brought to Kiev on July 17 and buried the same day here in the holy Monastery of the Caves."

TSAR SALTAN: INTRODUCTION

Tsar Saltan was written in the summer of 1831 during Pushkin's honeymoon at Tsarskoe Selo. It is both the largest and the finest example of Pushkin's experimentation with an essentially new genre, the folk tale closely following authentic plots but artistically transformed with varying degrees of metric elaboration.

The traditional *skazka* is a folk tale typically containing elements of fantastic adventure, burlesque, and supernatural intervention, and is often placed in a setting of courts and knights and wise men, peasants, sprites, and wizards. Pushkin's mind was saturated from childhood with samples of this ancient oral form. During his confinement at Mikhailovskoe near Pskov (1824-26) at the height of the European romantic revival of folk values and the legendary past, while in the close daily company of his old nurse, Arina Rodionovna, the poetic potential of the *skazka* struck him with renewed force, and he wrote down the plots of several tales from her dictation. The vehicle of the *skazka* was prose, marked by much formulaic material, recurrent epithets, and the kind of cozy repetitiousness demanded by the audience of oral literature; or non-tonic syllabic verse of variable line lengths and occasional use of rhyme. Pushkin employed the second vehicle in several of his own exercises in this genre in the early thirties; but in his most brilliant successes, *Tsar Saltan* and *The Golden Cockerel*, the fable is transposed into rhymed trochaic tetrameters of a gracefully stylized naïveté that is uniquely Pushkinian. The pregnant simplicity and subdued *espièglerie* of the diction partakes of the charms of both fairy tale and puppet play, and the combination of succinctness in detail and leisurely narrative pace contributes to an overall effect that is delightfully sophisticated and wholly original—a note last heard in that highly complex blend of classical European and native elements, Pushkin's early *opus mirabile, Ruslan and Liudmila* (1820). The harmonious permutations of the triple-structured plot are like a Mozartian dance suite in verse; and the whole is suffused with the luminous freshness, the pomp and gaiety in miniature of which a glimpse can be caught, in yet another medium of art, on the best of the Palekh lacquer boxes.

Prince Mirsky, the foremost admirer of Pushkin's folk tales among his critics, characterized them as follows in his biography:[1]

The charm of these tales lies in their beautiful consistency of style and fairy-tale logic, and in their absolute freedom from "meaning." They are pure creations out of a given material—things of beauty. Their peculiarity is that in making these things Pushkin did not make his personal and traditional tastes the criterion of their beauty, but subordinated their composition to the inherent laws discovered by him in the possibilities of the given folk tales. This is why, perhaps, after all, in spite of the argument being "borrowed," they are the most purely creative of Pushkin's works. The making of these stories was the making of a world obeying its own immanent laws and independent of this world of ours. The beautiful and logical consistency of these laws may be regarded as Pushkin's highest achievement and his greatest claim to poetical preeminence, and *King Saltan* and *The Golden Cockerel* as his most perfect creations. It is just because of the absence in it of all "human significance" that *King Saltan* is the most universally human of Pushkin's works. For it is pure form, and as accessible to all who understand Russian as pure ornament is to all those who have eyes. The child (I speak from personal experience) is as admiringly absorbed in the process of narration and in the flow of rhyme as is the sophisticated critic in the marvelous flawlessness of the workmanship and consistency of the "style." *King Saltan* is the only one of the three tales which quite answers to the definition of pure formal perfection. *The Golden Cockerel* is also full of charm, but it has a sting of irony in it, which enhances its intellectual, but perhaps diminishes its universal, appeal . . .

In his classic *A History of Russian Literature,*[2] Mirsky goes even further:

The longer one lives, the more one is inclined to regard *King Saltan* as the masterpiece of Russian poetry. It is purest art, free from all the irrelevancies of emotion and symbol, "a thing of beauty" and "a joy for ever.". . .It requires no understanding; its reception is immediate, direct, unquestionable. It is not frivolous, nor witty, nor humorous. But it is light, exhilarating, bracing. It has high seriousness, for what can be more highly serious than the creation of a world of perfect beauty and freedom, open to all?

I fully realize that the claim for *King Saltan* to be accepted as *the* masterpiece of Pushkin has little chance of getting a majority of votes. Such a majority is virtually pledged to the last great narrative poem of Pushkin— *The Bronze Horseman* . . . This poem certainly has very substantial claims to absolute preeminence. There is no conception of poetic greatness from the standpoint of which this preeminence could be challenged, except that (hypothetic) standpoint which would demand of all poetry that it be as free from human irrelevancies as is *King Saltan* . . .

THE TALE OF TSAR SALTAN, OF HIS SON, RENOWNED AND MIGHTY PRINCE GUIDON SALTANOVICH, AND OF THE FAIREST PRINCESS SWAN

Three young maidens sat one night
Spinning in the window-bight.
"If I were the Tsar's elected,"
One of these young maids reflected,
"I would spread a festive board
For all children of the Lord."
"If I were the Tsar's elected,"
Her young sister interjected,
"I'd weave linen cloth to spare
For all people everywhere."
"Had I been the Tsar's elected,"
Said the third, "I'd have expected
Soon to bear our father Tsar
A young hero famed afar."

Scarcely had she finished speaking,
When the door was softly creaking,
And the Tsar himself came in,
That whole country's sovereign.
He had heard behind the shuttered
Window every word they uttered,
And the third young sister's boast
Suited him by far the most.
"Fair my maid, your wish is answered,"
Said he, "you shall be my consort,
And by late September see
That you bear that prince for me.
As for you, good sisters, mind you
Leave this chamber, I consign you
To my retinue, and there
Serve me and your sister fair:
Serve us, one at weaving, stitching,
And the other in the kitchen."

Spoke and strode into the hall;
Off to court went one and all.
Soon to war the Tsar was heading,
That same night ordained the wedding
And was at the banquet seen
Seated with his youthful queen.
Then selected worthies led them
To their ivory couch to bed them,
And with ceremony due
Laid them down there and withdrew.
But the palace cook is grieving,
And the weaver weeps a-weaving,
Smarting both with envy keen
Of their sister, now their queen;
While our freshly purpled beauty,
Eager to discharge her duty,
That first night conceived an heir.

But the Tsar must leave her there.
On his goodly charger starting,
Tsar Saltan bade her at parting
Take good care, and not alone
For her sake but for his own.
While he leads his lusty yeomen
Fiercely battling far-off foemen,
God bestows on her the joy
Of an ell-long baby boy.
Perched above her offspring, regal,
Proudly like a mother eagle,
She sends off an envoy far
With a note to cheer the Tsar.
But the palace cook and seamstress,
Babarikha too, the schemestress,
Their perfidious plot all hatched,
Have the courier trailed and snatched.
In his place they send another
With false witness to their brother,
Saying that the Tsar had won
Neither daughter, neither son,

Nor of mouse or frog a litter,
But some quite unheard-of critter.

But the Father Tsar, apprised
Of the message thus devised,
Started raising blood and thunder,
Ready to string up the runner;
But, his fury once allayed,
He had this decree conveyed;
"Let the Tsar's return be waited
And the case adjudicated."

Off the envoy with this writ,
And at length returns with it.
But the palace cook and seamstress
Babarikha too, the schemestress,
Intercept the Tsar's command,
Lard the lad with liquor, and
In his empty pouch of leather
Slip another altogether;
So that day the fuddled slouch
Pulls this order from his pouch:
"Let the Tsar's decree be heeded:
With no more delay than needed,
Be the Queen and what she bore
Cast into the ocean's maw."

Powerless at this disaster
To the Empress and their Master,
All the nobles in dismay
Pressed into her room to say
What the Tsar's command was suing
For her son's and her undoing.
Orders duly read and seen,
They encased the prince and queen
In a keg at once brought forward,
Tarred it up and rolled it shoreward
And committed it to sea,
As by Tsar Saltan's decree.

Dark-blue skies and starlets flashing,
Dark-blue sea and wavelets plashing,
Cloud across the heaven slides,
Keg across the ocean glides.
Like a widow all bedraggled
In it wept the queen and struggled,
While the babe grew more, you'd say,
By the hour than by the day.
Gone the day, the queen is crying,
Pleads the babe, the rollers hying:
"Wave, my wave, I beg of thee,
Ever ranging, ever free,
Foaming far in feckless motion,
Rolling rocks beneath the ocean,
Coursing up the coastal crest,
Heaving hulks upon thy breast—
Do not let us perish, save us,
Up onto the mainland wave us!"
And the wave at once obeyed it,
Bore the barrel hence and laid it
(oh, so lightly and intently)
On the shore and ebbed off gently.
Queen and babe had safely reached
Land, the keg was firmly beached.
From the keg, though, who will see them?
Surely God alone may free them?
Up on tippy-toes the babe
Braced himself against a stave,
On the bottom bore a trifle
With his head, said: "Lest we stifle,
Why not break a window cleft?"
Burst the bottom out and left.

Free are now both son and mother,
See a mound across the heather,
All about, the dark-blue sea,
On the mound a green oak tree.
Son thought: solid food would beckon
To the two of us, I reckon.

From the oak a branch he breaks,
And a sturdy bow he makes,
Off his cross the silk he wrings it,
To the oaken bow he strings it;
Breaks a twiglet off a joint,
Fines it to an arrow point,
And goes down the yonder lea-side
Seeking game along the seaside.

    Barely as the shore he nears,
Something like a moan he hears . . .
He perceives the sea unquiet,
Looks, and sees some evil riot:
'Mid the waves a swan's astir
And a kite hangs over her;
Wildly that poor bird is thrashing,
All the sea churned up and splashing . . .
That one has its talons spread,
Bloody beak all sharp and red . . .
Twang! the arrow sang and whistled,
In the crop it struck and bristled—
Bow at ease he stood; the kite
Stained with blood the breakers bright;
Down it plunges, plumes asunder,
Groans unbirdlike going under;
Swimming shoreward sails the swan,
And the foul kite pecks upon,
And his near perdition speeding,
Wings him hard and drowns him bleeding.
Then unto the Tsarevich
In the Russian tongue she speaks:
"Prince, you are my potent savior,
My redeemer, no one braver!
Pine not lest you, lost my meat,
Have three days no food to eat,
Or no arrow on the morrow:
All this sorrow—is no sorrow.
Your high service I will earn,
And will serve you in my turn:
Not a swan-bird's rescue, know you,

But a maiden's life I owe you,
Not a kite you brought to earth,
Killed a warlock; of your worth
Never henceforth need remind me,
Ever by your side you'll find me.
Now then, let all sorrow cease,
Turn again and sleep in peace."

As the swan-bird soared to nesting,
Queen and prince, intent on resting
From the weary day they spent,
Settled and to slumber went.
On the morn the prince, awaking
And nocturnal visions shaking,
Marveled to behold ahead
A prodigious city spread,
Walls with crenellated arches,
Snowy bastions topped with churches,
Dazzling domes to heaven soar,
Holy monasteries galore.
"See what's there!" he wakes his mother,
She cries one Oh, then another,
"I can tell, my snowy bird
Is already well bestirred."
For the city making straightway,
Hardly have they passed the gateway,
Bells a-tolling peal tattoo
Fairly deafening our two;
Townsfolk throng to meet them, choirs
Sing Te Deums from the spires;
Gorgeous trains of courtiers wait,
Each in golden coach of state;
Every voice exalts them loudly,
And the prince is crested proudly
With a ducal diadem
As the sovereign over them.
With the Queen's consent attested,
There and then he is invested,
In his capital installed,

Duke Guidón[1] henceforward called.

Seawind saunters there and thither,
Drives a little vessel hither,
Bowling down the ocean trail,
Tautly bulging every sail.
All the sailormen a-sailing
Crowd amazed against her railing,
On the well-known isle they sight
Marvels in the noonday light:
A new city gold-enweltered,
Pier by sturdy barrier sheltered,
Cannon firing from the pier
To command a landing here.
As they fetch the mooring station,
Comes a ducal invitation,
They are furnished drink and food
And for course and parley sued:
"Guests, what goods may you be bearing,
Whither are you further faring?"
And the sailormen speak out:
"We have sailed the world about,
Fur of sable held our boxes,
Likewise coal-and-russet foxes;
Past the island of Buyan,
Feal to famous Tsar Saltan,
We are bound on eastward bearing,
For accomplished is our faring . . ."
Duke Guidon dismissed them then:
"Make in safety, gentlemen,
Down the ocean-sea your passage,
Carry Tsar Saltan a message,
Say I send my compliments."
Visitors despatched, the Prince
From the coast with spirit ailing
Follows far their distant sailing;
Lo! on drifting swells offshore
Swims the snowy swan once more.
"Hail, fair Prince! But why beclouded,
Like a rain-day still and shrouded?"

She addressed the royal lad,
"Has some sorrow turned you sad?"
Bleakly said the Duke, replying,
"Sadness-sorrow sends me sighing,
Eats my dauntless heart entire:
I so long to see my sire."
Swan to Prince: "So that's your worry!
Listen, would you care to hurry
Where that sloop is out at sea?
Then, my Prince, a gnat shalt be."
And she set her pinions flashing,
Whipped the water, sent it splashing
Over him from tip to toe.
And as he was standing so,
Faster than an eyelid's blinking
To a gnat she had him shrinking;
Off he flew with piping shrill,
Caught the sloop a-sailing still,
And discreetly downward gliding,
Found a crack and went in hiding.

Seawind blows a merry clip,
Merrily sails on the ship;
Past Buyan her passage gaining,
Where the famed Saltan is reigning,
They already sight the shore
Of the land they're destined for.
As they anchor in the shallows
They are summoned to the palace;
So they take the castle route;
Our bold lad flies in pursuit.
Tsar Saltan, all gold-ensheeted,
In his hall of state is seated
On his throne and in his crown,
Pensive sorrow in his frown.
But the palace cook and seamstress,
Babarikha too, the schemestress,
Near the Tsar have found a place
And sit gazing at his face.

Tsar Saltan commands them treated,
At his very table seated:
"Ho," he asks them, "Merchant Guests,
Long your voyage? Far your rest?
Are things sound abroad or parlous,
Can you tell us any marvels?"
"Everything is fairly sound there,
Here's a marvel we have found there:
Lay an island steep and bald,
All unpeopled and unwalled,
Plain and bare from crest to shingle,
On it grew an oak tree single;
Now upon this island dwell
A new town and citadel,
Rich in churches golden-headed,
Donjon chambers green-embedded,
Duke Guidon, their ruling prince,
Bade us bring you compliments."
Says Saltan: "If God will spare me,
To that island I will fare me,
Land upon that magic coast,
Duke Guidon will be my host."
But the palace cook and seamstress,
Babarikha too, the schemestress,
Do not wish to let him fare
To that isle of wonders there.
"I declare, astounding, brothers,"
Winking slyly at the others,
Sneers the palace cook, "dear me!
There's a city by the sea!
Here's a marvel, by Saint Cyril:
Wildwood spruce, beneath, a squirrel,
Squirrel sings a song and struts
Pawing, gnawing hazel nuts,
Not plain nuts he puts his paws on,
Golden shells the squirrel gnaws on,
Kernels of pure emerald:
Such are truly marvels called!"
Harks the Tsar with bated breathing,
But the gnat is seething, seething . . .

Swoops and sinks his stinger sly
Straight into his aunt's right eye.
Cook half fainted, turning white;
And that eye had lost its sight.
Servants, sister, and the shrew
Hunt the gnat with view-halloo:
"Oh, you thrice-accursed mosquito,
Just you wait!" He poohs their veto,
By the open window free
Homeward soars across the sea.

And again in restless motion
Scans the Duke the dark-blue ocean;
Lo! on drifting swells offshore
Swims the snow-white swan once more.
"Hail, fair Prince! But why beclouded,
Like drear day becalmed and shrouded?"
She addressed the royal lad,
"Has some sorrow made you sad?"
Said Guidon the Duke, replying,
"Sadness-sorrow sends me sighing,
There's a fabled fairy thing,
I should like to find and bring:
Lives a squirrel in the wildwood,
Magic past all dreams of childhood,
He sings songs, they say, and struts
Pawing, gnawing hazel nuts,
Not plain nuts he puts his paws on,
Golden shells the squirrel gnaws on,
Shells of gold with emerald core;
Folk, of course, have fibbed before."
"No," the swan assured the youthful
Prince, "that squirrel tale is truthful,
I have known of it long since;
Do not pine, my dearest Prince,
I will gladly give you token
Of our fellowship unbroken."
Cheered, the Duke betook him then
Back to his abode again.

For his central courtyard heading,
Lo! he sees a spruce a-spreading,
Squirrel nibbling 'neath the tree
Nuts of gold for all to see,
Little emerald cores extracting,
And the golden husks collecting
Neatly each upon its pile,
Whistling them this song the while,
To the good folk in the courtyard:
"In the garden, in the orchard."
"Well, I thank you," Duke Guidon
Said in wonder, looking on,
"Swan like none, may God be giving
You such joy as I am living."
Straightway for his squirrel sage
Built a crystal squirrel cage,
Put a watch on it unsleeping,
Set a deacon strictly keeping
Count of gems, and gold beside,
Prince's profit, squirrel's pride.

Seawind roaming there and thither
Blows a little vessel hither,
Bowling down the ocean swell,
All her canvas drawing well,
Past the craggy island fastness,
Past the wonder city's vastness:
Cannon firing from the pier
Bid the ship to anchor here.
As they fetch the mooring station,
Comes a ducal invitation;
They are served both drink and food,
And for course and converse sued:
"Guests, what goods may you be bearing,
Whither are you further faring?"
And the sailormen speak out:
"We have sailed the world about,
Trading steeds, both foal and filly,
Ponies from the Donland hilly,
Done our stint, it's homeward ho—

But we still have far to go:
Past Buyan the island sailing,
Tsar Saltan's dominions hailing..."
Duke Guidon addressed them then:
"Make in safety, gentlemen,
Down the ocean-sea your passage,
Carry Tsar Saltan a message,
Tell him Duke Guidon afar
Sends his duty to the Tsar."

Then the guests, farewells accorded,
Sought their ship and went aboard it.
For the shore makes Duke Guidon,
In the surf he spies the swan.
Pleads the Duke, his spirit yearning,
All with ache and anguish burning...
Swam the swan again ashore,
Splashed him soundly as before,
To a little housefly shrinking,
He flew off and, downward sinking,
Twixt the sea and sky on deck,
Tucked himself into a crack.

Seawind blows a merry clip,
Merrily sails on the ship;
Past Buyan her passage gaining,
Where the famed Saltan is reigning,
They already sight the shore
Of the land they're destined for.
As they anchor off the commons,
They receive a royal summons,
So they take the castle route;
Our bold lad flies in pursuit.
Tsar Saltan, all gold-ensheeted,
In his hall of state is seated
On his throne and in his crown,
Sorrow in his pensive frown.
But the one-eyed cook, the weaver,
And their gossip Babarikha,

Sit like angry toads not far
From the footstool of the Tsar.
By command the guests are greeted,
At the Tsar's own table seated;
"Ho," he asks them, "Merchant guests,
Long your voyage? Far from rest?
Are things sound abroad or parlous,
Can you tell us any marvels?"
So the sailormen speak out:
"We have sailed the world about,
Life is fair enough out yonder,
While abroad we saw this wonder:
There's an isle at sea out there,
On the isle a city fair,
Rich in churches golden-headed,
Donjon chambers green-embedded;
And a spruce tree shades the tower,
Underneath, a crystal bower;
In it lives a well-trained squirrel,
Nay, a wizard, by Saint Cyril!
Squirrel sings a song and struts
Pawing, gnawing hazel nuts,
Not plain nuts he puts his paws on,
Golden shells the squirrel gnaws on,
Emerald is every nut;
Servants guard the squirrel's hut,
Serve in sundry ways to suit it;
They make officers salute it,
Have a clerk for nothing but
Keeping tally of each nut;
Then the golden shells as nuggets
Go to mint and leave as ducats;
Maidens sift the emerald hoard
In a strong room to be stored.
On this isle they live in plenty,
All have mansions, never a shanty;
Duke Guidon, their reigning prince,
Bade us give you compliments."
Marvels Tsar Saltan: "So spare me,
To that island I will fare me,

Land upon that magic coast,
Duke Guidon shall be my host."
But the palace cook and seamstress,
Babarikha too, the schemestress,
Do not wish to let him fare
To that isle of wonders there.
Says the seamstress to His Highness,
Wreathed in sneering smirks and slyness;
"There's a squirrel—true or not—
Gnawing little stones—so what?
Nuggets out of nutshells making,
Little mounds of emerald raking,
This won't make us throw a fit,
Even if there's truth in it.
Here's what counts as marvel for me:
Where the ocean wild and stormy
Seethes up high with hiss and roar,
Foaming up an empty shore
And in rushing runs recoiling—
Rise from out the backwash boiling
Thirty-three young giants tall,
Bold of spirit one and all,
Comely heroes thrice eleven,
Mail aglow like blaze of heaven,
Muster-matched, and in the fore
Their old sword-coach,[2] Chernomor.
Talk of wonders, this one surely
Makes all others come off poorly!"
Mum, the prudent guests prefer
Not to bandy words with her;
Harks the Tsar with bated breathing,
But Guidon is seething, seething . . .
Up and with a buzzing cry
Lights upon his aunt's left eye.
And the weaver, turning white,
"Ai," One eye had lost its sight.
"Catch it, catch it," cried the lot,
"Snatch the sting-fly, snatch and swat,
Stay right there, hold still a little . . ."

But Guidon the Fly won't fiddle,
By the open window he
Soars back home across the sea.

    And the Duke in restless motion
Strides and scans the dark-blue ocean . . .
Lo! on drifting swells offshore
Swims the snowy swan once more.
"Hail, fair Prince! But why beclouded,
Silent like a rain-day shrouded?
Has some sorrow made you sad?"
She addressed the royal lad.
Said Guidon the Duke, replying,
"Sadness-sorrow sends me sighing,
Prodigies to overwhelm
I would bring into my realm."
"Pray, what portent brings such luster?"
"Somewhere there's a storm abluster,
Ocean breakers howl and roar
Foaming up a desert shore,
Back in rushing run recoiling,
Leaving in their backwash boiling
Thirty-three young giants tall,
Bold and mettlesome withal,
Comely heroes thrice eleven,
Mail aglow like blaze of heaven,
Muster-matched, and in the fore
Their old sword-coach, Chernomor."
Then the swan responded saying:
"So it's this you find dismaying!
Do not pine, my dearest Prince,
I have known of this long since.
Yonder sea-knights are no others
But my kin, my native brothers.
Don't you fret, but homeward fare,
They will wait upon you there."
Grief forgot, the Duke departed,
Climbed upon his keep and started
Gazing seaward; all at once,
'Gan the sea to heave and dance,

And in rushing runs retrieving
Surf and sough, retreated, leaving
Thrice eleven on the site,
Knights in blazing armor bright;
They approach in paired procession
And, his snowy floss a-flashing,
Chernomor in solemn state
Guides them to the city gate.
From the keep the Duke descended,
Greeting to his guests extended,
Forward flocked the city folk,
To the Duke the leader spoke:
"Aye, the Swan Princess despatched us
And as sentinels detached us,
Warders for your fair redoubt,
Walking guard the walls about.
Without fail we shall henceforward
Daily stride together shoreward,
Risen from the ocean wave
By your soaring bastions brave;
Shortly therefore you will sight us,
Meanwhile, though, the waves invite us,
For the air of earth is dense."
And they all went homeward thence.

      Seawind saunters there and thither
Drives a little vessel hither,
Bowling down the ocean swell,
All her canvas drawing well,
Past the craggy island fastness,
Past the wonder city's vastness;
Cannon firing from the pier
Bid the ship to anchor here.
As they fetch the mooring station,
Comes a ducal invitation.
They are furnished drink and food
And for course and parley sued;
"Guests, what goods may you be bearing,
Whither are you further faring?"
And the sailormen speak out:

"We have sailed the world about,
Trusty Damask steel we traded,
Gold and silver finely graded,
Done our stint, it's homeward ho—
But we still have far to go:
Past Buyan the island sailing,
Tsar Saltan's dominions hailing."
Duke Guidon addressed them then:
"Make in safety, gentlemen,
Down the ocean-sea your passage,
Carry Tsar Saltan a message,
Say the Duke Guidon afar
Sends his greetings to the Tsar."

    Then the guests, farewells accorded,
Sought their ship and went aboard it.
For the shore makes Duke Guidon,
In the surf he spies the swan.
And again he speaks his yearning,
Soul with ache and anguish burning . . .
Swam the swan ashore again,
Splashed him soundly there and then,
And at once he turned much smaller,
To a bumblebee, no taller;
Taking off with buzzing sound,
Out at sea the ship he found,
Straight upon her poop he glided,
Down a chink and there subsided.

    Seawind blows a merry clip,
Merrily sails on the ship;
Past Buyan their passage gaining,
Where the famed Saltan is reigning,
They already sight the shore
Of the land they're destined for.
As they anchor off the commons,
They receive a royal summons,
So they take the castle route;
Our bold lad flies in pursuit.

Tsar Saltan, all gold-ensheeted,
In his hall of state is seated
On his throne and in his crown,
Pensive sorrow in his frown.
But the palace cook and seamstress,
Babarikha too, the schemestress,
Sit near by him, and to see
Have four eyes among the three.
When the guests are duly greeted,
At the Tsar's own table seated,
"Ho," he asks them, "Merchant guests,
Long your voyage? Far your rest?
Are things sound abroad or parlous,
Can you tell us any marvels?"
And the sailormen speak out:
"We have sailed the world about,
Life is fair enough out yonder,
While abroad we saw this wonder:
There's an isle at sea out there,
On the isle a city fair,
Daily there befalls a wonder:
Ocean rollers seethe and thunder,
Rearing high with hiss and roar,
Foaming up a desert shore
And with rush and run resurging,
Leave from out their lee emerging
Thirty-three young giants hale,
Comely youths, their coats of mail
All with gold aglow and flashing,
Thrice eleven heroes dashing,
Like of choice recruits a crew;
Chernomor the Ancient too
Rises with them, marches forward,
And in pairs conducts them shoreward,
There to ward the isle redoubt,
Walking guard the walls about;
Watchful warders, none more ready,
None more dauntless or more steady.
Duke Guidon, residing there,

Bids Your Highness greetings fair."
Marvels Tsar Saltan: "So spare me,
To that island I will fare me,
Land upon that magic coast,
Duke Guidon shall be my host."
From the palace cook or seamstress
Not a murmur—but the schemestress
Snickers and will have her say:
"This is to amaze us, pray?
From the water watchmen amble,
Round and round an island shamble,
Truth or lie, I see in that
Nothing much to marvel at.
Here's what stuns the world astounded:
There is fame abroad, well-founded,
Of a princess far, far off
No one can adore enough,
Who the gleam of day outbrightens,
And the gloom of night enlightens;
In her hair the moon is borne,
On her brow the star of morn,
Forth she flows in splendor vested
Like a peacock fanned and crested,
And the words she utters seem
Murmurs from a purling stream.
Here you'd say without a blunder,
There's a wonder that's a wonder."
Mum, the prudent guests prefer
Not to bandy words with her,
Harks His Highness, barely breathing,
And the royal prince, though seething,
Hesitant to cast a blight
On the poor old granny's sight,
Bumbles buzzing with his muzzle,
Plummets plumb upon her nozzle,
Stings her right into the nose,
Where a monstrous bump arose.
And again they fuss and bustle:
"Help, for God's sake, hustle, hustle,
Guardsmen, catch the you-know-what,

Catch that sting-bee, snatch and swat!
Just you wait! Hold still a little,
Wait a while!"...All wasted spittle—
By the window wings the bee
Calmly home across the sea.

And the Duke in restless motion
Strides and scans the dark-blue ocean ...
Lo! on drifting swells offshore
Swims the snowy swan once more.
"Hail, fair Prince! But why beclouded,
Silent like a rain-day shrouded?
Has some sorrow made you sad?"
She addressed the royal lad.
Said Guidon the Duke replying,
"Sadness-sorrow sends me sighing,
Folk have wives; I look about:
I alone am left without."
"Whom then would you fain have courted,
May I ask?" "It is reported
That a princess lives far off
No one can adore enough,
Who of day the gleam outbrightens
And of night the gloom enlightens;
In her hair the moon is borne,
On her brow the star of morn,
Forth she steps in splendor vested
Like a peacock fanned and crested,
And her speeches sweet, it seems,
Murmur like the purl of streams.
Is this truth," he asks, "or error?"
And awaits her words in terror.
Still and thoughtful thereupon,
Says at length the snowy swan:
"Yes, there is just such a maiden,
Wiving, though, is not like trading,
Wives are not, like mitts of pelt,
Plucked and tucked behind your belt.
Here is some advice to ponder—
Think about this as you wander

Homeward, ponder long and hard,
Not to rue it afterward."
Swore Guidon, as God his witness,
Timeliness as well as fitness
Called for wedlock, he had brought
All the thought to bear he ought.
For this maid of fairy fashion
He stood ready, such his passion,
Starting forthwith to bestride
Thrice nine kingdoms far and wide.
Spoke the swan-bird, deeply sighing,
"Wherefore fare so far a-trying?
Know then, Prince, your fate is nigh,
For the princess fair—am I."
Then her pearly pinions spreading
And atop the breakers heading
For the shore in diving rush,
She alighted in the brush,
Shook and shed her plumage fluted,
To a princess stood transmuted,
Crescent in her tresses borne,
On her brow the star of morn;
Forth she steps in splendor vested
Like a peacock fanned and crested,
And the speech she utters seems
Murmurous like purling streams.
Duke Guidon, his bride enfolding
In his tender arms and holding,
Leads her as his rightful spouse
To his loving mother's house.
Brings her in and, humbly kneeling,
"Dearest Queen," entreats with feeling,
"I have found my consort true,
Your obedient child; we sue
Your consent in joint communion
And your blessings on our union:
Concord blissful, love serene
Wish us both." The Mother-Queen,
Shedding tears of fond complaisance
As they bow in deep obeisance

To her wondrous ikon, pleads:
"Children, God reward your deeds."
Then Guidon no longer tarried,
Duke and princess up and married,
Settled down and did their best
For their union to be blessed.

Seawind saunters there and thither,
Drives a little vessel hither,
Bowling down the ocean swell,
All her canvas drawing well,
Past the craggy island fastness,
Past the wonder city's vastness;
Cannon firing from the pier
Bid the ship to anchor here.
As they fetch the mooring station,
Comes a ducal invitation.
They are furnished drink and food
And for speech and answer sued:
"Guests, what goods may you be bearing,
Whither now are further faring?"
And the sailormen speak out:
"We have sailed the world about,
Sundry wares beyond our telling
None too cheaply were we selling,
Of our voyage home back east
What is left is not the least,
Past Buyan the island sailing,
Tsar Saltan's dominions hailing."
Duke Guidon addressed them then:
"Make in safety, gentlemen,
Down the ocean-sea your passage,
Carry Tsar Saltan my message,
And remind your Tsar once more
Of a visit twice before
Promised us in proper season—
Pledge neglected for some reason!
Then add greetings for the nonce."
Guests despatched, Guidon for once

Did not follow them but tarried,
Being but so lately married.

      Seawind blows a merry clip,
Merrily sails on the ship;
Past Buyan their passage gaining,
Where the famed Saltan is reigning,
They already sight the crest
Of the shore they know the best.
As they anchored in the shallows,
They were summoned to the palace,
Where the Tsar Saltan they found
Seated on his throne and crowned;
And the palace cook and seamstress,
Babarikha too, the schemestress,
Sit not far away and see
On four eyes among the three.
When the guests are duly greeted,
At the Tsar's own table seated,
"Ho," he asks them, "Merchant guests,
Long your voyage? Far your rest?
Are things sound abroad or parlous,
Can you tell us any marvels?"
And the sailormen speak out:
"We have sailed the world about,
Life is fair enough out yonder,
While abroad we saw this wonder:
There's an isle at sea out there,
On this isle a city fair,
Rich in churches golden-towered,
Donjon chambers busk-embowered;
And a spruce tree shades the tower,
Underneath, a squirrel bower;
In it lives a well-trained squirrel,
What a wizard, by Saint Cyril!
Squirrel sings a song and struts
Pawing, gnawing hazel nuts,
Not plain nuts he puts his paws on,
Golden shells the squirrel gnaws on,

Every nut an emerald bright;
And they tend him day and night.
There is still another wonder:
Ocean rollers seethe and thunder,
Rearing high with hiss and roar,
Foaming up a desert shore,
And with rush and run resurging,
Leave from out their lee emerging
Thirty-three young giants hale,
Comely youths, their coat of mail
All with gold aglow and flashing,
Thrice eleven heroes dashing,
Like of choice recruits a crew—
Chernomor the Ancient too.
Than this guard is none more ready,
None more dauntless or more steady.
And the Prince's little wife
You could look at all your life:
She of day the gleam outbrightens,
And of night the gloom enlightens,
Crescent in her tresses borne,
On her brow the star of morn.
Duke Guidon, who rules that country,
Warmly praised by all and sundry,
Charged us with good cheer to you,
But with plaint of grievance, too:
Of a visit in due season,
Undelivered for some reason."

      This was all Saltan could stand,
Bade the fleet cast off from land.
Yet the palace cook and seamstress,
Babarikha too, the schemestress,
Do not wish to let him fare
To that wonder island there.
But for once he did not heed them,
With a royal roar he treed them:
"Say, what am I, Tsar or child?"
He demanded, driven wild.

"Off I go!" With stomp and snortle
He stalked out and slammed the portal.

At his window Duke Guidon
Mutely gazed the sea upon:
Never roaring, never seething
Lies the ocean, barely breathing,
On the skyline azure-blue
White top-gallants heave in view:
Ocean's mirror-reaches bruising,
Comes the royal squadron cruising.
Duke Guidon then gave a leap,
Loudly shouted from his keep:
"Ho, my Mother, dearest Mother,
You, young Duchess, for another,
Look you over yonder, fast,
Here our Father comes at last!"
Guidon, through his spyglass peering
At the squadron swiftly nearing,
Spies the Tsar upon the stem
Gazing through his glass at them.
And the palace cook and seamstress,
Babarikha too, the schemestress,
Near him in amazement stand,
Staring at this unknown land.
Cannon boom from every barrel,
Carillons from belfries carol;
Lone, the Prince upon the pier
Greets the Tsar and at his rear
Both the palace cook and seamstress,
Babarikha too, the schemestress,
Leads them to the city wall,
Speaking not a word withal.

Now they pass the castle center,
Gorgets glisten as they enter,
And before the Sovereign's eyes
Thirty-three young giants rise,
Thrice eleven heroes dashing,
Comely knights in armor flashing,

Like of choice recruits a crew,
Chernomor the Ancient too.
And the Tsar steps in the spacious
Courtyard: lo, a squirrel gracious
'Neath a spruce tree sings and struts,
Gnawing golden hazel nuts,
Emerald kernels bright extracting
And into a pouch collecting,
All bestrewn the spacious yard
With the precious golden shard.
Hastening on, they meet, astounded,
Fair Her Grace and stand dumbfounded:
In her hair the moon is borne,
On her brow the star of morn;
On she walks in splendor vested,
Like a peacock fanned and crested,
Leading forth her Queen-in-law.
Tsar Saltan, he stares in awe . . .
Heart in throat, he marvels, ponders:
"By what magic? Signs and wonders!
How?" His pulses leaped and throbbed,
Then he burst in tears and sobbed,
In his open arms he caught her,
And his son, and his new daughter,
And they all sat down in strength
To a merry feast at length.
But the palace cook and seamstress,
Babarikha too, the schemestress,
Ran to hide in niche and nook;
Found at last and brought to book,
They confessed, all pale and pining,
Beat their breasts and started whining;
And the Tsar in his great glee
Let them all get off scot-free.
Late at night some subjects loyal
Helped to bed His Highness Royal.
I was there, had beer and mead,
Dip a whisker's all I did.

THE LITTLE HOUSE IN KOLOMNA: INTRODUCTION

Pushkin's note under the last octave of "The Little House in Kolomna" tells us that it was completed on October 9, 1830, in Boldino. In the years before the poem appeared in the almanac *Novosel'e* (vol. I, 1833)—offered to Pushkin's publisher, A. F. Smirdin, for the housewarming of his new shop on Nevsky Prospect opposite the Kazan Cathedral—the original forty-eight octaves were reduced to forty by Pushkin himself. Of the original forty-eight stanzas, fully one third had been devoted to the metaliterary introduction, Pushkin's playful musings about the attractions and pitfalls of the octave form, which had then barely attained citizenship in Russian verse. In the succinct forty-stanza version submitted in 1833, this portion, which the formalists considered the essence of the poem, still makes up one fifth (eight stanzas) of the whole. If one realizes that the plot does not really begin to develop until the thirteenth stanza, the proportion becomes thirty percent, much what it was at first.

Annenkov records that most contemporary literati regarded Push-kin's contribution as a mild jest, but also as an embarrassing sign of his irrevocable decay as a poet. Even Yazykov thought all the verse contributions to *Novosel'e* except Zhukovsky's and Krylov's were fit only for the wastebasket. This set a tone of patronizing neglect for some time and prompted absurd efforts to improve Pushkin's redaction by salvaging all the discarded "workshop" stanzas. But soon, perceptive hints were dropped by Belinsky, V. J. Bryusov, and M. L. Gofman, which went some way toward restoring the author's intentions and placing the puzzling work in the proper context of its literary associations, both ephemeral and lasting. The later formalists, while supplying little direct criticism of the poem, frequently drew upon it to illustrate their ideas about "art as device," about self-conscious literature, and about form as content. They made it the occasion for adducing much illuminating contemporary material. Foremost among those formalists were Shklovsky, Tomashevsky, Tyn-yanov, and Eikhenbaum.

Semionov[1] suggests that the figure of the disguised cook symbolizes Pushkin's intrusion, in the harmless guise of a *bonhomme*, into the well-guarded precincts of the Goncharov family. If this is so, there is good reason for Pushkin's leaving Parasha's complicity in the plot in some considerable doubt; for Natalia Goncharova surely never quite penetrated her fiancé's hymeneal, or her husband's uxorious, mask. However this may be, there certainly is autobiographical substance in the setting and in one of the two minor characters of "Domik v Kolomne." Pletnev, Pushkin's professorial friend and publisher, tells us in his correspondence with J. K. Grots that he became acquainted with Pushkin in 1818 after the poet's graduation from Tsarskoe Selo. At that time, Pushkin lived in the *petit bourgeois* quarter of St. Petersburg which provides the setting of the poem, "above the Korffs, near Kalinkin Bridge by the Fontanka, in the house then belonging to Klokachev." He further reports that Pushkin had received the plot of the transvestism story by way of a personal reminiscence from his friend, P. V. Nashchokin—the owner of the incredibly elaborate doll's apartment, a 1:20 scale model of his own dwelling. (The doll's apartment is now one of the more farfetched attractions of the Pushkin Museum at Tsarskoe Selo and reputedly cost its first owner far more than the original.) Nashchokin left this celebrated *domik*, complete with "a vessel into which hardly anyone but a Spanish fly could relieve himself," to Natalia Nikolaevna.

As Dostoevsky had all of Russian nineteenth-century prose emerge from Gogol's *Overcoat*, thus adding to the wearisome perplexities of scholars and teachers in that field, so it has been suggested that Russian poetry of the twentieth century has issued forth from Pushkin's "Little House in Kolomna"—perhaps an even taller tale. It is perhaps true, however, that "in this little masterpiece the major lines of development of Pushkin's *oeuvre* cross those of Russian literature."[2]   In its conscious search for new formal vehicles, groping more and more surely toward prose for a new social milieu—that of the Stationmaster and the clerk Eugene— and toward Gogolian farce and mystification, the little work foreshadows the far-reaching change in poetics and subject matter which were overtaking Russian verse by the middle of the nineteenth century.

THE LITTLE HOUSE IN KOLOMNA

I

The iambic quadruped has had full scope;
I'm sick of it. It should be relegated
To youngsters as a toy. My cherished hope
To write in octaves[1] has now germinated
For quite some time: and really, I could cope
With threefold rhyme; to work, with breath unbated!

Rhymes, after all, have lived with me like kin;
Two'll volunteer, the third will be dragged in.

II

To make their progress smooth and automatic,
I now unleash the verbs in -ate and -fy...
You know, whenever rhyming goes grammatic
There's righteous shuddering. I ask you, why?
Thus wrote Shikhmatov,[2] worshipful old vatic,
And just like that, most of the time, write I.
We're raggedy-poor and cannot do without it;
I'll rhyme on verbs and make no bones about it.

III

I'm not about to scrap words, like a snob,
As lame draftees who wangled some malfunction,
Or a new mount that's an ungainly job;
I'll sign 'em up, come adverb, come conjunction,
Recruit my outfit from the common mob.
I must have rhymes, I draft without compunction,
It's in the Unabridged, it's fit to call:[3]
We're not on dress inspection, after all.

IV

Well then, you words of male and female ending,
Let's say a prayer and start: Ten-shun!...here goes!
Dress ranks, let's have no fidgeting or fending,
Fall in by threes into the octave...close!
Don't be afraid, we shan't be too unbending;
You stand at ease, just see you don't break rows;
We'll all, praise God, get used to drill and tether
And soon will ride the level road together.

V

To lead one's verses, numbered, dressed just so,
Rank after rank, gives one such satisfaction,
And not to let them struggle out of row
Like some detachment blown to bits in action!
Here every syllable makes a brave show,

Heroic lines, bold feet in every section;
Who is the rhymester like, then, can you guess?
Like Tamerlane, Napoleon, no less!

VI

Let's pause a while at this point. *Con bravura*[4]
Ahead, I wonder, or into reverse?
I will confess I'm all for a caesura[5]
Each second foot of pentametric verse.
A pause like that makes any journey surer,
Else it's all ups and downs; though I rehearse
In bed, I seem to bump on springless barrows
At breakneck speed across hard-frozen furrows.

VII

Still, what's so bad? Is it all bliss to pace
The granite-clad Neva, to have cavorted
On polished ballroom floors, to mount and race
In the Kirghizian steppe? My taste's distorted,
I'll saunter at a walk from place to place,
Like that weird fellow who, it is reported,
Has trotted without feeding-stops, the crank,
From Moscow all the way to Neva's bank.

VIII

Some trotter! Why, the palfrey of Parnassus
Could not have caught him. Pegasus is hoar,
Toothless, the spring he dug is dry, and masses
Of nettles overgrow Parnassus' floor.
Phoebus is pensioned off, and the slow passus
Of senile Muses can enchant no more.
We've moved from classicism's lofty spaces
To pitch our camp upon the marketplaces.

IX

Sit down, my tomboy Muse, but quietly!
No fidgeting, hands folded, feet tucked under!
There lived a poor old widow (as you see,
We're off), eight years ago, I shouldn't wonder,
With just one girl. Her cottage used to be

By the Pokrov,[6] a humble hut, down yonder
Just past the sentry box. I see it still
The mansard, the three windows, porch and sill.

X

Out walking with a friend, I was affected
To see that spot again the other night.
Right where the cottage stood, they have erected
A three-floor tenement. For me that sight
Brought back to memory, quite unexpected,
The widow, the young daughter—as they might
Still sit beneath their window—and the season
Of youth. Were they alive yet? For no reason,

XI

I grew quite sorrowful: I looked askance
At that tall house, and if a conflagration
Had then engulfed it wholesale by some chance,
My spiteful eye with venomous elation
Would fair have gloated on it. Some weird trance
At times envelops our imagination;
Much nonsense clouds our reason as we wend
Our aimless way alone, or with a friend.

XII

Blessed he who curbs his words, contains his stable
Of swarming fancies in an iron grip,
He who has learnt to silence or disable
The hissing snake that lurks behind the lip;
While he who blabs will soon incur the label
Of miscreant . . . As for myself, I sip
My Lethe; grief is bad, says my physician:
So I will drop this—with your kind permission!

XIII

The crone wore specs and mobcap (in her guise,
To the last wrinkle, I've seen Rembrandt render
A score of beldames). But the daughter—eyes
And brows night-dark, herself as white and tender

As any dove—she was, I swear, a prize
Of gentle beauty. Further to commend her,
She was accomplished, too, her taste refined,
Emin's romances had improved her mind,

XIV

She sang "There mourns the purple dove," recited
"Shall I go forth,"[7] she played on the guitar,
Nor was that older repertory slighted
Which in drear autumn by the samovar,
Or when in winter dusk the stove is lighted,
Or walking in a vernal glade afar,
To doleful strains the Russian maiden uses,
Who is a grieving singer, like our Muses.

XV

Both plain and metaphorical, our tune,
From poet laureate to mere domestic,
Is in the minor keys. A wailing croon
Is Russia's song. Well-known characteristic:
What starts with merry toasts turns all too soon
To passing-bells. The chords of both majestic
And rustic Muses draw from grief their glow;
One likes the plaintive cadence even so.

XVI

Our little beauty—she was called Parasha—
Could wash and iron, sew and weave; she bore
All management unaided, scribe and usher
For household books and produce; furthermore,
She watched the boiling of the buckwheat *kasha*,
Though, to be sure, sustained in that grave chore
By Thekla, the old cook, old but endearing,
Who long had lost her sense of smell and hearing.

XVII

The mother, like old ladies, often sat
Beneath the window in the daytime, knitting
A stocking; in the evening she would chat
O'er fortune-telling cards, at table sitting,

The while her daughter walked this way and that,
From door to yard, from yard to window flitting,
And no one walking past or driving by
Escaped her sight (the sex has a sharp eye!).

XVIII

By winter dusk they had the shutters fastened,
But in the summer until late at night
The house stayed open. Pallid Dian's crescent
Long poured into the maiden's room her light.
(The writer's moon is never evanescent,
There is no novel where it's out of sight.)
At times the mother's snores had long been hissing
While daughter would still watch the moon, and listen

XIX

To sundry alley cats' meows and squeals
About the garrets—trysting calls unseemly—
To watchmen's far-off shouts, the clocks' rare peals,
No more. Nights in Kolomna are supremely
Pacific. From the doorways seldom steals
A twofold shade. The drowsy girl extremely
Distinctly heard her own heart's pulses beat
As it was pressed against the yielding sheet.

XX

On Sundays, any time of year or weather,
The widow went to the Pokrov with her
And took her stand, before a crowd could gather,
By the left screen. I live no longer there,
But once I did, and now, when I untether
My loyal dreams, the conscious mind a blur,
It's to Kolomna, the Pokrov, they're winging
To hear a Russian service with its singing.

XXI

That same church, I recall, the countess too
Used to attend (her name eludes me lately).[8]
This noble lady, young and well-to-do,

Used to come rustling in with progress stately
For her proud prayers (there was pride for you!),
And her proximity distracted greatly
This sinful wretch. Parasha, our poor miss,
Looked poorer still against a foil like this.

XXII

At times the countess from her grand position
Gave her a casual look. But she would pray,
And in untroubled stillness and submission
Seemed unaware of it in any way.
She was a touching image of contrition;
The countess was preoccupied, I'd say,
With her own self, her fashion-leader's duty,
And her austere and overweening beauty.

XXIII

Here was a goddess of the frigid creed
Of vanity, you would have joined in saying:
Through her outward hauteur, though, I could read
A different story: long-felt sorrow preying,
Complaint subdued . . . And it was these, I plead,
That touched my soul and kept my glances straying . . .
But this the countess could not know about;
She booked me as a conquest, I don't doubt.

XXIV

She suffered grief, though she was adulated
For youth and beauty, though her life flowed free
In easeful luxury, though fortune waited
Her mere command, though fashion would decree
Burnt offerings to her—she was ill-fated.
A hundredfold more fortunate was she,
My reader, the young friend I sought to usher
Into your heart, my simple, kind Parasha.

XXV

A swarm of reddish-golden ringlets tender
Uncoiling from a simple comb of horn,

On her slim neck a string of wax beads slender,
A little kerchief tied or crosswise worn—
A homely turnout; yet there would attend her
Black-whiskered guardsmen to the manner born.
The girl contrived to charm their eyes no less
For being unadorned by costly dress.

XXVI

Among these swains did any one more keenly
Engage her heart, or are we to report
Unbiased coolness? We shall see. Serenely
Meanwhile she lived her life and gave no thought
Be it to gala balls, be it to queenly
Paris, or to the court (although at court
Lived cousin Vera, consort to the able
Provisioner of the Imperial Stable).

XXVII

But once, back from a scalding bath, their cook—
Domestic grief here makes abrupt intrusion—
Came down with ague. Vainly she partook
Of tea, wine, vinegar, and mint infusion
For treatment, and on Christmas Eve forsook
This world. The same day brought to swift conclusion
Their last farewells. Before the sun was down,
The coffin was hauled off to Okhta town.

XXVIII

All in the household grieved, though to prostration
Vaska the cat alone. Three days, no less,
The old lady bravely bore the vacant station,
But cooking being not the kind of stress
One puts on the Almighty's dispensation,
She presently called out: "Parasha!" "Yes?"
"Where can we get a cook? Go ask the neighbor
Whom she might know. It's hard to find cheap labor."

XXIX

"I'll go and ask, Mama." And off she went
To get her wrap. The winter night was bitter,
The snow crunched, and the dark blue firmament
Hung unbeclouded, starred with frosty glitter.
Long did the widow wait; the old head bent
In sleep at last, Parasha found the sitter
When quietly she stepped into her nook
And said: "Here, I have brought you a new cook."

XXX

Advancing with a timid step, attired
In a short skirt, there entered at her back
A fine, tall girl, who, bowing low, retired
Into a corner with her apron sack.
"What wages will you take?" at once inquired
The widow as the cook undid her pack.
"Whatever suits; I know you will do rightly,"
Replied the woman modestly and lightly.

XXXI

This the old lady was much pleased to hear.
"What is the name?" "Why, Mavra." "Well, Mavrusha,
You come and live with us. You're young, my dear:
Keep clear of men. You know, my late Feklusha
Had served me as a cook for many a year,
Not once allowing anything to push her
Off the straight path. Just serve us with a will,
And, mind, no cheating on the grocer's bill."

XXXII

A few days passed. The cook proved far from clever:
She turned whole trays of crockery to sherd,
Burnt this dish, parboiled that one, and forever
Poured too much salt in everything she stirred.
Put her to sew—she couldn't thread or sever,
Take her to task—she'd never say a word;
All jobs she touched were somehow flubbed or fumbled,
For all Parasha tutored her and grumbled.

XXXIII

One Sunday the two ladies both had gone
To early morning service, thus forsaking
Luckless Mavrusha, who looked pale and wan,
An all-night toothache having left her shaken.
She was about to grind some cinnamon
To go into a cake that she was baking.
So she had stayed; but suddenly in church
The heart of the old widow gave a lurch.

XXXIV

A thought had struck her: "Why this sudden passion
In our resourceful cook for baking cake?
She may be making off with plate or ration;
What if she's out to rob us, not to bake?
Here's Christmas near, and we might in this fashion
Be stranded without help, for heaven's sake!"
Thus thinking, the old lady fussed and fluttered;
At last, unable to calm down, she muttered:

XXXV

"You stay, Parasha. I'll run home in haste,
I'm scared." She left the puzzled girl and, hitching
Her petticoats, she worriedly retraced
Her steps, in her great hurry all but pitching
Off the cathedral porch. Her pulses raced
As at some imminent doom. Here's home, the kitchen . . .
No Mavra. Off to her own room to see . . .
She entered . . . what a fright, oh mercy me!

XXXVI

Before Parasha's glass demurely seated,
The cook was shaving. Which the widow saw,
Gave two faint bleats and swooned away. Thus greeted,
The cook decamped in haste with lathered jaw,
In one rude leap cleared the prone lady, speeded
Into the hall, and crossing porch and field,
Made off at a brisk gallop, face concealed.[9]

XXXVII

Mass done, Parasha came about eleven.
"What is it, Mom?" "Oh, Pashenka, dear me:
Mavrushka . . . " "What about her?" "Cook . . .oh Heaven,
I can't get over it, I'm all at sea . . .
Before the glass . . .all soaped . . ." "Well, I'll let seven
Be even, but it makes no sense to me.
Where is Mavrusha then?" "Ah, the blackhearted . . .
Why, she was shaving here! . . .like my Departed!"

XXXVIII

If our Parasha blushed at this or not,
I cannot tell you; but of the outrageous
Young cook no trace remained upon that spot.
She left without a farthing of her wages,
And what small harm she did was soon forgot.
Who with her mistresses of unlike ages
Next took Mavrushka's place, that I for one
Don't know; besides, I'm eager to be done.

XXXIX

"What, is this all? You're joking?" "I assure you."
"So this is where your famous octaves strayed?
Look to what noble place you've let them lure you,
With all that spit and polish on parade,
All that brave show and bluster! I adjure you,
Was there no other tune you could have played?
Have you at least some moral admonition?"
"No . . .well, perhaps . . .I'll think, with your permission . . .

XL

Here is a moral for you: to my mind
A cook can be too frugally recruited
For safety; for a male to be inclined
To don a skirt is idle and ill-suited:
There surely comes a time when he must find
A chance to shave—a thing not instituted
By nature for the sex . . . Nothing more fine
Can be squeezed out of this plain tale of mine."

THE GOLDEN COCKEREL: INTRODUCTION

Washington Irving's story "Legend of the Arabian Astronomer" in his collection *Tales of the Alhambra* begins as follows:

> In old times, many hundred years ago, there was a Moorish king named Aben Habuz, who reigned over the kingdom of Granada. He was a retired conqueror, that is to say, one who, having in more youthful days led a life of constant foray and depredation, now that he was grown feeble and superannuated, "languished for repose," and desired nothing more than to live at peace with all the world, to husband his laurels, and to enjoy in quiet the possessions he had wrested from his neighbors.
>
> It so happened, however, that this most reasonable and pacific old monarch had young rivals to deal with; princes full of his early passion for fame and fighting, and who were disposed to call him to account for the scores he had run up with their fathers. Certain distant districts of his own territories, also, which during the days of his vigor he had treated with a high hand, were prone, now that he languished for repose, to rise in rebellion and threaten to invest him in his capital. Thus he had foes on every side; and as Granada is surrounded by wild and craggy mountains, which hide the approach of an enemy, the unfortunate Aben Habuz was kept in a constant state of vigilance and alarm, not knowing in what quarter hostilities might break out.
>
> It was in vain that he built watch-towers on the mountains, and stationed guards at every pass with orders to make fires by night and smoke by day, on the approach of an enemy. His alert foes, baffling every precaution, would break out of some unthought-of defile, ravage his lands beneath his very nose, and then make off with prisoners and booty to the mountains. Was ever peaceable and retired conqueror in a more uncomfortable predicament?
>
> While Aben Habuz was harassed by these perplexities and molestations, an ancient Arabian physician arrived at his court ...

No reader of Pushkin's *Golden Cockerel* on chancing to come across Irving's once-familiar tale could fail to be struck by the extraordinary resemblance between the two, which extends far into the plot. But by the time acquaintance with the "coq d'or" fable had spread in the West through Rimsky-Korsakov's opera, Irving's public had shrunk severely, so that in a hundred years no one seems to have noticed or called attention to this striking affinity until the great modern poet Anna Akhmatova, an ardent lover and disciple of Pushkin's, identified the forgotten tale from *The Alhambra* as Pushkin's source: *The Alhambra* had been published with a French translation in Paris in 1832. Her discovery remained unrewarded in her country, where Pushkin is of course revered and his sources are the object of constant painstaking research. But Akhmatova incurred the wrath of high-ranking Stalinist critics, who in the chauvinistic climate of the thirties could not bear or allow the thought of a contemporary foreign text behind what they claimed to be a blossom culled in the immemorial oak-groves of Russian folklore.

Pushkin's borrowing of Irving's fable is now beyond serious doubt. But in his brisk, wry-toned adaptation the story is stripped down to its essentials, bared of Irving's mechanical detail and slightly parodic Arabian Nights verbiage, and brought to a sharper dramatic finish. His poetic transformation endows the story with a flavor mingling sprightly folklore and burlesque, with a dash of the demonic. This last is precisely what lifts it out of the Russian *skazka* genre as well as the world of the romantic pseudo-oriental tales of the West. For what is lethal in Pushkin's stark *dénouement* is not so much the cynical abuse of power by which the royal pledge to the sorcerer is dishonored as the irresistible spell of exotic beauty, used with perfectly detached frivolity to ruin young and old. The chilling "hee-hee-hee and ha-ha-ha" of the young enchantress of Shamakhan is really the enunciation in styled-down folklore terms (post factum, to be sure) of the "mene, mene, tekel upharsin" which a ghostly hand wrote in fire on the wall of King Belshazzar's banquet hall.

In 1973 the Soviet literary scholar V. Nepomnyashchy published what is probably the most provacative study[1] of *The Golden Cockerel* since Anna Akhmatova's identification of its source. He seconded Akhmatova's interesting conjecture that the motif of the "breach of a monarch's word" had its origin in Tsar Nicholas I's perfidy towards Pushkin (he had impulsively befriended Pushkin in 1826 and promised to act henceforth as his sole censor, but had presently broken this pledge), and that this was the main clue to the underlying meaning of the tale. He agreed that this autobiographic fact lay close to the central mystery of the curiously bleak and arid poem but went on to develop several sets of internal clues inherent in the poem's isolated position among Pushkin's other fairy tales in verse and in similar notes of embattled detachment struck by other poems of the time around 1830. The following quotation shows some of the given data on which Nepomnyashchy's analysis proceeds.

> The lines which dispassionately draw the contours of the action begin, lead on to a certain point, and—remain uncompleted or stray aside; and in this incomplete drafting, this evasiveness, there is something alien, a little uncanny, and intriguing, like the capricious tracery of some magic ornament whose lines, now emerging, now vanishing, now rising, now falling, describe a strange pattern, abstract yet alluding dimly to some esoteric meaning.
>
> And why did Pushkin in a cycle of Russian fairy tales suddenly need an oriental legend? This question goes to the special structure of the fairy tale, its very flesh as a work of art.
>
> 'Flesh' clearly is not the right word here, of course—it lacks precisely *that*

more than anything else in comparison with the other stories, where the folktale "plan" was by contrast overgrown with living matter from human life and three-dimensional characters.

There is no flesh here, but a skeleton; not free-ranging fancy, but the chill of objectivity; not open emotion or even an underlying text, but the enigma of bare fact.

The oriental luxuriance and intricate painting of Irving's Arabic legend gives way to ascetic brevity, which produces a deceptive impression of unassuming simplemindedness: the content of the novella, which occupies 16 or 17 quarto pages, is severely cut down, connecting links are taken out, detail removed, the leisurely exposition compressed into 25 lines. The number of episodes is reduced to a minimum, the various parts of the action not developed in detail but, on the contrary, curtailed in treatment, enhancing the spring-loaded dynamics of the whole. The naked simplicity of expression, which makes a show of spontaneity and guilelessness, is driven to the limit of tension, the integuments of picturesque surface elements and psychological nuances are stripped away. And at the end of the line of Pushkin's full-blooded fairy-tale fantasies, his last tale looks like a skeleton, sardonically baring some grim underlying reality. And without in any way explaining this reality, the narrative rushes to its finale, where there ought to be, after all, some sort of resolution, some arcane meaning unsealed . . .

But the finale presents a new riddle; and the thought suggests itself that in hunting for the inner truth the reader, like Dadon, has been pursuing a phantom. What follows is a coda which makes one's head spin—the clanging flight of the Cockerel who has suddenly taken off from his perch, the instantaneous and horrifyingly natural death of Dadon: "Gave a wheeze and stretched his feet." And after this merciless execution—unexpected like a bolt from the blue, for which the reader, busy trying to penetrate all this mystery and taken aback by the pervasive tone of irony, is quite unprepared—the onward rush of events is choked off almost at half-sentence. Everything tumbles into the void—"just as though it never was." The enigmatic story runs headlong onto no less enigmatic a hint at "sense" which we are invited with a smile ("if not of truth") to discover, absorb, and even draw a "lesson" from.

But in order to do that, we have to understand everything from the very beginning.

The author proceeds to unravel strand after strand of a network of allusions behind Pushkin's sprightly frolic of death, using biographic and ergographic clues. Most of his arguments are convincing, but they do not lend themselves to summarization. Some broad hints may be given here which illustrate his line of approach without passing on his identifications or the conclusions they lead to. There is a monarch (among poets?) who after a boisterous youth craves peace of spirit (in a monastery? in some "far-off retreat of toil and pure delight," as Pushkin puts it in a poem of the same year?). If the "monarch" is to be taken literally, the situation fits Tsar Alexander I, who had been a war-lord in his prime, but in his later years sought repose and surrounded himself with "magi," i.e. sectarians, soothsayers, and religious cranks. But the monarch is beset on all sides by predatory neighbors, avengers of past transgressions. Then there is a sorcerer (among poets?) who provides magic redress, receives in return a blank cheque for royal favors, but in the end reaps ingratitude and death. The magus as well as the worldly tsar (they are separate now if they were not before) fall under the potent spell of a young enchantress (Pushkin's young wife, whom rumor linked with Alexander I) and clash, with fatal results to the magus. The magic bird (his reincarnation or surrogate?) exacts instant retribution . . .

Nepomnyashchy concludes in part as follows:

> Pushkin's last fairy tale is an "encoded" work, the sole product of the last Boldino autumn. It represents one of the most astonishing examples of Pushkinian terseness as applied to his larger form [the narrative poem is meant; tr.'s note]. It occupies a singular place of its own and is of uncommon significance for the poet's creative and spiritual biography. We have here, not a case of a design or "pattern" (as Akhmatova calls it) derived by Pushkin from Irving's oriental legend and used as a container to be "filled" with autobiographic "material" but on the contrary, a case of autobiographic material, personal life experience of mind and soul, endowing with meaning a schema of general significance.

Suggestive cross-connections between, on one hand, unusual features and qualities of this poem and, on the other hand, the poet's circumstances at the time of writing and the mood brought about by them as documented in letters, would be dismissed as irrelevant or at best marginal by many critics; and certainly they must not take the place of examination of the work of art in its own terms. Yet this case is a special one. Pushkin had already become a national poet unlike any before or since. His every work in this post-Decembrist era of repression was likely to be read not only for aesthetic pleasure but as a possible civic utterance and ultimately, a political document. Furthermore, the poet knew it would or could be so read, and he would carefully encode what extra-literary comment or message it might contain by metaphor, simile, allegory, or "Aesopian" language. Hence the linkages between the text and current circumstances, frame of mind, and concerns of state or society become, with this poet more properly than with most others, integral parts of the literary material. Thus Nepomnyashchy quite plausibly suggests that the main autobiographic nexus first pointed out by Akhmatova—the theme of the broken royal pledge—so far from being immaterial,"is merely the accurately observed surface stratum from which, once it has been discovered, one may penetrate farther and deeper, linking one's analysis not only to external facts influencing Pushkin's life but also to his 'internal biography' as a human being and an artist."

For all the sense of personal frustration and cultural pessimism which oppressed Pushkin in the late 1820s and early 1830s, which he shared with kindred poetic spirits like Baratynsky and Vyazemsky and often reflected in the works he produced (or failed to produce) in those years, he had found in his art and its austere standards a spiritual refuge; a safer one than in marriage. In the "Imitations from the Koran" which he wrote in this period of stress and bitter anger, he sounds here and there a new, gallant note of life affirmation, of a renascent faith in a viable world hospitable to free human creation—however baldly materialistic it seemed to have become (cf. "A Conversation between Bookseller and Poet" in this anthology, and the "Prelude in the Theatre" at the start of Goethe's *Faust*, which may have inspired the former). The following quatrain from the "imitations" is an instance of this resilient note:

> The earth is firm; the heavens' quarters,
> Upheld by Thee, o Lord, from fall,
> Will not collapse on earth and waters
> And in their ruin crush us all . . .

Commenting on this stanza of the 5th Imitation, Pushkin wrote: "Bad physics, but what spirited poetry!"

THE TALE OF THE GOLDEN COCKEREL

In the realm of Threeteenseventy,
Commonwealth of Thriceleventy,
Lived the famous Tsar Dadón.
Fierce he was from boyhood on,
And when scarcely more than twenty
Wrought his neighbors wrongs aplenty.
Aging now, he changed in mind,
Would give up the warlike grind
For a life serene and festive.
But his neighbors, growing restive,
Caused the grizzled Tsar alarm,
Dealing him a world of harm.
To protect the tsardom's borders
From the raids of bold marauders,
He was forced to raise and post
An unconscionable host.

Field commanders, never drowsing,
Still would scarce have finished dousing
Flames at left when, ho! at right
Hostile banners hove in sight.
These fought off, some visitation
Came by sea. The Tsar's frustration
Drove him wild enough to weep
And forgo the balm of sleep.
Who could thrive when thus infested?
So he pondered and requested
Succour from a gelding sage,
Planet-reckoner and mage;
Sent a runner to implore him
And the magus, brought before him,
From beneath his ample frock
Drew a golden weathercock.
"Let this golden bird," he chanted,
"High atop the spire be planted,
And my clever Cockerel
Be your faithful sentinel.
While there's naught of martial riot,
He will sit his perch in quiet;
Let there be on any side
Signs of war to be espied,
Of some squadron border-poaching,
Or some other ill approaching,
Straight my bird upon the dome
Will awaken, perk his comb,
Crow and veer, his ruff a-fluffing,
Point where harm is in the offing."
Rapt, the Tsar allowed the sage
Heaps of gold for ready wage.
"Such momentous boon afforded,"
He rejoiced,"shall be rewarded
By a wish, to be fulfilled
Like my own as soon as willed."

Cockerel atop the spire
Started guarding march and shire,
Scarce a danger reared its head,

Up he perked as though from bed,
Slewed about, his collar ruffled,
To that side and, wings unshuffled,
Crew aloud "Keeree-kookoo!
Reign abed, your guard is true."
Kings, the Tsar's domains investing,
Henceforth never dared molest him:
Tsar Dadon on every hand
Hurled them back by sea and land!

One year, two, the shrewd informant
Had been roosting all but dormant,
When one morning they broke in
On Dadon with fearful din.
"Tsar of ours! The realm's defender!"
Cries the household troop's commander,
"Majesty! Wake up! Alert!"
"Eh?...what's up?...Is someone hurt?"
Drawled the Tsar amid a double
Yawn, "who is this? What's the trouble?"
Answered him the Captain thus:
"Hark, the rooster's warning us;
Look below and see the people
Mill in fear, and on the steeple
See the rooster, ruffle-fleeced,
Crowing, pointing to the East."
"Up! No time to lose!" their Master
Spurred them on, "mount horses! Faster!"
Eastward thus a force he sped,
With his eldest at its head.
Cockerel gave over screaming,
And the Tsar continued dreaming.

Seven days go by and more,
But no message from the corps:
Has the march been rough or quiet—
Naught to tell it or deny it.
Cockerel goes off once more!
Tracking down the elder's corps,

Rides the younger with another
To the rescue of his brother.
Presently subsides the bird;
And again no more is heard!
And again the people, troubled,
Wait a week, their fears redoubled.
Yet again the cock is heard,
And Dadon sends out a third
Host, himself commander of it,
Though unsure what this might profit.

Day and night the columns wind,
Then it preys upon each mind:
Not a camp or battleground,
Not a warriors' burial mound,
Is encountered near or far.
"Strange and stranger," thinks the Tsar.
One week gone, the country changes,
Rising, high through hills and ranges,
Then, amid the peaks ahead,
Look! a silken tent is spread.
Wondrous hush enfolds the scene
Round the tent; a gaunt ravine
Cradles hosts in battle rent.
Now Dadon has reached the tent . . .
Staggers backward: sight appalling,
Hard before his eyes lie fallen,
Stripped of helm and armour chain,
Both his noble princes, slain,
Pierced each by the other's charge;
And their wandering mounts at large
On the mead all stamped and scored,
On the bloodied meadow-sward . . .
"Boys . . .my boys . . ." the father groaned,
"Strangled both my hawks," he moaned,
"Life is forfeit—woe is me . . .
Here were killed not two but three."
Wail of men and master merges
Soon resound with heavy dirges
Gorge and cliff, the mountain's heart

Shakes. Behold, the curtains part
On the tent . . .The prize of maidens,
Queen of Shamakhan, in radiance
Lambent like the morning star,
Quietly salutes the Tsar.
Silenced by her brilliant gaze
Like a nightbird by the day's,
Numb he stands—her sight outstuns
Aye! the death of both his sons.
Now she looked at him, beguiling,
Swept a graceful bow and, smiling,
Took his hand and drew him on—
To her tent came Tsar Dadon.
At her table did she seat him,
To all sorts of victuals treat him,
And for rest his body laid
On an othman of brocade.
Thus full seven days he lavished,
All enslaved by her and ravished,
On delight and merriment
In the royal maiden's tent.

At long last, though, forth he sallied,
His surviving forces rallied,
And, the maiden in his train,
Led his army home again.
Rumor started to outspeed him,
Tales of hap and no-hap breeding . . .
Throngs of subjects small and great
Swirl beyond the city gate
Round the coach of Tsar and Empress,
Fabled Shamakhanian temptress;
Tsar Dadon salutes them there . . .
All at once he is aware
Of his friend, the wise old eunuch,
In his white tarboosh and tunic,
Snowy-thatched now, like a swan.
"Father mine," exclaimed Dadon,
"Hail! How fare you? At your leisure

Come and speak; what is your pleasure?"
"Tsar!" replied the aged mage,
"Now we square desert and wage.
For the aid I once accorded,
You recall, I was awarded
My first wish—to be fulfilled,
Like your own, as soon as willed.
Let this maid be what I won,
This young queen of Shamakhan."
"What?" Dadon fell back, amazed.
"What possessed you? Are you crazed?
Does some wicked demon ride you?
Have your wits dried up inside you?
What's your game, in heaven's name?
Pledge I did; but all the same
There are limits, well you knew;
And—what use is she to you?
Kindly lodge it in your head
Who I am! Why, ask instead
For my mint, a magnate's sable,
Stallion from the royal stable,
Half my tsardom if you please!"
"No, I wish for none of these!
Just you give me what I won,
This young queen of Shamakhan,"
Piped the sage in former fashion.
"No!" the Tsar spat, in a passion;
"You yourself have brought this on!
You'll have nothing! There! Be gone
While you're in one piece! I say!
Drag the scarecrow from my way!"
Whitebeard wanted to pursue it,
But with some, you're apt to rue it;
With an angry scepter blow
Tsar Dadon has laid him low,
Not to breathe again.—The city
Gave a shudder, but our pretty:
"Ha-ha-ha" and "hi-hi-hi,"
Not a pious thought, you see.
Tsar Dadon, though greatly flustered,

Smiled at her, as soft as custard,
And proceeded cityward.
Then a tiny sound was heard,
And in sight of all the people,
Look! The cock whirred off the steeple,
Swooped upon the coach of state,
Perched upon the monarch's pate,
Fluffed his ruff and pecked and clink!
Soared aloft...Without a blink
Tsar Dadon slid off his seat,
Gave a wheeze and stretched his feet.
Gone the empress sight unseen,
Just as though she'd never been.
Tale of sense, if not of truth!
Food for thought to honest youth.

THE BRONZE HORSEMAN: INTRODUCTION

The Bronze Horseman, although overpraised by some, is perhaps the most significant of Pushkin's narrative poems, and certainly the most original among those that are not what the Soviet scholiasts blushingly call "indecorous." It was completed in 1833 and published posthumously, with some omissions due to censorship, in 1837, the year of Pushkin's death. The Prologue with the celebrated accolade to St. Petersburg and homage to Peter I is intriguingly at odds with the import of the poem as a whole. The setting, and part of the symbolic energizer of the poem on its historic-philosophical plane, is of course the great flood of the Nevá River in 1824—and it also carries the human plot on to its tragic conclusion.

The Bronze Horseman was previously translated into English some sixty years ago by Oliver Elton, who sought to preserve the metric form of the original, and later by Edmund Wilson, who did not. By far the best critical work on the poem was done by the distinguished Polish scholar, Wacław Lednicki. Lednicki was the first to perceive and document fully the poem's central significance in the ambivalent relationship between its author and his admired friend and political antagonist, the great Polish poet Adam Mickiewicz, and thus, indirectly, in the century-old rivalry between Poland and Russia; between the emerging Western commitment to pluralistic liberalism and humanism and Russia's instinctive revulsion against it, of which we witnessed the latest tragic examples in Czechosolovakia and Poland. The poem may be legitimately read, in one of its aspects, as part of a complex long-distance dialogue in verse across an unbridgeable political gulf between two estranged friends, the hero-poets (in Carlyle's sense) of their estranged nations. Specifically, it is in this sense an attempted rebuttal of Mickiewicz's far more passionate and poetically opulent indictment of St. Petersburg in the "Digression" of his verse drama of 1832, *Forefather's Eve, Part III.* In a magnificent blast of hot fury and cold contempt, Mickiewicz, in this cycle of poems, assails and morally annihilates St. Petersburg, which he sees as a prime symbol of the tasteless megalomania and brutish malignity of imperial Russia. Mickiewicz's "Digression" and Pushkin's *Bronze Horseman* are so intimately linked that from the viewpoint of comparative literature and Slavic political history one would wish that they were always printed as companion pieces. Marjorie Beatrice Peacock has created a distinguished English translation of the former, which I believe is most accessible in the appendix to Lednicki's monograph, *Pushkin's Bronze Horseman: The Story of a Masterpiece* (Berkeley: University of California Press, 1955). Even this is now a rare book.

The tenor of Pushkin's private pronouncements about St. Petersburg in the thirties differs startlingly from the panegyric tone adopted in *The Bronze Horseman*. The records of his correspondence and conversation in the period from 1833 to 1837 are poignant testimony to his settled disgust with the "repulsive" city; a feeling not wholly attributable to the maddening frustrations of his professional and personal situation there, though admittedly it is more its society and court than the city itself that he abominates. Here are some typical examples from his letters, mostly to his wife; many more were collected fifty years ago by Andrei Bely and published with his study of Pushkin's diction in *The Bronze Horseman*[1] :

> Petersburg is dreadfully depressing . . .

> I spit and do my best to get out of Petersburg . . .

> God, how I should like to light out for the fresh air . . .

> You don't think by any chance that swinish Petersburg is not repulsive to me? That I enjoy living there among libels and denunciations? . . .

> I am angry with Petersburg and rejoice in every sickening thing about it . . .

> Brjulov is just leaving me for Petersburg, bracing his heart; he is afraid of the climate and the lack of freedom. I try to console him . . .(while) my own heart sinks to my boots . . .

The Bronze Horseman, then, derives much of its troubling impact and its lasting freshness from a profound ambiguity. This is the sustained tension between the claims of *raison d'état*—lately in America more deceptively labeled the "national interest"—which in the poem are most overtly endorsed in the sonorous cadences of the Prologue; and the equally strong and more appealing claims of the humble (a key word of Pushkin's later poetry) individual in whose ostensible interest, but at whose crucial expense, the imposing edifice of the state is created and maintained. The external elements of authoritatively enforced law, discipline, and progress merge in the poetic mind into an aesthetic effect: the kind of ordered beauty, imposed on an ill-favored nature, which is still persuasive to the foreigner under the changeful sky over the water-mirrored pastel neoclassic of Leningrad.

Yet in numerous subtle ways Pushkin also identifies himself with his lowly, tormented, déclassé hero, Eugene. The green-cream-and-magenta charms of palaces and spires harbor nameless terrors and paralyzing frustration; the patterned grace of wrought-iron railings and granite banks confines not only classicist statuary and leafy parks but also private liberty and private need for fulfillment; and in this, Peter's city was and is ominously unlike Brühl's Dresden, William III's Amsterdam, or Canaletto's Venice, all of which seem to share collaterally in its urban pedigree. Peter the Great, Atarus, is both hero and anti-hero of *The Bronze Horseman*. With a combination of paternalistic ruthlessness, often faddish xenophilia, and deeply flawed success that is highly reminiscent of his pupil, Atatürk, in the 1920s, Peter had unfrocked, unbeavered, and unpriested his bewildered Russians. He had "made the trains run on time" like the bloated little Caesar of Fascist Italy whom so many befuddled foreign intellectuals fawned on before Ethiopia. But he and his imperial descendants, Alexander I of this poem, Nicholas I who was Pushkin's jailer and censor ("a lot of the staff sergeant in him, and a little of Peter the Great"), and their unanointed disciples of the last half-century have unalterably ranged against them the forces of intractable nature and elusive human privacy. This is what Mickiewicz's superb poems in the "Digression" are about; and this is what, despite Pushkin's conscious intentions, *The Bronze Horseman* came to be about also, under the compulsion of the Polish poet's fraternal genius.[2]

THE BRONZE HORSEMAN

A Tale of Petersburg

The occurrence described in this narrative is based on truth. The details of the flood are drawn from journals of the time. The curious may consult the account composed by V. N. Berkh.

PROLOGUE

Upon a shore of desolate waves
Stood *he*, with lofty musings grave,
And gazed afar. Before him spreading
Rolled the broad river, empty save
For one lone skiff stream-downward heading.
Strewn on the marshy, moss-grown bank,
Rare huts, the Finn's poor shelter, shrank,
Black smudges from the fog protruding;

Beyond, dark forest ramparts drank
The shrouded sun's rays and stood brooding
And murmuring all about.

He thought;
"Here, Swede, beware—soon by our labor
Here a new city shall be wrought,
Defiance to the haughty neighbor.
Here we at Nature's own behest
Shall break a window to the West,
Stand planted on the ocean level;
Here flags of foreign nations all
By waters new to them will call,
And unencumbered we shall revel."

A century passed, and there shone forth
From swamps and gloomy forest prison,
Crown gem and marvel of the North,
The proud young city newly risen.
Where Finnish fisherman before,
Harsh Nature's wretched waif, was plying,
Forlorn upon that shallow shore,
His trade, with brittle net-gear trying
Uncharted tides—now bustling banks
Stand serried in well-ordered ranks
Of palaces and towers; converging
From the four corners of the earth,
Sails press to seek the opulent berth,
To anchorage in squadrons merging;
Nevá is cased in granite clean,
Atop its waters bridges hover,
Between its channels, gardens cover
The river isles with darkling green.
Outshone, old Moscow had to render
The younger sister pride of place,
As by a new queen's fresh-blown splendor
In purple fades Her Dowager Grace.

I love you, work of Peter's warrant,
I love your stern and comely face,
The broad Nevá's majestic current,
Her bankments' granite carapace,
The patterns laced by iron railing,
And of your meditative night
The lucent dusk, the moonless paling;
When in my room I read and write
Lampless, and street on street stand dreaming,
Vast luminous gulfs, and, slimly gleaming,
The Admiralty's needle bright;
And rather than let darkness smother
The lustrous heavens' golden light,
One twilight glow speeds on the other
To grant but half an hour to night.

I love your winter's fierce embraces
That leave the air all chilled and hushed,
The sleighs by broad Nevá, girls' faces
More brightly than the roses flushed,
The ballroom's sparkle, noise, and chatter,
And at the bachelor rendezvous
The foaming beakers' hiss and spatter,
The flaming punch's flickering blue.
I love the verve of drilling duty
Upon the playing fields of Mars,[1]
Where troops of riflemen and horse
Turn massed precision into beauty,
Where laureled flags in tatters stream
Above formations finely junctured,
And brazen helmets sway and gleam,
In storied battles scarred and punctured.
I love, war-queen, your fortress pieces
In smoke and thunder booming forth
When the imperial spouse increases
The sovereign lineage of the North,
Or when their muzzles roar in token
Of one more Russian victory,
Or scenting spring, Nevá with glee,
Her ice-blue armor newly broken,

In sparkling floes runs out to sea.

Thrive, Peter's city, flaunt your beauty,
Stand like unshaken Russian fast,
Till floods and storms from chafing duty
May turn to peace with you at last;
The very tides of Finland's deep
Their long-pent rancor then may bury,
And cease with feckless spite to harry
Tsar Peter's everlasting sleep.

There was a time—our memories keep
Its horrors ever fresh and near us . . .
Of this a tale now suffer me
To tell before you, gentle hearers.
A grievous story it will be.

PART ONE

Through Peter's darkened city rolled
November's breath of autumn cold.
Nevá, her clamorous waters splashing
Against the crest of either dike,
Tossed in her shapely ramparts, like
A patient on his sickbed thrashing.
Already dark it was and late;
A rainstorm pressed its angry spate
At windowpanes, with moaning driven
By dismal winds. Just then was seen,
Back from a friend's house, young Eugene—
(A pleasant name that we have given
The hero of our tale; what's more,
My pen was friends with it before.)
His surname may go unrecorded;
Though once, who knows but it was lauded
In native lore, its luster keen
Blazed by the pen of Karamzin,[2]
By now the world and rumor held

No trace of it. Our hero dwelled
In poor Kolomna,[3] humbly serving
Some office, found the great unnerving,
And cared for neither buried kin
Nor legend-woven origin.

    And so tonight Eugene had wandered
Back home, slipped off his cloak, undressed,
Composed himself, but found no rest,
As ill at ease he lay and pondered.
What were his thoughts? That he was poor,
And by his labor must secure
A portion of esteem and treasure;
That God might well have eased his pains
With wit and cash; that men of leisure,
Endowed with luck if not with brains,
Could idly leave him at a distance,
And lead so carefree an existence!
He thought that in the post he held
He had attained but two years' rating;
That still the storm was not abating,
And that the banked-up river swelled
Still more—and since by now they surely
Had struck the bridges down securely,
He and Parasha must, he knew,
Be parted for a day or two.
And poet-like, Eugene, exhaling
A sigh, fell musing on his lot:

    "Get married? I? And, yet, why not?
Of course, it won't be easy sailing,
But what of that? I'm young and strong,
Content to labor hard and long,
I'll build us soon, if not tomorrow,
A simple nest for sweet repose
And keep Parasha free of sorrow,
And in a year or two, who knows,
I may obtain a snug position,
And it shall be Parasha's mission
To tend and rear our children . . .yes,

So we will live, and so forever
Will be as one, till death us sever,
And grandsons lay us both to rest . . ."
Thus ran his reverie. Yet sadly
He wished that night the wind would still
Its mournful wail, the rain less madly
Be rattling at the windowsill.
At last his eyelids, heavy-laden
Droop into slumber . . .soon away
The night's tempestuous gloom is fading
And washes into pallid day . . .
Disastrous day! Nevá all night
Has seaward strained, in hopeless muster
Of strength against the gale's wild bluster,
But now at last must yield the fight.

From morning, throngs of people line
The banks and marvel at the fountains
Of spray, the foam-tipped rolling mountains
Thrust up by the envenomed brine;
For now Nevá, her flow arrested
By the relentless sea-wind's force,
Reared up in fury, backward-crested,
And drowned the islands in her course.
The storm more fiercely yet upsoaring,
Nevá, engorged, with swell and roaring
As from a cauldron's swirl released,
Abruptly like a frenzied beast
Leaped on the city. At her onrush
All scattered, every place was swept
An instant void, swift waters crept
Into the deeply hollowed basements,
Canals rose gushing to the casements,
There streamed Petropolis, foam-laced,
Like Triton foundered to the waist.

Beset! Besieged! The vile surf charges
Through window frames like thieves, loose barges
Crush window panes, stern forward wrenched.

Street-hawkers' trays, their covers drenched,
Smashed cabins, roofing, rafters reeling,
The stock-in-trade of thrifty dealing,
The wretched gain of misery pale,
Whole bridges loosened by the gale,
Coffins unearthed, in horrid welter
Float down the streets.
                            In stricken gloom
All see God's wrath and bide their doom.
Alas! All founders, food and shelter!
Where now to turn?
                            That fateful year
Our famed late sovereign still was sitting
On Russia's throne—and sadly he
Appeared upon his balcony
And owned: "For tsars there is no pitting
Their power against the Lord's." His mien
All grief, he sat and contemplated
The fell disaster's desolate scene.
Into the squares to lakes dilated,
Debouched, like riverbeds inflated,
What had been streets. The palace stood
Like a lone cliff the waters riding.
The Tsar spoke out: and where they could,
By roadways near and distant gliding,
Upon their stormy path propelled,
The Emperor's generals went speeding
To save the people, who, unheeding
With fear, were drowning where they dwelled.

        That night, where on Tsar Peter's square
A corner-house[4] new-risen there
Had lately on its high porch shown—
One paw raised, as in live defiance—
A marble pair of guardian lions:
Astride upon the beast of stone
There sat, his arms crossed tight, alone,
Unmoving, deathly pale of feature,
Eugene. He was afraid, poor creature,
Not for himself. He did not hear

The evil breakers crest and rear,
His soles with greedy lashes seeking,
Nor feel the rain splash in his face,
Nor yet the gale with boisterous shrieking
Tear off his hat. Impaled in space,
His eyes held fast a distant border
And there in frozen anguish gazed.
There, mountainous, in wild disorder
From depths of chaos skyward raised,
Huge waves were towering and gloating,
There howled the storm and played with floating
Wreckage . . .God, God! Just there should be,
Set hard upon the inland sea,
Close, ah, too close to that mad billow,
A fence unpainted, and a willow,
And a frail hut: there dwelt those two,
Her mother and she, his bride bespoken,
Long dreamed-of . . .or was all he knew
A dream, naught but an empty token
All life, a wraith and no more worth,
But Heaven's mockery at Earth?

    And he, as by a spell enfolded,
By irons to the marble bolted,
Could not descend; all within sight
Was an unending watery blight.
And o'er Nevá all spray-ensheeted,
Its back to where Eugene still clung,
There towered immobile, undefeated,
Upon its bronzen charger seated,
The Idol with its arm outflung.

PART TWO

    With rack and ruin satiated,
Nevá, her wanton frenzy spent,
At last drew back her element—
By her own tumult still elated—
And nonchalantly abdicated

Her plunder. Thus a highwayman
Comes bursting with his vicious clan
Into some village, wrecking, slashing,
Destroying, robbing—shrieks and gnashing
Of teeth, alarms, oaths, outrage, roar—
Then, heavily with booty weighted,
Fearing pursuers, enervated,
The band of robbers homeward pour
And strew the wayside with their plunder.

  The waters fell, and as thereunder
Dry footing showed, Eugene, heartsore,
Benumbed with sorrow, fear, and wonder,
Made headlong for the riverside,
Close on the barely ebbing tide.
For still Nevá, high triumph breathing,
Sent angry billows upward seething
As from live coals beneath her course,
And still the whitecaps heaved and slanted,
And heavily the river panted
As will a battle-winded horse.
Eugene looks round: a boat on station!
He greets it like a revelation,
Calls to the wherryman—and he,
With daring unconcern, is willing
To take him for a quarter-shilling
Across that formidable sea.

  And long he struggled hard to counter
The turmoil with his practiced strength;
Time after time their craft, aflounder
Between banked waves, seemed sure to founder
With its rash crew—until at length
They reached the shore.

    Eugene, fear-stricken,
Runs down the long-familiar lane,
By long-dear places, looks—in vain:
Unknowable, a sight to sicken
The heart, all stares in disarray,

This flung aside, that swept away,
Here half-uprooted cabins listed,
There others lay all crushed and twisted,
Still others stood misplaced—all round,
Strewn as upon a battleground,
Were scattered corpses. Barely living,
Eugene flies onward arrow-straight,
Worn-out with terror and misgiving,
Onward to where he knows his fate
Awaits him with a secret message,
As it might be a sealed despatch.
Here is the suburb now, the passage
Down to the bay, and here the thatch . . .
But what is this?
                    He stopped, confounded.
Retraced his steps and once more rounded
That corner . . . stared . . . half raised a hand:
Here is the place where it should stand,
Here is the willow. There, remember,
The gate stood—razed, no doubt. And where,
Where is the house? Distraught and somber,
He paces back and forward there,
Talks to himself aloud, soon after
Bursts out abruptly into laughter
And slaps his forehead.

                    Night sank down
Upon the horror-shaken town;
But few found sleep, in every dwelling
They sat up telling and retelling
About the day just past.

                    Dawn's ray
From pallid banks of weary gray
Gleamed down upon the silent city
And found of yesterday's alarm
No trace. The purple cloak[5] of pity
Already covered recent harm
And all returned to former calm.
Down streets re-won for old endeavor

Men walk as callously as ever,
The morning's civil service troops,
Emerged from their nocturnal coops,
Are off to work. Cool tradesmen labor
To open cellar, vault, and store,
Robbed by Nevá the night before,
The sooner to surcharge their neighbor
For their grave loss. They carted off
Boats from the courtyards.

            (Count Khvostov,
A poet whom Parnassus nurses,
Lamented in immortal verses
The blight Nevá had left behind.)

     My pitiful Eugene, though—evil
His lot; alas, his clouded mind
Could not withstand the brute upheaval
Just wrought on it. The clash and strain
Of flood and storm forever thundered
Upon his ear; his thoughts a train
Of horrors, wordlessly he wandered;
Some secret vision seemed to chill
His mind. A week—a month—and still
Astray from home he roved and pondered.
As for the homestead he forsook,
The landlord let his vacant nook
To some poor poet. Eugene never
Returned to claim it back, nor took
His left possessions. Growing ever
More alien to the world, he strayed
All day on foot till nightfall led him
Down to the wharves to sleep. He made
His meals of morsels people fed him
Through windows. His poor clothing frayed
And moldered off him. Wicked urchins
Threw pebbles at his back. The searching
Coachwhips not seldom struck him when,
As often now, he would be lurching
Uncertain of his course; but then

He did not feel it for the pain
Of some loud anguish in his brain.
Thus he wore on his luckless span,
A moot thing, neither beast nor man,
Who knew if this world's child, or whether
A caller from the next.

               He slept
One night by the Nevá. The weather
Was autumn-bent. An ill wind swept
The river. Sullen swells had crept
Up banks and steps with plash and rumble,
As a petitioner might grumble
Unheard outside the judge's gate.
Eugene woke up. The light was failing,
The rain dripped, and the wind was wailing
And traded through the darkness late
Sad echoes with the watchman's hailing . . .

      Eugene sprang up, appeared to waken
To those remembered terrors; shaken,
He hurried off at random, then
Came to a sudden stop; again
Uncertainly his glances shifted
All round, wild panic marked his face.
Above him the great mansion lifted
Its columns. On the terrace-space,
One paw raised as in live defiance,
Stood sentinel those guardian lions,
And high above those rails, as if
Of altitude and darkness blended,
There rode in bronze, one arm extended,
The Idol on its granite cliff.

      Eugene's heart shrank. His mind unclouding
In dread, he knew the place again
Where the great flood had sported then,
Where those rapacious waves were crowding
And round about him raged and spun—

That square, the lions, and him—the one
Who, bronzen countenance upslanted
Into the dusk aloft, sat still,
The one by whose portentous will
The city by the sea was planted . . .
How awesome in the gloom he rides!
What thought upon his brow resides!
His charger with what fiery mettle,
His form with what dark strength endowed!
Where will you gallop, charger proud,
Where next your plunging hoofbeats settle?
Oh, Destiny's great potentate!
Was it not thus, a towering idol
Hard by the chasm, with iron bridle
You reared up Russia to her fate?

The piteous madman fell to prowling
About the statue's granite berth,
And furtively with savage scowling
He eyed the lord of half the earth.
His breath congealed in him, he pressed
His brow against the chilly railing,
A blur of darkness overveiling
His eyes; a flame shot through his breast
And made his blood seethe. Grimly louring,
He faced the haughty image towering
On high, and fingers clawed, teeth clenched,
As if by some black spirit wrenched,
He hissed, spite shaking him: "Up there,
Great wonder-worker you, beware! . . ."
And then abruptly wheeled to race
Away full tilt. The dread Tsar's face,
With instantaneous fury burning,
It seemed to him, was slowly turning . . .
Across these empty spaces bound,
Behind his back he heard resound,
Like thunderclouds in rumbling anger,
The deep reverberating clangor
Of pounding hoofs that shook the ground.
And in the moonlight's pallid glamor

Rides high upon his charging brute,
One hand stretched out, 'mid echoing clamor
The Bronzen Horseman in pursuit.
And all through that long night, no matter
What road the frantic wretch might take,
There still would pound with ponderous clatter
The Bronzen Horseman in his wake.

And ever since, when in his erring
He chanced upon that square again,
They saw a sick confusion blurring
His features. One hand swiftly then
Flew to his breast, as if containing
The anguished heart's affrighted straining;
His worn-out cap he then would raise,
Cast to the ground a troubled gaze
And slink aside.

A little island
Lies off the coast. There now and then
A stray belated fisherman
Will beach his net at dusk and, silent,
Cook his poor supper by the shore,
Or, on his Sunday recreation
A boating clerk might rest his oar
By that bleak isle. There no green thing
Will grow; and there the inundation
Had washed up in its frolicking
A frail old cottage. It lay stranded
Above the tide like weathered brush,
Until last spring a barge was landed
To haul it off. It was all crushed
And bare. Against the threshold pressed,
My madman's chilly corpse was found,
And forthwith in this very ground
For love of God was laid to rest.

EUGENE ONEGIN: INTRODUCTION

Pushkin's mature art is concrete and of this world, humanly dimensioned, capable even of homey simplicity, though never petty or stuffy. It remains craftsmanlike and lucid even in the noblest flights of his early and, occasionally, late mode of Schilleresque pathos—the vein of "The Dagger," "Liberty," "From Pindemonte," and of the prologue to *The Bronze Horseman.* It does not shroud itself in the draperies of diffuse idealism and shuns the metaphysical kitsch that marks much of contemporary romanticism and inheres, to name a prominent example, in the very conceptual structure of Goethe's *Faust.* Although Pushkin pays Goethe the tribute of a distant and in large part, one suspects, hearsay admiration, he would have snorted unprintably at such oddities of Goethean invention as Homunculus in his flood-lit sputnik, that amphibious montgolfière of hot air, or that even less buoyant classicist yeast cake, the hop-skip-and-jump-to-glory skirt-chaser, Euphorion-Byron. The murky and infelicitous threnode to Byron in *Faust II* (lines 9907 to 9938) contrasts very instructively with Pushkin's terse and inspired lines to the same Continental idol in "To the Sea," conceived roughly simultaneously and presented in the present anthology.

Not that Pushkin is always simple in form or earthbound in conception. Some of his structures, large and small, notably *Tsar Saltan* and *Eugene Onegin*, partake of the involute intricacy of a Chinese chess set; but they remain free of any cargo of symbolisms or any cast of cerebral pallor. Their complexity of structure and viewpoint is reminiscent rather— in a more purposeful and less mannered way—of the conceits that amused certain artists of the seventeenth and eighteenth centuries; those painted vistas, say, of the interior perspectives of a picture gallery. You enter the frame of the painting, as Alice entered her looking glass, and gain a limited, doubly abstracted, but infinitely suggestive view of a world of little worlds: foreshortened corridors alive with miniature portraits and landscapes and interiors in every manner and style, usually authentic and recognizable works, with mirrors placed here and there to double and quadruple, remove and ironize the sights, and doors half-open to glimpses of receding halls and cabinets and more corridors. There is a modest example of the kind in the Hermitage, and some finer ones in West European galleries. The finest of them all is *Eugene Onegin.*

For expert and far-ranging commentary on Pushkin's central work, *Eugene Onegin*, see volumes II and III of Vladimir Nabokov's *Aleksandr*

Pushkin, Eugene Onegin, Bollingen Series, LXXII (New York: Pantheon Books, 1964 and Princeton Univ. Press, 1975). A succinct introduction to the work, critical studies by R. Jakobson and others, and a full translation in the metric form of the original are found in my own *Alexander Pushkin: Eugene Onegin*; The Bollingen Prize Translation in the Onegin Stanza (New York: Dutton Paperbacks, 1981, 2nd edition, revised and expanded).

First published in the present anthology are the surviving complete stanzas of *Onegin's Journey*, which was originally to constitute Canto VIII of the novel.

SELECTED STANZAS FROM *EUGENE ONEGIN*

A Novel in Verse

I, 1

"Now that he is in grave condition,
My uncle, principled old dunce, [1]
Has won respectful recognition
And done the perfect thing for once.
His act should be a guide to others;
But what a bore, I ask you, brothers,
To tend a patient night and day
And venture not a step away!
Is there hypocrisy more glaring
Than to amuse one all-but-dead,
Fluff up the pillow for his head,
Dose him with melancholy bearing,
And think behind a public sigh:
Deuce take you, step on it and die!"

I, 2

Thus a young good-for-nothing muses,
As in the dust his post-wheels spin,

By a decree of sovereign Zeus's
The extant heir to all his kin.
Friends of Ruslan and of Liudmila!
Allow me, with no cautious feeler
Or foreword, to present at once
The hero of my new romance:
Onegin, a dear friend of mine,
Born where Nevá flows, and where you,
I daresay, gentle reader, too
Were born, or once were wont to shine;
There I myself once used to be:
The North, though, disagrees with me.[2]

II, 1

The manor where Onegin fretted
Was so enchanting a retreat,
No simple soul would have regretted
Exile so pastoral and sweet:
The hall, well sheltered from intrusion
Of world and wind, stood in seclusion
Upon a stream-bank; and away
There stretched a shimmering array
Of meads and cornfields gold-brocaded,
And hamlets winked; across the grass
A wandering herd would slowly pass;
And leafy clusters densely shaded
The park, far-rambling and unkempt,
Where pensive dryads dwelt and dreamt.

II, 2

The hall was built on unpretentious
But solid lines, such as befit
The plain good taste and conscientious
Design of timeless mother-wit.
Room after room with lofty ceiling,
A tapestried *salon*, revealing

Ancestral portraits hung in file[3]
And stoves of many-colored tile.
All this has now been superseded,
Exactly why, I never learned;
But where Onegin was concerned
In any case it went unheeded,
Because he yawned with equal gloom
In any style of drawing room.

III, 22

With beauties have I been acquainted
As pure as winter and as kind,
Untouched, untempted, and untainted
Inviolate even to the mind;
I have admired their self-possession,
Their innate virtue and discretion,
And run for cover, I avow,
As if beholding at their brow
The dread inscription over Hades:
"Abandon hope who enter here."
To kindle feeling strikes with fear,
And to repel, delights these ladies.
On the Nevá have some of you
Not come across such Vestals too?

III, 23

And others shine there, proudly wielding
Adherents to their service bent,
Themselves complacently unyielding
To passion's plea and blandishment.
And what was I amazed to witness?
When with a show of rigid fitness
They've driven bashful love away,
They lure it back into the fray
By a judicious use of kindness:

The words at any rate appear
At times less formal and severe—
And with impressionable blindness
The love-game's innocent recruit
Returns to the inane pursuit.

III, 25

A flirt allures with calculation,
Tatyana's love is his to keep,
Without reserve or hesitation,
As dear as children's and as deep.
She has not learned to whisper: tarry—
With choicer bait to trap the quarry
The more securely in the net,
Designing here with hope to whet
Vainglory, there to leave suspended
The doubting heart, then stoke desire
To higher blaze with jealous fire,
Lest, ardor in fulfillment ended,
The cunning slave should entertain
A restless urge to slip his chain.

IV, 38, 39

Reposeful slumber, reading, rambling,
The purl of brooks, the sylvan shades,
Betweentimes fresh young kisses sampling
From creamy-skinned and black-eyed maids,
An eager mount, to rein obedient,
Light dinner taken when expedient,
A glass or two of gleaming wine,
Seclusion, hush: thus in divine
Simplicity his life proceeded;
Unfeelingly, without a care,
He sipped its sweetness, unaware
Of summer's shining gait; unheeded

Alike his urban friends and treats
And tedious holiday conceits.

IV, 40

But then, our northern summer season
Like southern winter comes, and lo,
Is gone, and though for some odd reason
We won't admit it, it is so.
Autumn was in the air already,
The sun's gay sparkle grew unsteady,
The timeless day became more brief;
The forest, long in darkling leaf,
Unclothed itself with mournful rustle;
The fields were wrapped in misty fleece,
A raucous caravan of geese
Winged southward; after summer's bustle
A duller season was at hand:
November hovered overland.

IV, 41

Through frigid haze the dawn resurges,
Abroad the harvest sounds abate;
And soon the hungry wolf emerges
Upon the highway with his mate.
His scent scares into snorting flurries
The trudging horse; the traveler hurries
His way uphill in wary haste.
No longer are the cattle chased
Out of the byre at dawn, the thinning
Horn notes of cowherds cease the tune
That rounds them up again at noon.
Indoors the maiden sings at spinning
Before the crackling pine-flare light
Companion of the winter night.

IV, 42

At last a crackling frost enfolded
Fields silvered o'er with early snows:
(All right—who am I to withhold it,
The rhyme you knew was coming—*rose*!)
The ice-clad river's polished luster
No stylish ballroom floor could muster;
A joyous swarm of urchins grates
The frozen sheet with ringing skates.
A cumbrous goose on ruddy paddies
Comes waddling down the bank to swim,
Steps gingerly across the rim,
Slithers and falls; in swirling eddies
Descends the virgin snow and pranks
And showers stars upon the banks.

IV, 43

What in those winterbound recesses
To do? Take walks? One must agree,
The somber countryside depresses
With its austere monotony.
Across the frozen steppes to gallop?
Your horse, its iron's blunted scallop
Caught on a vicious icy clot,
Will have a fall, as like as not.
Stay in your cell and read: the highlights
Are Pradt and Walter Scott. No good?
Not interested? Well, you could
Check ledgers, sulk, drink—the long twilights
Will somehow pass, tomorrow's too,
And so the whole gay winter through!

V, I

Fall lingered on as if it never
Would leave the countryside that year,

While Nature seemed to wait forever
For winter. Snow did not appear
Till the third January morning.
Up early, Tanya without warning
Finds roofs and fences overnight
Turned to exhilarating white,
Her window laced with subtle etching,
The trees with wintry silver starred,
Pert magpies sporting in the yard,
The softly covered hilltops stretching
'Neath winter's scintillating pall . . . .
And clear is all, and white is all.

V, 2

Winter . . . the peasant, feeling festive,
Breaks in a track with sledge and horse;
Sensing the snow, his nag is restive
And manages a trot of sorts;
Here passes, powdery furrows tracing,
A spirited kibítka,[4] racing,
The coachman on his box a flash
Of sheepskin coat and crimson sash.
There runs a yard-boy, having chosen
To seat his "Rover" on a sled,
Himself hitched up in charger's stead;
The rascal rubs one finger, frozen
Already, with a wince and grin,
While Mother shakes her fist within.

V, 11

And dreams a dream of wondrous strangeness.
She seems to walk a wintry field,
A clearing set in snowy ranges,
By dreary vapors half concealed.
Ahead, between the snowdrifts rushing,

Its angry waters, swirling, gushing,
In somber grayness roars and strains
A stream, still free of winter's chains.
Two boughs which ice has fused together
Here form a parlous swaying plank
To join the near and further bank;
Distraught, uncertain where and whether
To dare the roaring torrent's wrath,
Tatyana halted in her path.

V, 12

The stream, like rankling separation,
Moves her to chide it, as it were;
There's no one at the further station
To stretch a helping hand to her;
But there—a snowdrift heaves and surges,
And from beneath it who emerges?
A bear, disheveled all and swarth;
Tanya cries out, he stretches forth
A mighty paw with razor talons
And growls; she with a shrinking hand
Supports herself upon it, and
In tremulously halting balance
Is borne across the torrent there;
And then—the bear comes after her!

V, 13

She dares no backward glance, unable
To spur her hurried steps enough,
And still the groom in shaggy sable
Refuses to be shaken off;
Still onward crashed the fiend and shuffled.
Woods loom ahead; tall firs unruffled
In their beclouded beauty frown,
Their sloping branches all weighed down
With pads of snow. Through the denuded

Treetops of linden, birch, and ash
The rays of heaven's lanterns flash.
No path leads here; all blurred and hooded,
The brush and hillsides rise and fall,
Enveloped deep in snowy pall.

VI, 44

With new temptations I am lusting,
With yet untasted sorrow sad;
The first I find myself mistrusting,
And hanker for the grief I had.
Oh, dreams, my dreams, where is your sweetness?
Oh, youth's (the rhyme fair beckons) fleetness!
Can it be really true at last,
Its lovely bloom is past, is past,
In truth, in sober earnest ended?
All elegiac pose aside,
The springtime of my days has hied
(As hitherto I just pretended)?
Is it irrevocably noon?
Shall I be really thirty soon?

VI, 45

The afternoon of life is starting,
I see I must confront this truth.
So be it: friendly be our parting,
Oh, nimble season of my youth!
For your delights my thanks I render,
For suffering, for torments tender,
For turmoil, tempest, revelry,
For all the bounty proffered me,
I render thanks. In full, aye, doubled,
Alike in tumult and in calm
I quaffed you, without stint or qualm.
Enough! And now I set, untroubled,

My course for quite another shore
To rest from what I knew before.

VI, 46

One backward glance; farewell, dear settings
Where my lone days were used to roll,
Instinct with ease and passion's frettings
And musings of the pensive soul.
But you, my verdant inspiration,
Keep ever green imagination,
Come winging oftener to this part;
Come quickening the slumbrous heart,
Let not the poet's soul grow frigid,
Or coarsen to a cruder cast
And turn to lifeless stone at last,
With worldly stupor numb and rigid,
In that vile quicksand where we lie
And wallow, brothers, you and I!

VII, 1

The snows from the surrounding mountains,
By spring's insistent rays beset,
By now cascade in turbid fountains
On meads already glistening wet,
And Nature from her slumber breaking
Greets with a smile the year's awaking.
The sky renews its azure sheen,
And with a downy haze of green
The still transparent forest rallies,
While from her waxen cell the bee
Goes gathering the meadow-fee.
Gay hues invade the drying valleys,
Herds rustle, and the twilight hush
Has thrilled to nightingale and thrush.

VII, 2

How I am saddened by your coming,
Oh time of love, oh time of bud!
What languid throb you send benumbing
Into my soul, into my blood!
What painful-tender feeling seizes
The heart, as spring's returning breezes
Waft to my face in silken rush
Here in the lap of rural hush!
Have I become so alienated
From all things that exult and glow,
All things that joy and life bestow,
That now they find me dull and sated,
And all seems pale as burnt-out coal
To the long-since insentient soul?

VII, 6

By rolling mountains half-surrounded,
Come, let us wander where one sees
A brook meander, meadow-bounded,
Across a grove of linden trees.
Nightlong, the nightingale, spring's lover,
Sings there, and heather roses hover
Above the coursing water's drone;
And here a tomb and graven stone—
Two venerable firs impart it
Their shadow—tell the passing guest:
"Vladimir Lensky here found rest,
Who met death young and eager-hearted;
Such was the year, *so long* his lease.
Fair youth and poet, sleep in peace."

VII, 7

There, for a time, when night had ended,
On a low branch one might discern
A wreath, by unknown hand suspended,
Asway above the tranquil urn;
And for a time, two maidens yonder
At leisured eventide would wander
And by the rising moon be found
In mingled tears upon the mound.
But now . . . the mournful shrine is never
Sought out; the trail that passed beneath,
Untrod; the fir branch bears no wreath.
Alone the shepherd sings as ever,
Grizzled and frail, his simple air
And plaits his artless sandal there.

ONEGIN'S JOURNEY

The Complete Stanzas[5]

XII

He sees the willful Térek scour
Its gorges, twisting to and fro,
Sees a majestic eagle tower,
A standing buck, its antlers low;
A camel rests in cliffside shadows,
Circassian steeds percourse the meadows,
And Kalmyk sheep at pasture stray
By nomad tentments; far away
Show dimly piled Caucasian masses,
Now free of access: war has pried
Apart their natural divide,
Has swept across their frowning passes;
Now Russian bivouacs line in ranks

Kurá's and swift Arágva's banks.

XIII

By then Beshtú, pent by a cordon
Of lesser mountains close about,
The craggy-peaked eternal warden
Of arid wilderness, stands out;
And green Mashúk, profuse with courses
Of healing streams; to its blest sources
In pallid swarms the patients pour
To cure, now honest wounds of war,
Now sores of Haemorrhoid or Venus;
The sufferer dearly hopes to slow
Life's passing in the wondrous flow,
The jade, to sink her years of heinous
Offence in it; and agèd men,
To grow, if briefly, young again.

XIV

Engrossed in bitter meditations
Amidst this melancholy crew,
Onegin looks with wry impatience
Upon the waters dim with dew
And thinks: why could not I be blessed
With such a bullet in my chest?
Why am I not a senile coot
Like that poor sack of landed loot?
Why, like the alderman from Tula,
May I not lie there stiff with gout?
Could not at least my shoulder sprout
Rheumatic pains? O Lord and Ruler,
I'm young, and life is strong in me,
And what's ahead? Ennui, ennui!

[XV]

XVI

Fair are you, Tauris' shores, at dawning
Beheld from shipboard when you climb
In view beneath the star of morning,
As I beheld you that first time.
Revealed as if in nuptial lustre,
Your shining massive mountain-cluster,
And valleys, trees, and hamlets traced
Against the blue and limpid waste,
Spread to my gazes in their turning.
There, 'mid the huts of **Tartary**...
What inner glow was lit in me!
What magical constraint of yearning
Was on my ardent bosom cast!
But, Muse, forbear—forget the past!

XVII

Whatever feelings then were hidden
Within me, they are there no more:
They suffered change or left unbidden.
Peace unto you, wild pangs of yore!
I felt I had to pay addresses
To pearly wave-crests, wildernesses,
What ocean voice and cliffs reveal,
And that "proud maiden," my ideal,
And inarticulate afflictions . . .
New days, though, new imaginings;
You have subsided now, my spring's
Daydreaming and exalted fictions;
The juice in my poetic pot
Has since been watered down a lot.

XVIII

I feel the need for other sketches . . .
I like a sloping sandy track,
A wicker gate, neglected hedges,
Two rowans by a peasant shack,
A clouded sky with grayish hatching,
A threshing yard with piles of thatching,
A village pond with willows thick,
Young ducklings' rightful bailiwick.
I now enjoy the balalaika,
The jig's inebriated whoop
And thumping at the tavern stoop;
Now my ideal is the *khozaika*, [6]
My wish, just to be left alone:
"A pot of *shchi*, and me my own."

XIX

The other day, in rainy weather,
I happened into my stockade—
But fie on me! What prosy blather,
The Flemands' piebald stock-in-trade!
Was this my way when sap was mounting?
Speak up, Bakhchisarayan Fountain!
Was this the kind of specimen
Drawn from your ceaseless purling then,
When silently I sat and pondered
Zarema's tale in front of you?
Those proud forsaken halls I knew—
Onegin in my footsteps wandered
There also after three years' lapse
And recollected me perhaps.

XX

I know Odessa's dusty summers . . .
There cloudless skies for long prevail,
There bustles an abundant commerce,
Outfitting sail on busy sail;
It blends with Western flair and fashion
Mediterranean glamor, flashing
With animate variety;
The tongue of golden Italy
Resounds with cheer across the paving;
With haughty Slavs parade the streets
Armenians, Frenchmen, Spaniards, Greeks,
Besides the ponderous Moldavian,
And the Egyptian, Moralí,
Emeritus of piracy.

XXI

Our friend Tumansky has depicted
Odessa in resounding rhyme,
But he must clearly be convicted
Of being partial at the time.
For he arrived fresh from Parnassus
And wandered with his spying-glasses
Alone above the sea, and then
With his intoxicating pen
Extolled "the gardens of Odessa."
But he ignored the facts: to wit,
There's naked steppe surrounding it;
But seldom toil and water pressure
Has dabbed some artificial green
Upon the calcinated scene.

XXII

But let me take my ramble farther . . .
I called Odessa dusty then;

I might have called in muddy rather
And told no more than truth again.
Six weeks a year, the heaven's sluices
By a decree of Stormy Zeus's
Flood, bog, and choke the place entire
In thick impenetrable mire.
Half-fathom deep the houses wallow,
Pedestrians must lift their feet
On stilts to get across the street,
Men are engulfed and coaches follow,
And oxen, straining shanks and necks,
Replace the broken-winded hacks.

XXIII

But stone is being crushed by hammer
To lay a ringing pavement down,
Which like an iron suit of armor
Will rehabilitate the town.
But then another, hardly lesser,
Defect bedevils moist Odessa.
What shortage? Water, if you please;
Which takes a deal of toil to ease . . .
What of it, though? You see, the beauty
Of this is that in water's place
A cask of wine will meet the case,
Which is imported free of duty.
And then, the sun, the sea . . . It's still
A blessèd spot, say what you will!

XXIV

There was a season when no sooner
I'd heard the sunrise cannon roar
Its signal from an anchored schooner
Than I would scamper down to shore.
My hot chibúk blue trailers drifting,

The briny surf my spirits lifting,
Black coffee, thick and sweet, I quaff,
A muslim at his blissful *keyf*.
I take a stroll. There clinks already
The kind Casino's crockery,
And high upon the balcony
The billiard-marker wields, unsteady
With sleep, his broom, while on the stair
There waits an early merchant pair.

XXV

When next you look, the square is zestful
With life and color. To and fro
They stream, on business or restful,
The first more than the second, though.
The child of pluck and calculation,
The merchant, scans the mooring station
And wonders if the heavens chose
To send him back a sail he knows.
What cargoes might they now examine
In storage under quarantine?
Has he been sent the ordered wine?
What war has broken out? What famine?
What news of fire or pestilence
Or similar intelligence?

XXVI

But we young fellows, never fretting,
Unlike the watchful merchantdom,
Have only to await a setting
Of oysters from Byzantium.
They've come, you say? What joy amongst us!
Off scamper the voracious youngsters
To swallow from the sea-wet shell
The chubby hermit, live and well,
Caressed with juice from lemon slivers.

Discussion, noise; there comes aboard
Light wine, which from the cellar hoard
The prompt Monsieur Automne[7] delivers.
Time flies, the while the fearsome bill
Invisibly grows longer still.

XXVII

But now the evening blue is fading,
It's close to opera time, we're pressed!
Rossini waits, the scintillating
Orpheus and darling of the West.
Cantankerous reviews ignoring,
He stays the same, yet never boring;
He pours out music, and it breathes,
It coolly flows, it hotly seethes,
It turns the mind to youthful kissing,
All languid with the senses' bloom;
To Aï's spurt and golden spume
Caught in the goblet, cool and hissing . . .
But, friends—to mix do-re-mi-so
With wine is hardly *comme il faut?*

XXVIII

How rich a spread for our elation!
What of the spyglass's foray?
What of the backstage assignation?
The Primadonna? The ballet?
The box where, in young beauty shining,
The merchant's wife is seen reclining,
Complacent and inured to raves,
Surrounded by her troop of slaves?
She both takes in and pays no mind to
Melodious serenade or plea,
Or jest disguising flattery.
Her husband in the chair behind her

Cries out a drowsy "bravo," then
Completes a yawn and snores again.

XXIX

Finale storms; the crowd retraces
Its entrance, loud and pent up tight,
Then bursts into the public places;
With streetlamps and the stars for light,
Sons of Ausonia[8] the placid
Strike up the kind of catchy passage
Which charms the mind and never leaves,
While we belt out recitatives.
It's late, though. All Odessa slumbers,
Alike inanimate and warm
Its soundless night. The lunar form
Shows through a gossamer penumbra
Which mists the sky. All nature rests
But for the murmuring Black Sea crests.

[End of *Onegin's Travels*]

VIII, I

When in the parks of the Lyceum
A carefree flower life I led,
And eagerly read *Apuleium*,
But *Ciceronem* left unread,
In springtime, when the stillness brought us
But swan calls over gleaming waters,
In valleys charged with mystery
The Muse began to visit me.
Into my monkish study breaking
Like sudden dawn, she would ignite
The sparkling trails of fancy-flight
And sing of childish merrymaking,

Our glorious dawn's heroic themes,
The heart's first palpitating dreams.

VIII, 2

And lo, the public smiled, and served us
The fairy food of early fame;
Derzhavin in old age observed us
And, gravebound, with his blessings came . . .

. . . .
. . . .
. . . .
. . . .
. . . .
. . . .
. . . .
. . . .
. . . .
. . . .

VIII, 3

And I, adopting for sole canons
The passions' arbitrary cues,
Confiding all to chance companions,—
I brought my enterprising muse
To noisy feasts and disputations,
Patrolmen's midnight imprecations,
And at such giddy feasts she flung
Her gifts among the boisterous throng,
A young bacchante—joined their revels
And, singing to the clink of glass,
Was wooed with many an ardent pass
By those now middle-aged young devils;
And I was happy to show off
My volatile young lady love.

VIII, 4

But angry fortune glared upon me
And drove me far . . . She left me not,
My tender maid, and often won me
Sweet respite with a wondrous plot
That charmed the burden off my shoulders.
How often 'mid Caucasian boulders
On moonlit gallops it was she
Who, like Lenore, rode with me!
How often by the Tauris' waters
She led the way through misty caves
Of night, to hear the murmuring waves,
The endless lisp of Nereus' daughters,
The breakers' deep, eternal choir
In praise of all creation's sire!

VIII, 5

The capital's ado and glitter
Forsworn as soon as left behind,
She roamed the humble tents of bitter
Moldavia, and found them kind.
In that bleak wilderness she rambled
With wandering tribes, and soon resembled
Her hosts, forgot for their scant tongue
That of the gods whence she had sprung,
And learned the airs of that steppe pleasance.
Then—sudden shift of scene all round—
In my own garden she was found,
Clothed in a country damsel's presence,
In wistful musing steeped her glance,
And in her hand a book from France.

NOTES

NOTES TO THE INTRODUCTION

1. Like Samuel Cross, Leo Wiener, Leonid Strakhovsky, Albert Parry, and A. P. Coleman; Ernest Simmons, René Wellek, and Roman Jakobson, Michael Karpovich, Renato Poggioli, and Wiktor Weintraub, Isaiah Berlin, Gleb Struve, Dimitri von Mohrenschildt, and Wacław Lednicki.

2. *The Works of Alexander Pushkin: Lyrics, Narrative Poems, Folktales, Plays, Prose.* Selected and edited, with an introduction, by Avram Yarmolinsky (New York: Random House, 1936). Reissued later as a "Borzoi" volume under the title *The Poems, Plays, and Prose of Pushkin.*

NOTES TO LYRIC POEMS

To Chaadaev

1. Petr Yakovlevich Chaadaev or Chadaev (1793-1856), Western-oriented Russian philosopher who in his late twenties began to circulate, in French manuscript, his *Lettres philosophiques*. They contained a profound critique of Russian historical evolution on premises of a quasi-Catholic world view. The first of these *Lettres*, published in Russian in 1836, caused the journal *Telescope* to be shut down, and Chaadaev to be declared insane and put under house arrest. Pushkin had known and admired him ever since Chaadaev was stationed at Tsarskoe Selo as a young officer.

To the Author of History of the Russian State

1. N. M. Karamzin (1766-1826), the noted stylist and pioneer of new literary movements, whose famous *History* was conservative and strongly monarchist in tone.

The Dagger

1. Hephaistos, in charge of Metallurgy, Thermodynamics, and Mechanical Engineering.

2. The border stream between Cisalpine Gaul and Italy. Caesar crossed it with his army, violating the terms of his senatorial mandate and precipitating the civil war that ended the Republic.

3. The propitiatory term for the dreaded Erinyes (the Latin Furies), the ancient divinities of retribution.

4. The German nationalist student Karl Ludwig Sand (1795-1820), who in 1819 shot the reactionary German playwright and Russian official August Friedrich von Kotzebue (1761-1819), who was also an intermittent Bonapartist. Sand was executed in 1820, and thus became a martyr to anti-Napoleonic Europe.

Napoleon

1. The iron crown of Lombardy, dating back to the 5th century A.D., which Napoleon had assumed some time after the Italian campaigns. It seems unlikely that he fingered it, like Nero his lyre, while Moscow burned.

To Ovid

1. Consult the notes to the narrative poem *The Gypsies* in this volume. Here Pushkin uses

alexandrines—the traditional classicist form of the ode, in six-footed couplets—a form never naturalized in English.

2. Ivid's *cognomen* or nickname, *Nose*.

3. Augustus' *nomen gentile* (clan name), used before his elevation to monarchic statue.

Epigram on A. A. Davydova

1. Agláya Davydova, née Duchesse de Grammont, (the promiscuous wife of General Alexander Davydov, the southern Decembrist's brother), whose favors Pushkin also enjoyed briefly.

2. Cleon and Damis are shepherds' names in 17th and 18th century pastoral poetry. They probably stand for Davydova's lovers without any personal reference.

From a Letter to Wiegel

1. F. F. Vigel', writer and memoirist, was among Pushkin's companions in the St. Petersburg literary coterie, Arzamas.

On Count Vorontsov

1. Count Vorontsov was provincial governor and Pushkin's ex officio guardian at Odessa in 1923-24. He was noted for his commercial interests, his anglophilia, and his beautiful wife's androphilia.

To A. N. Wulf

1. A. N. Wulf was a dissolute young man from the Baltic provinces, a relative and frequent visitor to Pushkin's neighbors at Trigorskoe, near his own place of confinement, Mikhailovskoe.

2. N. M. Yazykov (1803-46) was one of the leading poets of Pushkin's circle.

Conversation between Bookseller and Poet

1. For information on Zhukovsky see the Introduction to *Ruslan and Liudmila* in this volume.

2. Korinna was a 6th century lyric poet from Boeotia in central Greece, by tradition the teacher of the great odist, Pindar.

To the Sea

1. Lord Byron, who had perished at Missolonghi that year.

Cleopatra

1. This is the earliest of Pushkin's several treatments of the fiction of Cleopatra's testing her admirers' passion.

To Yazykov

1. Camoenae or Camenae were soothsaying nymphs of the springs in ancient Italic folklore, equated since Livius Andronicus with the Greek Muses. The one most often cited, Egeria, came to stand in a general sense for "the Muse" who inspired the poet.

2. Hippocrene is the source that, according to Greek legend, sprang up under the hoofbeat of Pegasus and was thought of as the fount of poetic imagination.

To I. I. Pushchin

1. Ivan Ivanovich Pushchin had been P.'s close friend ever since they were classmates at Tsarskoe Selo (1811-17). Undeterred by P.'s latest official disgrace, Pushchin used a convenient family connection at Pskov to visit P. in January, 1825, at the nearby family estate

of Mikhailovskoe, which P. inhabited under surveillance from both state and church authorities from 1824 to 1826. This was especially risky in view of Pushchin's own active role in the inner circle of the Decembrist conspiracy. The friends had a heartwarming reunion, both fearing, correctly, that under the circumstances it might be their last. Pushchin was condemned to Siberia after the Decembrist revolt, and on arriving at the remote prison camp, three years after that visit, was handed the present poem.

We owe to Pushchin an invaluable set of sensitive and penetrating memoirs covering the fourteen years of their close association.

Stanzas

1. (On the accession of Nicholas I.)

2. Count Vasily Lukich Dolgoruki (1672-1739) was among the first young Russians to be sent abroad by Peter I to be educated. He served for a time as his foremost ministerial counselor and was entrusted with several important embassies. His later career was both less fortunate and less savory.

Winter Journey

1. Both in metric form and lyrical atmosphere this poem oddly resembles Nikolaus Lenau's "Der Postillon," conceived in the same general period, although there can scarcely be any connection between the two.

To Dawe, Esq.

1. George Dawe (1781-1829), English portrait painter and mezzotint engraver in the manner of Sir Joshua Reynolds. Went to Russia and was named First Painter in the Court of Russia by Alexander I, who had him paint about 400 portraits of officers who served in the Napoleonic Wars. Several of Dawe's paintings hang in the Hermitage Musuem in Leningrad.

Remembrance

1. A continuation of this poem, to more than double its length in print, exists in a manuscript version that shows a few single-word gaps. These, and an unexplained reference to "two dear shades, angels given me by fate in bygone days," may explain Pushkin's decision not to include the rest of the poem in editions printed in his lifetime.

Egyptian Nights

1. In Pushkin's prose sketch "Egyptian Nights" (now available in English in Paul Debreczeny's *Alexander Pushkin: Complete Prose Fiction,* Stanford University Press, 1983), an Italian improvisor of poetry first recites the present poem on a set subject as proof of his powers. Later he proceeds before a larger company to improvise the Cleopatra poem next following. The "first improvisation" took shape originally as stanzas 12 and 13 of Pushkin's fragmentary narrative poem, *Ezersky,* in 1832-33. But since it was inserted into "Egyptian Nights" (1835?) logically preceding the Cleopatra poem (1828), we have chosen this order of presentation.

As down the noisy streets I wander

1. This query is echoed by, among many others, Heinrich Heine when he asks ca. 1825 in "Wo?":

Wo wird einst des Wandermüden/ Letzte Ruhestätte sein?/ Unter Palmen in dem Süden?/ Unter Linden an dem Rhein?// Werd' ich wo in einer Wüste/ Eingescharrt von fremder Hand?/ Oder ruh' ich an der Küste/ Eines Meeres in dem Sand?// Immerhin! Mich wird umgeben/ Gotteshimmel, dort wie hier,/ Und als Totenlampen schweben/ Nachts die Sterne über mir.

At the Bust of a Conqueror
   1. Directed at Alexander I.

What use my name to you, what good?
   1. Written in response to a request to write his name in the album of the Polish beauty, Countess Karolina Sobańska, already immortalized by the love of Mickiewicz.

Conjury
   1. Barry Cornwall (pseudonym for the minor English dramatist and poet B. W. Procter, 1787-1874) published a poem with a similar title which, like other works of his, had some influence on Pushkin in this period.

To the Slanderers of Russia
   1. This poem is Pushkin's angry reply to the clamor of indignation and calls for intervention generated in Western Europe by the brutal suppression of the Polish uprising of 1831, of which his friend Mickiewicz became the spokesman and spiritual leader abroad.
   2. The suburb of Warsaw where the insurgents made their last desperate stand.
   3. The Turkish fortress in Bessarabia stormed by Suvorov in 1790.

Echo
   1. The motif of this lyric appears to have been drawn from Barry Cornwall, see note to "Conjury."

The Commander
   1. The maligned *Commander* of this poem is Field Marshal Barclay de Tolly, Russian commander-in-chief during the first phase of Napoleon's Russian campaign in 1812. Barclay de Tolly, who was the strategist behind the ultimately successful campaign, had been abruptly relieved of his command as a concession to mob chauvinism, which took umbrage at his French name and hinted at treason.

From Pindemonte
   1. Italian poet (1753-1828), to whom Pushkin ascribed this ode to privacy solely in order to hoodwink the censorship.

NOTES TO *RUSLAN AND LIUDMILA*

Introduction
   1. This last reference is a little puzzling. The octave is part of Genevra's tale of her infatuation with a young courtier, but is totally unrewarding for the seeker of titillation. It contains nothing more heating than the young lady's admission that she did her best to lure the gentleman into her bed.
   2. Consider *Spiess* 'roasting spit; pike,' whence prob. *Spiesser* 'militiaman, pawn,' then 'lowbrow, philistine, *pošljak;* cf. Eng. piker.

Ruslan and Liudmila
   1. The best known of the Russian witches. Pushkin gives her a free ride here, but tradition has her paddle a mortar with a pestle and sweep behind her with a broom.
   2. Kashchey or Koshchey, usually called "deathless" in fairy tales and byliny, plays the role of a grasping guardian of treasure, hostile to the hero. So does the serpent or dragon, and

they often interchange roles in parallel versions of tales. Although Kashchey is mentioned in the preface, it is Chernomor who takes his part in the poem, and Naina, who significantly adopts a serpent's guise, seconds him in defending the treasures—Liudmila and the Beard. But Kashchey is a far more durable nuisance than Chernomor. To kill him, one must find the island of Buyan (cf. Pushkin's *Tsar Saltan*), from under a green oak tree dig up an iron casket, wherein a hare, in which a duck, wherein an egg. If this egg be squeezed, the ogre will feel a mortal agony; if squashed, it will be his death.

3. The folklore embodiment of Vladimir I Svyatoslavich, Prince of Novgorod (970-979) and Great Prince of Kiev (979-1015), in-law of the East Roman Emperor, and Christianizer of Rus'.

4. Alexander Orlowski (1777-1832), Polish genre and battle painter, active in Warsaw under the patronage of Princess Czartoryski and Prince Józef Poniatowski, in Petersburg a protégé of the later Polish Viceroy, Grand Duke Konstantin Pavlovich; admired for his dashing way with combat scenes.

5. Zoilos of Amphipolis, 4th c. B.C. rhetorician and critic, whose name became synonymous with carper for having filled nine books with niggling strictures on Homer's logic and grammar.

6. Names of this sort of flavor are often adopted by Pushkin for masked or fictitious persons; they may or may not have an original in French erotic or pastoral writing.

7. Here follows a plot summary of Zhukovsky's *The Twelve Sleeping Maidens*, cf. Introduction.

8. An allusion, earnestly "veiled" so as to leave the girl all but naked, to the liberated heroine of Mme. de Staël's famous novel *Delphine* (1802).

NOTES TO *THE GYPSIES*

1. The legend alludes to Ovid, the Roman poet banished by Augustus in A.D. 8 to Tomi on the Black Sea, not far from Bessarabia, the setting of *The Gypsies* and Pushkin's own temporary place of exile.

2. Derogatory Slavic, especially Polish, term for "Muscovite."

3. The Budzhak (Turkish: *bucak*, "corner," probably from the angle between the Prut and the Danube) is the extensive *puszta*-like prairieland of southern Bessarabia.

NOTES TO *COUNT NULIN*

1. François Guizot (1787-1874), French conservative statesman and historian, elected to the Academy. "Little books," as the original has it, were not Guizot's forte; some of his studies and memoirs ran from eight to thirty-one volumes. The diminutive here denotes contempt.

2. Pierre Jean de Béranger (1780-1857), most popular writer of *chansons* of the century.

3. Ferdinando Paer (1771-1839), Italian composer (Venice, Vienna, Dresden, Paris) of over forty operas.

4. François Joseph Talma (1763-1826), brilliant tragedian (French classical drama and Shakespeare); chosen by Napoleon to play before a *parterre de rois* at Erfurt in 1808.

5. Stage name of Anne Françoise Hippolyte Boutet (1779-1847), celebrated Paris actress, active for forty-seven years, like Talma a favorite of Napoleon's.

6. Charles Potier (1775-1838), veteran Paris actor of the time, father of the prominent vaudeville playwright of the forties by the same name.

7. Charles Victor Prévot, Vicomte d'Arlincourt (1789-1856), French poet, dramatist, and historical novelist.

8. Corresponds to *Piter*, a later colloquialism for St. Petersburg, not used in the original.

9. No rhyme to this line in the original.

NOTES TO *POLTAVA*

Introduction

1. As published by Borschak and Martel, v. i.

2. The works chiefly consulted by Pushkin, besides his contemporary's, D. N. Bantysh-Kamensky's, *History of Little Russia* (1822), seem to have been M. M. Shcherbatov's *Diary of Peter the Great* as published in 1770; Prokopovich's well-known *History of the Russians* (Rusov); Voltaire's *History of Charles XII* (1728) and *History of the Russian Empire under Peter the Great* (1759), both written without access to Ukrainian sources; I. I. Golikov's *The Deeds (Deianiia, res gestae) of Peter the Great* (1789); and D. P. Buturlin's outline of military history of the 18th century, published ca. 1820. Some of the above in turn are grounded in extensive Russian archival and documentary materials; the documents printed in the appendix to the Bantysh-Kamensky history influenced Pushkin noticeably in shaping the would-be historical parts of *Poltava*. The all-important contents of the Hetmanate's archives at Baturyn, though, perished when Menshikov, on Peter's orders, destroyed the city and exterminated its population, soldiers and civilian alike, in 1708.

One foreign source of importance, besides Voltaire's treatises, was Charles-Louis Lesur's *Histoire des Kozaques*, 2 vols., Paris, 1814. Pushkin had the more pertinent volume in his library (No. 1095 by B. L. Modzalevsky's annotated register). For Pushkin sources one may consult N. V. Izmailov's *Ocherki tvorchestva Pushkina*, Nauka, Leningrad, 1975, and for his use of Lesur in particular, G. P. Blok, *Pushkin v rabote nad istoricheskimi istochnikami*, M.-L., 1949, ch. 8, pp. 163 ff.

Poltava

The numbered notes in *Poltava* are Pushkin's and follow the text.

NOTES TO *TSAR SALTAN*

Introduction

1. D. S. Mirsky, *Pushkin* (New York: Dutton Paperbacks, 1963).

2. Ed. Whitefield (New York: Knopf, 1926, 1927, 1949, 1958).

Tsar Saltan

1. The prince's name transliterated would be *Gvidon*, but since it was originally borrowed from the Italian, it is here restored to Guidon, which is as half-exotic as Gvidon is to Russian. The stress is, as shown above, on the second syllable, but the mark will be omitted henceforth.

2. The Russian term *diad'ka*, dimin. from 'uncle' and also 'tutor of young nobles', seems to be a loan translation from a similar 'elder relation' term in Selçuk Turkish for sword-master, drill sergeant. "Sword-coach," or "little uncle" if one is a Selçuk Turk, therefore fits the context better than the term 'tutor' recommended by S. Karlinsky.

NOTES TO *THE LITTLE HOUSE IN KOLOMNA*

Introduction

1. Jury Semionov, *"Das Häuschen in Kolomna" in der poetischen Erbschaft A. S. Puschkins*, Uppsala, 1965.

2. Ibid.,p. 5.

The Little House in Kolomna

1. The iambic tetrameter is the line used in over half of Pushkin's verse, including *Eugene Onegin* and virtually all his narrative poems. The *ottava rima* à la Tasso was a new form not only to Pushkin, who used it a few times after "Domik v Kolomne," but to Russian metrics in general, both in its pentametric form, which Küchelbecker adopted, and in its tetrametric form, which Zhukovsky had pioneered.

2. Prince Shirinksy-Shikhmatov (1783-1837), versifier, translator, and academician, who had just entered a monastery. Pushkin had poked gentle fun at him before, citing him as Rifmatov, "rhymester," and the like in Lyceum poems.

3. Semionov in his excellent monograph on "Domik v Kolomne" (see the note in the introduction to this work), to which I am much indebted, documents the more than casual relationship between this poem and Byron's *Beppo* with such striking parallels as this:

> But I am but a nameless sort of person
> (A broken dandy lately on my travels)
> And take for rhyme, to hook my rambling verse on,
> The first that Walker's Lexicon unravels . . .

4. *Con bravura* here renders *pustit' na pe*, a term drawn from the Pharao (faro) game and indicating the situation when winnings are left "in peace" (*en paix*) along with the original stake, i.e., the player "goes for broke" to double or quadruple his winnings.

5. Pushkin had discussed the question of the caesura in the octave and its lately ignored constraints in the original ninth stanza, later omitted.

6. The church of St. Mary Protectress in Kolomna.

7. *Stonet sizyi golubok* is the first line of the saccharine pseudo-folk poem written by I. I. Dimitriev (1760-1837) in seven quatrains of rhymed trochaic tetrameter. The poem had almost become a true folk song. *Vyidu l' ia* is the beginning of an eleven-stanza sentimental romance by Yu. A. Meletsky (1752-1828), which had also become popular among both ladies and lasses, as Vyazemsky tells us.

8. Pletnev tells us that this proud, outwardly imperturbable beauty, in her regal bearing and secret grief so reminiscent of Pushkin's Tatyana, was Ekaterina Aleksandrovna née Budkevich, who as a young girl married the wealthy septuagenarian Count Stroynovsky in order to save her family from bankruptcy. Pushkin—when he, like the Countess, lived in Kolomna—supposedly used to go to St. Mary's to admire the bride and evidently knew her poignant history.

9. Octave XXXVI in the original lacks the last line of its sestet.

NOTES TO *THE GOLDEN COCKEREL*

Introduction
1. "K tvorcheskoi evoliutsii Pushkina v 30-e gody," *Voprosy literatury*, XI (1973), pp. 124-68.

NOTES TO *THE BRONZE HORSEMAN*

Introduction

1. Andrei Bely, *Ritm kak dialektika i Mednyi Vsadnik: Issledovanie*. Izdatel'stvo "Federaciia" (Moskva, 1929), cf. p. 266 ff.
2. A few excerpts from Mickiewicz's "St. Petersburg," in the Peacock translation, will serve to illustrate the extraordinary parallelism between the two works at certain key junctures:

> The ladies gleam like splendid butterflies/ With bright-hued cloaks and hats of brave design;/ Each glitters in Parisian elegance,/ Her small foot twinkling in a fur-lined shoe,/ Her face crab-red and snowy white of hue.—// ...Pale-lipped with hate,/ He laughed, raised his clenched fist, and struck the stone,/ As though he summoned down a vengeful fate...// His charger's reins Tsar Peter has released;/ He has been flying down the road, perchance,/ And here the precipice checks his advance./ With hoofs aloft now stands the maddened beast,/ Champing its bit unchecked, with slackened rein:/ You guess that it will fall and be destroyed./ Thus it has galloped long, with tossing mane,/ Like a cascade, leaping into the void,/ That, fettered by the frost, hangs dizzily./ But soon will shine the sun of liberty,/ And from the West a wind will warm this land.—/ Will the cascade of tyranny then stand?//

The Bronze Horseman

1. The parade grounds of St.Petersburg are called Mars Field.
2. Allusion to Karamzin's monumental *History of the Russian State*.
3. Then an outlying faubourg of St. Petersburg.
4. The new edifice of the Ministry of War.
5. This is assumed to refer either to imperial charity or to the calm dawn, or ambiguously to both.

NOTES TO *EUGENE ONEGIN*

1. See Introduction, p. 26.
2. Allusion to Pushkin's recent banishment from St. Petersburg for writing subversive poetry.
3. The manuscripts have either "tsars" or "ancestors" here; presumably it was suspected that the censor might take umbrage at the notion that displaying portraits of tsars was old-fashioned.
4. Light cart or sleigh with a hood.
5. According to M. A. Tsiavlovskii and S. M. Petrov, *A. S. Pushkin, Sochineniia*, Ogiz, 1949, pp. 372-75.

6. "Housewife."
7. Odessa restaurateur.
8. A poetic name for Italy.

Walter Arndt, translator of Pushkin's Eugene Onegin, *the present anthology, and Goethe's* Faust, *was born at Constantinople in 1916 as a citizen of the Free and Hanseatic City of Hamburg. He had nine years of classical schooling at Breslau, Silesia (now restored to Poland as Wrocław), and in 1934 moved to Oxford, where in the intervals of rowing for Oriel College he read Economics and Political Science.*

After Oxford, Mr. Arndt went to Poland for graduate study at Warsaw, and after learning Polish began his study of Russian. In 1939 he resigned his German citizenship and volunteered for the Polish army. After the peripatetic campaign of 1939 he escaped from a German POW camp, spent a year in the Polish underground at Warsaw forging Nazi documents, and made his way to Istanbul by way of Berlin in 1940. Here, in an enforced civilian interlude, he took a degree in mechanical engineering at Robert College and resumed intensive study of Russian language and literature.

Between 1942 and 1945, Mr. Arndt was active in political, military, and economic intelligence with the U.S. Office of Strategic Services and, later, O.W.I. in the Aegean theater. He taught at Robert College and worked in U.N. refugee resettlement between 1944 and 1949, when he emigrated to the United States. There he taught Classics and modern languages (French, German and Russian) at Guilford College in North Carolina until 1956, when he received his doctorate in Comparative Linguistics and Classics at the University of North Carolina.

After Ford fellowships at Ann Arbor and Harvard, Mr. Arndt held successive appointments in linguistics and Slavic languages and literatures at Chapel Hill. He left in 1966 as Chairman of the Department of Linguistics, Slavic, and Oriental Languages to take up a professorship in Russian and linguistics at Dartmouth.

Mr. Arndt's verse translation of Pushkin's Eugene Onegin *was published in 1963 (2nd expanded edition in 1982), and awarded a Bollingen Prize. His verse translation of Goethe's* Faust *in the metric forms of the original and an anthology of Anna Akhmatova's poetry in English were published in 1976. He has also translated from Lermontov, Tyutchev, Fet, Pasternak, Heine, Morgenstern, and Rilke, and published studies in linguistic theory and glottochronology. His latest book,* The Genius of Wilhelm Busch: Comedy of Frustration, *was published by the University of California Press in 1982.*